More praise for *Trail Tested*

"One of the most comprehensive looks into the world of hiking ever created by one of the sport's most accomplished athletes. *Trail Tested* is an excellent guide for any hiking enthusiast from beginner to expert. Learn in one exciting read what it took Trauma thousands and thousands of hard-earned miles to learn."

—Eric Larsen, polar explorer, educator, and lecturer, *Outside* magazine's Eco All Star (2008)

"*Trail Tested* is a visually stunning foray into the realities of long-distance hiking. Justin Lichter's 35,000 miles of hiking experience and trail-tested wisdom come through in every page. *Trail Tested* is great for both day hikers and hikers that will be out for many days!"

—Lawton "Disco" Grinter, Triple Crowner, directed and edited *The Walkumentary*, author of *I Hike*

"In *Trail Tested*, Justin has distilled thru-hiking to its very core. Justin shares his knowledge backed by nearly 40,000 miles on the trail in a concise and thoroughly enjoyable format. For every thru- and section hiker, whether it's your first hike or you've had your trail name for years, this book is a must read."

—Rob Coughlin, general manager, Granite Gear

"This book is probably the most important outdoor field guide since the first release of *The Complete Walker* by Colin Fletcher in 1968. These pages will save you time, money, and many exhausting nights of confusion from surfing mindless internet threads . . . job well done."

—Winton Porter, Georgia author of the year 2010 for *Just Passin' Thru*; former owner of Mountain Crossings at Neels Gap on the Appalachian Trail

Viewing Mount Everest, Lhotse, and Nuptse
from Renjo La (17,520 feet), Nepal
Photo by Shawn Forry

Taking a break and reading on the Great Divide Trail in the Canadian Rockies. Sometimes ultralight isn't always right! Other things can take priority, like when the new Harry Potter book came out.

Cover photo: Hiking above treeline on Mt. Kenya, Kenya, Africa

Facing page: Almost to the top of Cho La Pass, 17,782 feet, with Ama Dablam in the background; Nepal Himalayas
Photo by Shawn Forry

TRAIL TESTED

A Thru-Hiker's Guide to Ultralight Hiking and Backpacking

Second Edition

Justin Lichter

FALCON®

An imprint of The Rowman & Littlefield Publishing Group, Inc.
4501 Forbes Blvd., Ste. 200
Lanham, MD 20706
www.rowman.com
Falcon and FalconGuides are registered trademarks and Make Adventure Your Story is a trademark of The Rowman & Littlefield Publishing Group, Inc.

Distributed by NATIONAL BOOK NETWORK

British Library Cataloguing in Publication Information available

Library of Congress Cataloging-in-Publication Data

Names: Lichter, Justin, author.
Title: Trail tested : a thru-hiker's guide to ultralight hiking and backpacking / Justin Lichter.
Description: Second edition. | Guilford, Connecticut : FalconGuides, [2020] | Includes index. | Summary: "Hundreds of valuable tips and advice based on Justin Lichter's more than 35,000 miles of hiking across the country and beyond"— Provided by publisher.
Identifiers: LCCN 2020012930 (print) | LCCN 2020012931 (ebook) | ISBN 9781493052097 (paperback) | ISBN 9781493052103 (epub)
Subjects: LCSH: Hiking—Handbooks, manuals, etc. | Backpacking—Handbooks, manuals, etc. | Backpacking—Equipment and supplies—Handbooks, manuals, etc.
Classification: LCC GV199.5 .L34 2020 (print) | LCC GV199.5 (ebook) | DDC 796.51—dc23
LC record available at https://lccn.loc.gov/2020012930
LC ebook record available at https://lccn.loc.gov/2020012931

∞™ The paper used in this publication meets the minimum requirements of American National Standard for Information Sciences—Permanence of Paper for Printed Library Materials, ANSI/NISO Z39.48-1992.

CONTENTS

Cameron Lake, Waterton Lakes National Park, Canada

INTRODUCTION

WHAT THIS BOOK IS AND IS NOT

This is not a typical how-to book. There is a lot of information inside, from small "micro-tips" to larger picture items. This book will hopefully get you feeling comfortable in the backcountry faster and also provide help as an ongoing reference. It may help you learn some things faster and hopefully speed up the learning curve, as well as save you money and time when buying gear. The goal is to make this an easy, fun-to-read learning tool and reference for all ability levels. Hopefully it will make it easier for you to get outside, experience the outdoors, and overcome situations that might previously have turned you back. Sometimes the unexpected makes trips more rewarding.

The goal of this book is to give you useful tips and reduce the time you spend learning so you can enjoy more time in the wilderness. Almost every page has a tip or two that I've picked up along the way. Some of the tips are personal preferences, so keep in mind it's an outline about the topic in question, its pros and cons, and my opinions.

Getting outside and hiking and camping can change your life. You may even start to want to change some of your priorities and reduce some things you don't need in your life. Streamlining the gear selection process to essentials and planning to get outdoors help keep your enthusiasm going. You'll quickly learn to live with what's on your back!

This book is purely to prepare for the journey. Enjoy the read while at home or en route to the trailhead. Use the information here to prepare and remember what you can on the trail. Adding weight with a book is counterintuitive to this book's purpose. Let me instead help you shed weight from your pack.

In building on the first edition, I'm adding trends in gear, planning, and where I see the ultralight hiking world moving in the future. There are countless new tips and chapters on the future of the sport and multisport adventures—the direction of fun I've been pivoting to and think the future of long-distance adventuring is headed.

Now let's go hiking!

GETTING STARTED

Near Red Pass, Washington, on the original, washed-out
Pacific Crest Trail route in 2004 (disposable camera)

EARLY DAYS

Windsong, Ottie, Yoni, and I crossing the Bear Mountain Parkway, New York

You can always learn to hike, backpack, and camp. You may not go on a 1,000-mile hike or be out in the mountains for six months, but you can experience the calm of disconnecting, unplugging, simplifying life, and being with nature. There's nothing like being out in the backcountry and thinking only about the beauty, where/when you're going to reach the next water source, how much you can eat out of your food bag, and where you're going to camp.

I started hiking when I was young, and I can't imagine life without hiking. What you do when you hike is up to you. Some people love sitting by a lake. Others like hiking fast and far, looking at flowers, or summiting peaks. You'll find what you like. Age and skill don't matter. This is an activity for everyone. The more you get out, the more you'll learn, and you'll learn more than you even realize.

There is a beauty to a simple hike. You really don't need anything that you don't already have. You don't need to start out by buying a lot of gear.

Going on a day hike is simply going on a nice walk through the woods. You can wear your sneakers or running shoes. Use your school backpack. Grab an empty soda bottle; it's your water bottle. Grab some food from the cupboard. Find a destination to go to—that's all you need for a hike.

If you like it and want to go on more day hikes or go out on overnight trips, cover more miles, and mix in cross-country (lingo for off-trail) travel, this book will help you find what you need and learn the necessary skills.

Windsong and I atop Avery Peak, Maine, on the Appalachian Trail

Windsong and I atop Mount Katahdin, northern terminus of the AT

Sometimes you just need to take a nap to stay mentally fresh.

PREPARATION

MENTAL PREPARATION

Mental preparation is an integral part of planning and, in some ways, probably even more so than physical preparation. Long-distance hiking, backpacking, multisport adventures, and other adventures are a big transition from most people's normal routines. It is important to start thinking and planning ahead for not checking your e-mails daily or being able to pick up the phone and call or text friends or family at a whim. You will most likely be disconnected, or at best have limited connectivity. Less so on the Appalachian Trail and certain sections of other major trails, but you also may choose to limit yourself to connection during town stops or just at nighttime to save your battery or be respectful to other people seeking solace in the wilderness. Sometimes it takes a day or two or more to get used to the new routine that places more value on maps, food, and movement than checking your calls, texts, and e-mails. Practicing self-control the first few days of the trip will help ease the transition and help get you into a routine that doesn't revolve around checking your devices.

It is also important to transition into a routine that revolves around motion and movement all day long. This is not easy, and the first couple weeks can be exhausting, even painful. It is critical to take this in stride and not go too hard out of the gate. Ease into it, even if you are in good shape heading out. No matter the time of year, you'll likely have at least 8 hours of daylight, a lot more in summer. Pace yourself. Take breaks. Have fun.

Don't turn it into a death march. If you're not having fun, there's no reason to be out there. It might be type-2 fun, but still make sure you're having fun. And it is important to acknowledge beforehand that you won't be having fun every minute of every day. There will be terrible, miserable times, and painful moments. There will be cold, wet, soggy days, but also beautiful, perfect sunny days. Don't make the decision to quit on a bad-weather day. It's the journey, not the destination. Without the highs and lows, the trip won't be as rewarding. Just know there will be some very tough times, emotionally and physically. It's not all rainbows.

PHYSICAL PREPARATION

Mental preparation is key, but physical preparation is the foundation for success. You will break in easier to long days of movement and travel if you are in shape and ready for it. Starting a hike "off the couch" is never easy. It can lead to injuries and bruising on your shoulders and hips from a weighted backpack. It is important to work up in weight and start wearing a weighted backpack before a trip. Get your hips, shoulders, and leg muscles used to carrying the extra weight. Don't expect cross-training to prepare you for the sport you'll be doing. At least start to build up in that same activity, even if you don't have the time to put in 8 or 12 hours doing the type of walking you will be doing. This will help get your feet ready for the shoes, calluses in place with the equipment you'll be using, and also help the mental transition.

Let me give you some background for what I'm talking about in this section. I'm normally thru-hiking or long-distance hiking by myself, with my dog, with Pepper, or with someone else I met on one of the long trails. We know each other's tendencies, goals, and capabilities. However, this time I went with my girlfriend to hike a few-hundred-mile section of the Pacific Crest Trail (PCT) southbound from the Canadian border through Washington. I tried to ease into the mileage, or what I thought was easy mileage. I thought 10–15 miles per day was pretty reasonable to start. After all, she was in shape and frequently day hiking. We started late the first afternoon, and all was good. We got about 6 or 7 miles in and set up camp. The next day we were about 12 miles in when she started to bonk. We took a long break and then started hiking again. We needed to get a few more miles to camp so we could fill up water for cooking. When she got to camp, she lay down and couldn't move. I told her to soak her legs in the water, since that would help tremendously. The water source was 1,000 feet away, but she couldn't move, never mind get over to the water. Finally, after a couple hours of her lying there, I insisted she go soak her legs. She was sore and completely spent. Not a good way to start the hike—she still had to wake up

and hike the next six or seven days until a resupply day. It's hard to fully recover until there's a rest day. To this day, she says the last few miles and that hiking day were the hardest of her life and the sorest she's ever been.

I typically look at physical preparation as including the first few weeks of the hike, not just pre-hike. I don't usually have time before a hike to devote 8- to 12-hour days to preparation, training, and hiking. That time may be limited to an hour or two or day hikes. Sometimes I'm coming off ski season, so there may be a little cross-training with backcountry skiing, but not apples to apples. It is very hard to start going 8 hours plus per day without ramping up. If you've done a long hiking trip before, you may find it easier; your body may be used to it, but it is crucial to ramp up and not overdo it. Wherever you are with training, try not to go over 5 miles more than that right away. For example, depending on trail conditions, I try not to go more than 20–25 miles per day for the first week or ten days; then I might have a smaller day at a resupply to provide some rest and recovery. After that I may ramp up to 23–28 miles per day for about a week or so then have a shorter recovery day at a resupply before increasing to 28–35 miles per day. I think the shorter, recovery days or complete rest days are very important in the ramp-up progression.

Just as important is the daily flow. This gets more and more challenging in cold or bad weather. When I first hiked the Appalachian Trail, I hiked 5-plus hours at a time, with an hour or hour-and-a-half lunch break. I continued this for my first thru-hikes on the Pacific Crest and Continental Divide Trails. I would be on the trail by 6 or 7 a.m. and would go until noon. Same in the afternoon until dinner, then maybe even get a couple hours of hiking in after dinner if there was still daylight. I would pack snacks in outside pockets of my backpack and eat snacks about halfway through the five-plus-hour session while hiking. I called it "snack-packing." I no longer think this is the best system. I changed up the routine a long time ago. Consistent calories are key to not bonking.

The routine I think works best is 3 hours on and then a break. You can extend or shorten your break based on temperatures, weather conditions, or where in the trip you are. For example, if you're at the beginning of a trip, you may want to take a longer break to help spread out the exertion periods and help break in. Typically I'll break for an hour at the beginning of the trip then reduce to 30 or 45 minutes when in shape—enough time to eat, get your shoes off, dry out some wet gear, and recharge a bit mentally. Then rinse and repeat for the length of the day. If you're breaking in, you may also want to stop a little earlier or break the last session into a partial session when you find a good campsite. In summary for a typical summer hike: I wake up early and am out hiking around dawn (6:30 a.m.), hike until 9:30 a.m., break/second breakfast until 10:15 a.m., hike until 1:15 p.m., break for lunch until 2 p.m., hike until 5 p.m., snack/break until 5:30 or 5:45 p.m., hike until dark, find a campsite and cook dinner. If the days are short, dinner might be cooked at the last break.

FINANCIAL PREPARATION/ BUDGETING

A lot of people ask what it costs to thru-hike. There is no true mathematical equation for this, since it depends on your budget. I think the single biggest cost of a hike is how many hotel rooms you get. Hotel rooms can range from $50 (in the Southeast on the AT or if you are sharing with another hiker) up to $250+ per night in summer in the touristy

Getting ready to head to rural areas where they don't accept credit cards. Be prepared with cash!

towns near the trails or near national parks. That definitely skews the equation. I used to be able to hike a trail and budget $1 per mile, including food, restaurant meals, hotels, and replacement gear. Keep in mind that I don't drink alcohol, which can add a considerable amount to your budget. In the past ten years I've seen my cost increase to more like $2 per mile because of increased food costs, not including transportation to and from the trail. Your cost could be as much has $5 to $10 per mile, depending on how often you're staying in town and eating at restaurants, or if you have any dietary limitations. That being said, thru-hiking is still relatively inexpensive—$5,000–$20,000 for a 2,500-mile hike that might last five to six months. If you are able to minimize other expenses, including expenses you're paying "at home" while out on the trail, this can be pretty obtainable in a season or two of working.

Getting the lowdown in one of the great specialty outdoor stores, Midwest Mountaineering, Minneapolis, Minnesota

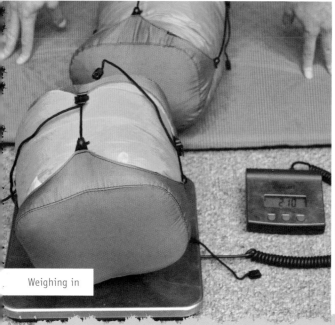

Weighing in

Scoping out some hidden pockets.

CHOOSING GEAR

Gear is a personal preference, and preferences can only be gained from experience and trial and error. I know exactly what gear I prefer for certain situations and places. For the past ten years, the majority of what I carry stays the same. I swap certain things for different trips based on the conditions I expect to encounter. It's important to pack properly for the conditions you expect and for potential changes or setbacks. After a few trips you'll start to learn exactly what you want with you on your journeys. Until then, here's what you need to know about getting started.

I can't say this strongly enough: Don't go out and buy hundreds of dollars' worth of new gear when you're just getting started. Research the gear by reading reviews in magazines, in forums, and on the internet. But, be advised, you'll hear a million different opinions on the same pieces of equipment, and many times they'll contradict. Also, always keep in mind your intentions for the equipment and what types of trips you plan to be doing. For example, I'll rarely trust *Backpacker* magazine on a gear review for a thru-hike or other long-distance adventure unless the writer or correspondent has long-distance experience, since typically they're only using brand-new gear for a few days or a week and covering less distance each day.

I have seen it happen a hundred times. A family wants to go camping. They go into a store to get outfitted with gear. The salesperson sells them tons of stuff he or she likes and thinks they also will like. The salesperson may be trying to upsell you

on expensive equipment and will probably suggest things that likely aren't essential.

Figure out what you think you really need before making purchases. Go camping and hiking with friends that have gear, and ask about it. Ask questions at stores and look around for discounts, online or on Craigslist. It's likely that as you get used to the outdoors, your gear will change quickly. With experience, your comfort level will change. The first few times I went backpacking, I never would have thought that I'd be completely comfortable in a small, flat tarp with no bug netting in certain conditions. Once you have figured out your "go to" gear choices, you can add different gear to your quiver for different seasons or situations.

I have seen countless people start the Appalachian Trail (AT) with 50- to 60-pound backpacks and a bunch of brand-new gear. (I was one of them, even though I had backpacked in southern Utah for three months the year before.) Then everyone

Photos by Russ Sackson

learns in the next few weeks that they don't need most of the stuff they're carrying. They bought all this new gear just for the trip. Many AT hikers end up buying everything all over again within a few weeks of setting out. Tents (or any gear for that matter) are like cars: Once off the dealer's lot, you'll be lucky to get two-thirds of what you paid for it.

When considering buying hiking or backpacking gear, keep the weight in mind. It's not so important for car camping. Your tent and other backpacking gear could cross over for car camping. Remember, you will be carrying everything you have on your back. Ounces quickly add up to pounds, and pounds add up to a heavy pack. You may or may not want to be an ultralight hiker. However, it's important to keep weight as a main consideration in order to be comfortable. The second part of that is learning what you actually need so you can limit what you are carrying.

Lighter loads:

- Are more comfortable.
- Are faster to pack up.
- Are easier, faster, and more agile to move with.
- Are more organized and simplified.
- Mean less energy is exerted, so you can travel farther and faster.
- Are often less expensive than heavier gear.

The lightweight way also crosses over to other sports like climbing, mountaineering, backcountry skiing, even into everyday life!

When picking out gear, try to keep an ultralight or lightweight mindset. A rough estimate of your base weight (backpack, sleeping bag, and tent) for backpacking should be 10 pounds or less. This will help your pack stay relatively light. However, you do not want to try to cut weight on the backpack itself if you know the weight of your gear is going to be above the pack's recommended weight limit. The weight rating is for your comfort. You don't want to cut corners on the pack and end up with thin padding in an effort to shave base weight. You will end up being uncomfortable on the trail. Countless times I have seen people hit the trail with an ultralight backpack and be miserable in just an hour. An ultralight pack works for a lot of people. If you're going out for just five days, your food alone might weigh more than some packs' recommended capacity.

I have seen people head out on 5-day trips in an ultralight pack with about 50 pounds in their pack. A pack that has no hip belt and small mesh shoulder straps can't support that amount of weight. The shoulder straps always end up cleaving into the hiker's shoulders from the weight. I saw one hiker who had wrapped duct tape around huge squares of open cell foam underneath each shoulder strap. The tape probably made it a little more comfortable, but

TRAUMA TIP

I wouldn't recommend buying certain items used. Be careful with climbing equipment. You never know how many falls someone has put onto a rope, a carabiner, or a harness, which can greatly affect their performance. Rain gear and items with DWR (durable water repellency) also can have a short useful life.

Checking packability and compressibility.
Photos by Russ Sackson

Light, lighter, lightest. This guy carried this cabinet for four days up the valley. I'd much rather be wearing our ultralight packs than either of these!

it was definitely not the ideal situation. He added weight to his ultralight pack to make it more comfortable. His goal of being ultralight backfired!

BUYING GEAR

There are a few good places where you can get outdoor gear. You can buy directly from the manufacturer. Some manufacturers sell directly to customers; others sell only from their website. Manufacturers and their customer service crews are also a great place to get information on the products you're interested in. They should know everything about their products. If you have any questions, ask them before and after your purchase.

You can often find really good prices on gear and almost any product you're looking for online. However, you lose that personal, interactive contact and often the ability to get feedback or ask questions. I know some online stores have LiveChat features. It just doesn't feel the same, though, and you don't really even know if the person that you are talking to has any clue about the gear you are asking about.

Then of course there are the local outfitters and major outdoor retailers, like REI. You get personalized service, a good vibe, and can get some really helpful salespeople. Some of the most amazing backpacking stores I've been in are locally owned specialty outdoor stores, especially along some of the main long-distance hiking trails. It is a trade-off, however; the price might be higher in store than online.

Other options to consider are Craigslist, eBay, and hiking forums like backpackinglight.com and whiteblaze.net. These websites have "gear for sale" or "gear swap" forums, which will have some more-specialized gear than REI. You can access them for free.

Now on to the nitty-gritty . . .

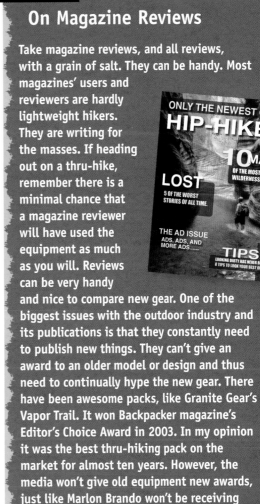

TIP

On Magazine Reviews

Take magazine reviews, and all reviews, with a grain of salt. They can be handy. Most magazines' users and reviewers are hardly lightweight hikers. They are writing for the masses. If heading out on a thru-hike, remember there is a minimal chance that a magazine reviewer will have used the equipment as much as you will. Reviews can be very handy and nice to compare new gear. One of the biggest issues with the outdoor industry and its publications is that they constantly need to publish new things. They can't give an award to an older model or design and thus need to continually hype the new gear. There have been awesome packs, like Granite Gear's Vapor Trail. It won Backpacker magazine's Editor's Choice Award in 2003. In my opinion it was the best thru-hiking pack on the market for almost ten years. However, the media won't give old equipment new awards, just like Marlon Brando won't be receiving an Oscar for *The Godfather* this year. Keep that in mind when you are reading current reviews and trying to pick the best gear for you. You might find that your best choice is a pack model that is a couple of years old. You won't find a review in the latest magazine because they won't keep repeating the same gear reviews. They also may favor items with new colors and new catchphrases instead of real meaningful additions—or the companies buying advertising in their publications and thus paying their bills.

Checking compressibility at a display
at the Outdoor Retailer trade show
Photo by Russ Sackson

AND MATERIALS

Twice per year, thousands of manufacturers go to the Outdoor Retailer trade show to introduce new fabrics, hardware, and technologies. The textile manufacturers attend to show their latest and greatest innovations to manufacturers in the industry. They hope to get these new materials into up-and-coming outdoor products. Here are the basic, common ultralight materials. This section will also help explain why some products are more expensive than others and which will likely last longer.

FABRICS

Nylon and polyester are standard fabrics. Nylon is a little lighter, tougher, and more abrasion-resistant. The weight of fabric is measured in denier, written like this: 40D. It is a measurement of a yarn's weight, in grams, based on a 9,000-meter length of that yarn. Higher numbers represent more rugged fabric; lower numbers are less rugged.

RIPSTOP NYLON: A nylon woven with a doubled thread at regular intervals. This helps prevent rips from spreading.

CORDURA: A nylon brand name. Cordura yarns are of the highest quality. The name Cordura represents high-tenacity (strength) yarns, and the fabrics coming from the mills producing those yarns are rigorously tested to ensure they meet Cordura standards.

SPINNAKER: An ultralightweight sailcloth. From my experience, it doesn't seem to last as long nor is it as durable as DCF. Has pretty much gone by the wayside with the introduction of DCF.

DCF (DYNEEMA COMPOSITE FABRIC)/FORMERLY KNOWN AS CUBEN FIBER: Another material that originated in the sailing industry. This is Spectra laminated with Mylar. It's very strong but susceptible to damage from abrasions. However, for its strength-to-weight ratio, it is fantastic and probably the most durable option for the weight. It's also very pricey. The proliferation of DCF Is probably the single most important technological advance in the ultralight industry in the past ten years.

HYPALON: A heavy but strong material often used in high-abrasion areas, like underneath crampon storage areas.

MESH: Mesh comes in different forms. It's handy to have mesh pockets because they stretch and you can see into them. Most people think mesh is lighter than other fabrics. This is not true if compared

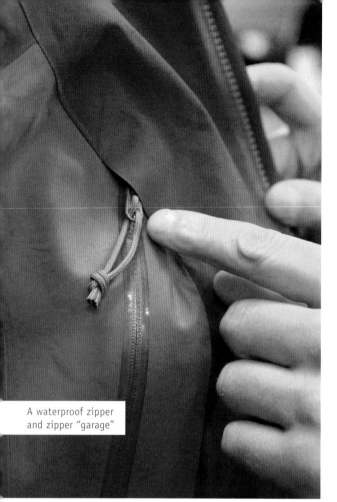

A waterproof zipper and zipper "garage"

to lightweight silnylon or other ultralight fabrics like DCF. Mesh absorbs a lot of water and gets heavier when wet. Also, if it gets nicked, it can unravel over time.

DURASTRETCH OR STRETCH MESH: Another option for outside pockets or back panels. It's a great substitute for regular mesh. It's less transparent but doesn't absorb as much water and holds up better to heavy use.

ZIPPERS

Zippers come in different sizes and types (waterproof or regular). Most waterproof zippers are merely water resistant, but at least they shed some water. Don't be fooled by an inverted slider; this does not mean it is a waterproof zipper. YKK is one of the most widely used zippers. I have noticed that YKK "taped" waterproof zippers start to "peel" in the middle over time and with a lot of usage. The peeling leaves a little area where water can get in once you have used the zipper. Another way

Photos by Russ Sackson

Laminated jacket

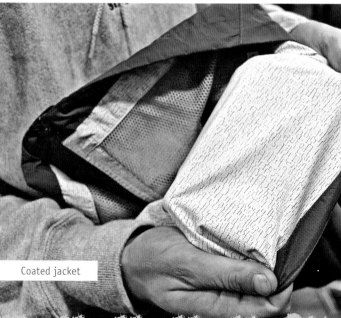

Coated jacket

manufacturers waterproof zippers is by "welding" the teeth to the rubberized fabric and having little offsets in the teeth. All zippers need maintenance when dirty, especially after being in gritty conditions. Heads up: Curved zipper runs wear out faster than straight zippers.

LAMINATE VS. COATINGS

Here's a nutshell comparison of waterproof and/or breathable technologies used in rain gear and on other waterproof products. A laminate is like adding wallpaper to a fabric; a coating is like painting a wall. Laminates are often more breathable and expensive.

Dan, from Granite Gear, and I chatting about new ideas and prototypes

TRAUMA TIP

Most people think mesh is light because you can see through it and it has holes. Mesh is heavier than many fabrics, including ultralight silnylon and DCF.

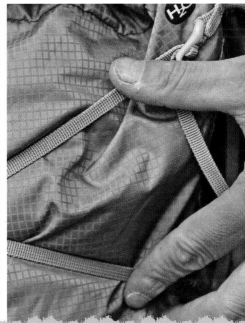

Scoping out Midwest Mountaineering's pack wall

Getting fitted for my torso length

BACKPACKS

There are tons of packs out there. Here's the lowdown on packs.

TYPES OF PACKS

The standard terminology for referencing the "front" of a backpack is the side that faces away from your back.

DAY PACKS: These are usually smaller, so you don't need to worry much about the weight of a day pack. Most companies make them with a bunch of bells and whistles. (Literally! Check the sternum strap for an emergency whistle!)

Features may include water-bottle pockets, hydration-system compatibility, stretch pocket or helmet pocket on the pack's front, ventilated back panel, hip-belt pockets for a camera or an energy bar, ice ax loops, and other zippered pockets. People aren't carrying much weight in a day pack, so there's really no need for a suspension system in the back panel or for a real weight-bearing hip belt. If you're looking for a day pack, find the features, price, and colors you like. Check the fit carefully. There isn't much else to it.

OVERNIGHT PACKS: Overnight packs are a different animal. Some are full-featured; others are stripped down. Packs are made for different-size torsos and waist belts. Overnight packs also have different capacities and load or weight classifications. Fit and comfort are the most important things to me.

Photos by Russ Sackson

Some packs save weight by skimping on features that make the pack comfortable and entice you to buy it because it's light. I don't mind a backpack that's a few ounces heavier than another when it's much more comfortable.

Most overnight packs are available in multiple sizes and have adjustable torso lengths and different-size hip belts to make the pack fit better.

GENDER- AND AGE-SPECIFIC PACKS

YOUTH BACKPACKS: These packs offer smaller volumes so that they fit a youth's body better and do not overburden the child with too much weight in the pack. They also include a more adjustable suspension to accommodate a child's growth. Several brands design packs for children. Women's backpacks, because of their smaller frame sizes, often work well for young backpackers of either gender. Small versions of some men's packs also work for children and teenagers.

WOMEN'S BACKPACKS: Women-specific designs are engineered to conform to the female frame. Their torso dimensions are generally shorter and narrower than men's. Hip belts and shoulder straps are contoured with the female form in mind.

TO GET THE RIGHT FIT

Torso length, not height, determines your pack size. Here's how to measure yours:

Measure torso length:

1. Have a friend locate the bony bump at the base of your neck, where the slope of your shoulder meets your neck. This is your seventh cervical (or C7) vertebrae. Tilt your head forward to locate it more easily.

2. Using a flexible tape measure, have your friend start at that spot and measure downward along your spine.

The progression of packs and trekking poles! I'll take my comfortable lightweight pack any day of the week.

3. Place your hands on your hips so you can feel your iliac crest, those two pointy bones just above the front pockets on your pants, which serves as the "shelf" of your pelvic girdle. (It's the first hard thing you feel when you run your fingers down from the sides of your rib cage.) Position your hands so that your thumbs are pointing toward your backbone.

4. Have your friend finish measuring at the point where the tape crosses an imaginary line drawn between your thumbs. That is your torso length.

5. Use your torso length to find the best pack size for you. Generally, manufacturers size their pack frames like this:

- **Extra small:** Fits torsos up to 15½"
- **Small:** Fits torsos 16" to 17½"
- **Regular:** Fits torsos 18" to 19½"
- **Large/Tall:** Fits torsos 20" and up

Measure belt size:

Take the tape measure and wrap it around the top of your hips, where you can feel your iliac crest. Use this measurement to get a properly fitting hip belt. A properly positioned and fitted hip belt will straddle your iliac crest, about an inch above and below that line.

Three possible choices for lightweight backpacks
Photo by Russ Sackson

TYPES OF PACK SUSPENSION

EXTERNAL SUSPENSION BACKPACKS: These seem to be going by the wayside, but I will mention them briefly. These were the standard back in the 1970s. They have a metal frame that surrounds the exterior of the pack. These packs carry weight well but are bigger, heavier, and not nearly as agile as other packs. They are pretty antiquated because the internal suspension packs have progressed so much. External frame packs make everyone look like SpongeBob SquarePants from behind.

INTERNAL SUSPENSION BACKPACKS: These are the more popular option these days. Hundreds of models are available. They have a stay to provide stiffness to the pack, allowing it to handle the weight of a load. The suspension can vary from lightweight metal stays around a back panel, to metal or aluminum rods placed vertically along the pack's sides, to plastic or composite frame sheets. Generally, the stiffer the rod, stay, or frame sheet, the more weight the pack can carry comfortably. Stiffer suspensions makes for heavier packs.

NO SUSPENSION/FRAMELESS BACKPACKS: These are usually the lightest weight packs, but they also support the least amount of weight. Typically, a pack without a suspension isn't recommended to carry more than 25 pounds. If you want to carry more with one of these packs, a good way to create some rigidity along the back panel is to fold your sleeping pad and slide it on the inside along the back panel. If you're using an inflatable pad, leaving a little bit of air in it offers more comfort and extra support. With a foam pad you can fold it along the back panel or curl it around the whole inside of the pack and place items inside the curve of the pad.

VENTILATED BACK PANELS

These are making headway in the market, and a lot of people like the extra breathability they offer your back. Your back will sweat when hiking with a pack on. These various styles of breathable back panels are supposed to aid in airflow along your back to help keep it cooler. These can really help cool your back if the conditions are right and there is a cool breeze blowing. If it's hot and you're in 100 percent humidity, like on the AT in summertime, I don't think there is anything that will really prevent you from getting hot and sweaty.

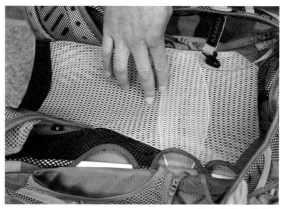

Photo by Russ Sackson

Many packs have ventilation channels built into back panels and, in some cases, even into the frame sheet as well. A few packs have engineered a permanent air channel between you and the pack, using a trampoline-like mesh panel. Your back rests against the mesh back panel, and the mesh provides improved breathability. With these, the frame-supported pack rides a few inches off the back.

Certain ventilation features seem to have inherent flaws. Packs with mesh back panels have a number of drawbacks:

1. The mesh absorbs and holds more water than other materials, so a mesh back panel can both keep your back wet and add weight to the pack.

2. It is fairly abrasive, so it can wear out shirts and other clothing faster.

3. It has no real ripstop properties. If you snag the back panel on something, you risk having it run and continue to unravel.

4. In trampoline-style systems, the air channel between the pack and the mesh takes up valuable space between your back and the pack itself. It loses volume while adding weight because of the trampoline.

5. Trampoline-style packs add additional space between your back and the pack itself. It moves the weight of the pack from your center of gravity, which could make the pack less comfortable or agile when fully loaded.

PACK LOADING SYSTEMS

PANEL LOADER: A panel loading backpack is anything with a zipper or access point up and down the pack. It allows you to access the body of the pack through a panel.

TOP LOADER: Any pack with primary access through the top, even if it has a lid. Top-loading packs generally have a zipper or roll-top closure system. These packs are normally some of the lightest weight packs on the market. Some have access zippers on the front panel or side to allow easy access to items at the bottom of the pack. You don't have to dig from the top to the bottom to grab something. The zippers are nice but add a few ounces.

HYBRID/NONTRADITIONAL: Packs that don't fit the top or panel-loader description. Granite Gear's Core and Flatbed are good examples of hybrid or nontraditional packs. They are designed for specific needs and work better for trail crews, handling bear canisters, or carrying odd shapes and sizes that won't easily fit in a normal pack. They are usually heavier than a traditional top loader.

STRAPS

About 75 percent of the weight of a backpack should rest on your hips. Your back, shoulders, and upper chest area should carry minimal amounts of weight. To optimize pack comfort and stability, tinker with the various adjustment straps.

LOAD-LIFTER STRAPS: These are stitched into the top of your pack's shoulder straps and the top of the pack frame. Ideally, they should form a 45-degree angle between your shoulder straps and the pack.

The straps should be snug, but not too tight. They prevent the upper portion of a pack from pulling away from the body and causing it to sag on your lumbar area. If straps are left too loose, the pack can tip backward, compromising balance and comfort.

If load-lifters are angled higher than 60 degrees or lower than 30 degrees, the pack is likely not the correct torso size. Shoulder straps on many packs can also be adjusted on the frame sheet to make the pack fit your torso better.

Some ultralight packs don't have load-lifter straps. If you get a good fit from the shoulder straps and you aren't carrying much weight, they're not strictly necessary.

HIP STABILIZER STRAPS: These are on the side of the hip belt. They connect the belt to the lower pack body. They keep it close to your body to prevent the pack's weight from swaying.

As with load-lifters, some ultralight packs don't have hip-belt stabilizer straps. If you get a good fit from the hip belt and aren't carrying much weight, they're not strictly necessary.

TRAUMA TIP

Unless on a trip where I think a lid will be worthwhile for convenience or some other reason, I find it is not worth the added weight for the space provided. Lids add zippers, buckles, and a bunch of fabric for a relatively small amount of useful space. I'd rather just have an ultralight stuff sack that I pack at the top of my top-loading backpack with the items I want handy—some snacks, extra maps if needed, and gloves or other items I might need to grab quickly.

STERNUM STRAP: This allows you to connect your shoulder straps across your chest, increasing the stability of the load. It helps you and your pack move as one. Don't overtighten the sternum strap. It can constrict your breathing, particularly when going up hills.

Photos by Russ Sackson

WEARING YOUR PACK

After shouldering your pack, in order to fit it properly, the straps should be put on and adjusted in the following order (bottom up):

1. Hip belt
2. Hip-belt stabilizer straps
3. Shoulder straps (beneath armpit)
4. Sternum strap
5. Load-lifter straps (cinched down but not cranked on)

HOW TO LOAD A BACKPACK

This is very important in order to get the most out of your backpack and keep it comfortable and. The comfort rating, or weight rating, is irrelevant if you do not pack it properly. If a pack is packed improperly, it will always be uncomfortable.

Always place heavy items against the pack's back (against the frame or hydration sleeve) and not on the outside of your pack. This helps keep the center of gravity close to your body and helps keep everything stable.

I pack like this:

1. I line my pack with a trash compactor bag or pack liner.
2. I stuff my sleeping bag and clothes I don't anticipate needing until camp into the bottom of the trash bag. (I don't use a compression sack because it adds weight, but some people like them.) I pack a roll-down DCF ultralight stuff sack for my sleeping bag and put this at the bottom also. If the trail section is longer than four days and I need to gain volume in my pack because of the amount of food I'm packing, I'll stuff my sleeping bag in the stuff sack. I then pack it inside the trash bag and against the back panel, filling the void in front and on the side with other clothes I will only need in camp.

3. I set aside my trail snacks and other food for the day, then drop my food bag on top of that.

4. I shove spare clothing around the front of the food bag to fill empty spaces in the pack.

5. I stuff my shelter on top of the food bag and put my pot and stove toward the front of the pack, at the same level as my shelter. I then roll my liner down to seal it.

6. I place my food for the day on top of everything so it's easily accessible during breaks. If my shelter is wet, I put all my food inside the liner bag and seal it. Then I stuff the shelter on top.

7. I'll fill outside pockets and my hip-belt pockets with my water bottle, water treatment, maps, sunscreen, bug repellent, a couple snack bars, a camera, and any other items I may need throughout the day at easy reach.

PACK COVERS

Pack covers are a lightweight fabric that is designed to cover your backpack in wet weather and keep your gear dry. Many people like them and consider them a necessity. I would rather let my pack get wet and just use a trash bag liner on the inside to keep my equipment dry. When your backpack gets wet it also gets heavier, since it is absorbing water. I would rather be 100 percent confident that my sleeping bag and insulation layers are not getting wet inside my backpack. If you are bushwhacking, a pack cover can get snagged on things and tear. It also has a tendency to accumulate water in the bottom.

BEAR CANISTERS

Bear canisters make packing your backpack a lot harder, since they never seem to fit well inside a pack. Here are a few tips for using them.

Photos by Russ Sackson

1. Always fill your canister to the max when it's in your pack. If you're running low on food, put other items in the canister to fill it. Don't waste space.

2. Put the canister where you normally put your food bag. It helps with weight distribution in your pack.

3. Pack things as tightly as you can around the canister to take up the dead space, since your backpack is not exactly cylindrical. This will keep the canister from shifting while you walk, keeping your pack more stable as well as preventing "pack on legs" syndrome, where your pack is huge vertically (so people can't actually see the person carrying the backpack except for his or her legs).

4. Remember to put any scented items in your bear canister at night. Bears are attracted to scented items like toothpaste and deodorant.

When you are planning to hike in a national park or wilderness area, make sure to research if a hard-sided bear canisters is required. This is becoming more and more common, and many places have specific instructions and details on what products can and can't be used to meet their requirements. Many locations don't accept the Ursack as an option, even though it is easier to pack.

TRAUMA TIP

Waterproof your pack for next to nothing in weight or cost: Line your pack with a plastic trash bag, trash compactor bag, or pack liner. Pack everything inside that to keep the interior waterproof and your gear dry. I use a trash compactor bag. It's thicker and more durable, even though it's a bit heavier. Make sure the seal is good by overlapping, rolling, or spinning and tucking (aka donkey tailing) in the top so no water can get in.

HIP-BELT POCKETS:
A nice feature that keeps a camera, energy bar, or Aquamira handy. Most packs without hip-belt pockets are designed to allow aftermarket pockets to be added on.

SIDE POCKETS (AKA WAND POCKETS): These are a staple on any pack I use. I like accessing my water bottle, maps, food, and water treatment easily, without taking off my pack. Stretchy side pockets are essential to me. Climbing packs don't have side pockets because climbers don't want things to fall out. I like the accessibility of side pockets. If you don't want to use them or it is raining, put everything inside the pack.

SHOVEL POCKET (ALSO CAN BE A FRONT MESH POCKET): Some people love having a shovel pocket and wouldn't buy a pack without it, while others couldn't care less. A lot of ultralight backpacks include it because Ray Jardine's original ultralight pack design had one. I think it's a handy feature, but I don't care too much if a pack doesn't have it.

If your pack does have a stretch shovel pocket on the back, you're generally sacrificing straps on the front of your pack for your sleeping pad or crampons. If you use an inflatable pad, it isn't a big issue because you can pack it in by the back panel. If you use a foamie (foam mattress) then the front of the pack is a nice place to carry it. When a shovel pocket doesn't have straps, you often end up attaching crampons or the foamie atop your pack and fumble with the mess every time you want to get into your pack.

Those are the trade-offs. Having that big stretch pocket to throw stuff in without opening your pack much during the day is handy. It's especially nice when you have wet stuff. You can throw whatever is wet on the outside in the shovel pocket so it doesn't contaminate your other stuff. If it's wet when you wake up, you can seal up your pack while in your shelter. When you're ready to go, you can throw the wet shelter in the shovel pocket so you don't have to open up the pack liner in the elements at all. Make sure the shovel pocket isn't too loose and floppy. It can suck back and hug into the pack. It can also snag on things and not carry itself well.

COMPRESSION: Compression is essential to stabilize the load in a pack and bring it closer to your body. The number of compression straps needed on a pack depends on its size. Compression straps are either webbing straps or LineLoc cord. LineLoc is much lighter, but it doesn't compress as broad an area as webbing. The LineLocs are easily changed if they break. Webbing is sewn into the pack and is a bit more difficult to change.

DAISY CHAIN: A daisy chain is a sewn-on piece of material, usually webbing, with loops for clipping or attaching things to the outside. They're a handy feature but not absolutely necessary. Usually there are plenty of other places on a pack for clipping extra stuff onto, so you don't really need a separate daisy chain.

HYDRATION PORT/HYDRATION COMPATIBLE: This is standard in modern packs. It's a system or sleeve that houses a hydration bladder and a port for a drinking tube. I don't like to use a hydration bladder for a number of reasons. I'll explain them later. Some hydration systems are easier to use than others.

If you are a fan of a hydration system, make sure the port for the tube is big enough to easily slide your drinking tube through. Make sure it is not a hassle to feed it through every time you fill up. That gets old fast. You can carefully cut out the material or port to widen it.

LID: Many people like having a pack lid to keep a lot of little things you might use on a hiking break handy. Lids are handy but they can often add about 10 ounces, almost the weight of a full can of soda, to the

pack's weight. If I get a pack with a lid, I want one that is removable. I often don't need the extra capacity or need to keep gear organized or handy in the lid. When I don't need it, I use the pack without the lid to save weight.

You can often use your lid as a hip pack or shoulder bag in town or when not on your backpack. I often use my lid like a messenger bag. Here's how to do it on many packs. Completely unclip the lid from the pack. On the underside of the lid there's often a pocket where extra webbing is hidden. This webbing is used for a shoulder or waist strap. Unclip the harness on the webbing and pull both sides out. (If a lid doesn't have this strap, it's often designed to be used with the pack's hip belt as a pack strap. Remove the hip belt and run it through the fabric or webbing on the lid's underside to create the day pack.) Flip the extra material, which connected the lid to the pack, over toward the lid's top and thread webbing through the ladder lock (loops) on the lid. You can use those straps to compress the bag.

SEAM-TAPED/WELDED/WATERPROOF PACKS:
Very few packs are seam taped and truly waterproof. Most packs are water resistant because they're made of waterproof materials. If the seams are not taped, the pack is not completely waterproof. Welded seams are more waterproof, but they make a pack more expensive and harder to repair.

If any of my gear is wet, I pack it outside the trash bag so it won't contaminate the rest of my stuff. Remember that your sleeping bag is your lifeline. It is the most important thing in your pack because it keeps you alive when you're cold and wet. Keeping wet stuff from my sleeping bag means my sleeping bag will always be dry.

OTHER POCKETS:
A lot of packs have pockets all around the pack. People love pockets! Pockets are a good way for people to organize their stuff. I think too many pockets are a hassle. They don't add any necessary function to the pack and make it heavier.

SLEEPING BAG COMPARTMENT:
Almost every pack used to have a zippered compartment at the bottom of the pack for a sleeping bag; today, just traditionally styled packs do. I think they're useless.

Sleeping bags have progressed so far that it's hard to fill the entire compartment with just your sleeping bag. As a result, the compartment makes it hard to pack a pack well, get things into all the pack's empty spaces, and waterproof a pack with just one garbage bag. Also the U-shaped zippers that kept the sleeping bag compartment closed are prone to blowing out.

HEAT-MOLDABLE HIP BELTS:
Some companies like Osprey offer customers a heat-moldable hip-belt system. Retail stores with Osprey packs usually have a little oven that they bake the hip belt in and then fit it to you. This technology came from ski boot liners. While it is essential to get a good fit on your hip belt, I think the heat-moldable hip belt is more of a sales gimmick than a necessity.

Hip belts will conform to your hips as you use them. It is like breaking in a pair of shoes; but, unlike shoes or boots, most hip belts are not uncomfortable out of the box. Maybe heat molding speeds up the break-in process (nice in ski boots because they can be so uncomfortable), but it also causes the foam to pack out in certain areas. That's usually what happens when you're fitted with a heated belt.

ICE-AX LOOPS:
There's usually at least one on every pack. For me this is a necessity. While it's important to carry an ice ax when you need one, it's more important to me to carry my trekking poles when it's raining. Stashing your poles when it's raining helps keep your hands warmer.

Ice ax loops are kind of counterintuitive. You feed the ax through the loops from the top, then flip them back up and strap them in.

PADDING:
In the race to lower pack weight, some companies have sacrificed padding in hip belts and lumbar pads. If you keep your pack weight low, this isn't an issue. Overloading a lightweight pack that has a minimalistic hip belt and lumbar pad can cause hot spots. When looking for a pack, be realistic about how much weight you plan to carry. You should be comfortable in your weighted pack when you are carrying it up to 10 or more hours a day. When lightening your load, the last piece of gear you should lighten is your backpack.

trail tested

From November 1, 2005, to October 23, 2006 (356 days) I hiked more than 10,000 miles. I averaged more than 26 miles per day for the entire trip. Equally as impressive to this personal accomplishment is that my pack lasted the entire trip! A little sun-faded and well-used, my pack was still completely functional after all of those miles. In comparison, I went through loads of other gear, including twenty-four pairs of shoes (as you can see from the picture with me standing next to all my worn-out equipment). This page has some pointers to help keep your backpack working for the long haul.

10 Tips to Make Your Pack Last Longer

TRAUMA PICK

Pack comfort is the most important thing for me. If my pack is uncomfortable, it makes the whole trip uncomfortable. The last place I want to cut weight is from my backpack. Once I know my other gear and expected food weight is light enough, I will downsize and choose a lighter pack. I'd much rather have a little heavier backpack and be comfortable than cut weight in the backpack prematurely.

Depending on where I'm headed. I typically choose a pack that is capable of carrying about four to five days' worth of food comfortably, for me usually around 3,200–3,600 cubic inches (about 45–55 liters). Since most of my pack weight is food and on most trails in the United States my average resupply time is four to five days (except the Appalachian Trail), this means my pack will be comfortable on the bulk of the trip. If the segment is longer than four to five days, I may be slightly out of the weight class of the backpack for a few days, but I am OK with that. I also don't mind carrying the extra weight of the pack that can support the 4- to 5-day load. I can easily carry an unframed pack for a 4- to 5-day stretch and be comfortable for three-season camping. A minimal frame or removable frame sheet is also a nice option.

For most trips, I like a lightweight pack that weighs less than 2.5 pounds and has side (wand) pockets so I can stash my water bottle, maps, water treatment, snacks, and a few other odds and ends. I also like a pack that has some sort of attachment system on the front or a big stretch pocket. These can come in handy for keeping your wet shelter on the outside of your pack or just making more items handy during the day.

RECOMMENDED PACKS: Volume depends on the trip, season, and distance between resupplies, but my go-tos are: Granite Gear Crown, Granite Gear Leopard (for trips with technical equipment), Granite Gear Virga, Mountain Laurel Designs, ULA, Gossamer Gear, and Z Packs (model preferences vary depending on capacity and needs for the trip).

1. Do not pack a backpack beyond its recommended weight limit.

2. Do not constantly stuff a backpack to its collar's capacity. The roll-top collar is intended to make a backpack more waterproof. If you find yourself constantly filling your pack to the collar's brim, you need to get a backpack with more volume.

3. Do not pack sharp, unprotected objects near the pack's fabric. They can pierce it.

4. Do not place objects tightly near the outside of the pack. If fabric on the outside of the pack is tight, it's being stretched. Stretched fabric is easier to rip.

5. Most backpacks are meant to stand upright when set down. The bottom of the backpack has the strongest fabric on the pack, and it's intended to take that wear. Do not sit on the pack when it's on the ground. It stretches and abrades the pack's fabric.

6. Do not force backpack zippers closed. If the zipper doesn't zip easily, readjust the contents of the backpack to allow the zipper to close easily.

7. Do not pack a backpack so there is anything protruding in the zipper's path. If an item creates an abnormal kink in the zipper, it's putting additional stress on the zipper. This can cause the zipper to fail.

8. Do not cross-load webbing straps with heavy objects. This pulls down at the seams where the webbing is sewn in and puts unnecessary stress on the seams.

9. If bushwhacking, do not lead with the backpack. It's not designed to be the first line of attack in shielding or protecting a backpacker from invasive materials.

10. There is no need to use excessive force when tightening compression straps. Doing so creates unnecessary stress on the seams. Tightening them loosely doesn't affect the pack's performance or shift or dislodge any packed items. By using loose yet secure methods in tightening the compression straps on a backpack, the seams last longer and wear much less over time.

TRAUMA
TIP

If you are going to purchase your first sleeping bag or only have one bag in your quiver, think about what time of year and where you will most likely be hiking. For most people a 20-degree bag is a good trade-off and a good temperature rating that will work most of the year. If you sleep warm and wear some clothes in the bag, you may be able to use a 30-degree bag as a three-season bag. A 30-degree sleeping bag is what I use the most.

SLEEPING BAGS

There is nothing like getting into your sleeping bag after a tough day on the trail. Get a sleeping bag that's right for you and right for the conditions you'll be in. Everybody sleeps differently and has different comfort levels. Here's what you need to know to choose a good bag.

FILL MATERIALS

DOWN: This is the fluffy under-plumage from a goose or duck. Down is a great insulator. Most down in outdoor gear is goose down because it has a higher fill power. Fill power is the number of cubic inches that 1 ounce of down will displace. The higher the fill power, the less down is needed to meet a given temperature rating.

The manufacturer needs less down to make a higher-fill-power sleeping bag, but the price will usually be higher. The higher the fill power, the less the bag will weigh. (Depending on their fill power, two different sleeping bag models with identical temperature ratings can have different weights.)

Down fill pros:

✓ Very light.

✓ Highly compressible.

✓ Durable.

✓ Breathable.

✓ Lasts a long time if you treat it right. The loft lasts longer than synthetic fill.

Down fill cons:

✗ Initially more expensive.

✗ When wet it loses loft and therefore its insulating properties. Most quality down bags will

Photos by Russ Sackson

have a nylon fabric with a durable water repellent (DWR) coating to help keep water out; the shell of a few bags is made of a completely waterproof, breathable membrane.

SYNTHETIC: There are many different brands of synthetic fill, however, they all fall under two main categories: short staple fills and continuous filament fills.

Short staple fills, like PrimaLoft, are the most common. They use densely packed strands of fine denier filaments to insulate. That means little fibers are packed together to create loft and insulation. The small filaments allow for a flexible and fairly compressible synthetic bag. However, the fibers break and lose performance easier.

Continuous filament fills, like Climashield, are typically stronger and more durable. They are made from thicker continuous fibers. Continuous-filament fills have a good loft, but because of that, they are less compressible.

Synthetic fill pros:

✓ Cheaper.

✓ Fill is very evenly distributed.

✓ Completely nonallergenic.

✓ Maintains some insulating properties even when wet.

Synthetic fill cons:

- x Heavier than down, lower warmth-to-weight ratio.
- x Less compressible.
- x Made out of polyester, petroleum-based, and less sustainable.
- x Usually doesn't last as long as down and doesn't fluff up as well.

TEMPERATURE RATINGS

Choose a sleeping bag rated for the coldest temperature you expect to encounter. There are a few ways to save weight and use a lighter-weight and warmer bag. The bad news is that ratings are usually subjective to the manufacturer.

However, the new European Norm (EN) is helping to standardize the rating system. Not many manufacturers have adopted it. Hopefully it will become more common, because traditionally a bag's temperature rating has been the lowest temperature at which the average sleeper is comfortable. This is tricky, because everybody sleeps differently and has different metabolic rates. I am a warm sleeper and have used a summer sleeping bag liner down to 15°F (not ideal, but it worked and I didn't freeze).

A QUICK NOTE ABOUT EN RATINGS:

EN/ISO ratings take into account that women sleep colder than men. There is a gender-specific rating specifying the lowest comfortable temperature that a standard man or woman would sleep comfortably. Keep in mind that the EN ratings take into consideration that the sleeper uses a sleeping pad and wears a base layer and a hat. As the system has become more popular, EN/ISO ratings have helped to standardize the temperature testing and ratings. One impediment is that it costs additional money to test bags with this system and all the ratings are certified by a third-party laboratory. That said, the system is used throughout Europe and catching on. There is hope for standardization.

Women usually sleep colder. And my friend and hiking partner on a few trips, Pepper, sleeps colder than a lot of women. On a few hikes I have used a 40°F sleeping bag comfortably while he was using a 20°F bag. Essentially, manufacturer's ratings are based on their own research and categorization. These numbers should be considered more of a guide than a guarantee.

SHAPE

The shape of a bag, as well as your shape, can affect how you sleep. Most high-quality sleeping bags for backpacking are mummy-shaped. Roomier mummy-shaped bags are sometimes referred to as semi-rectangular. Summer sleeping bags and a lot of low-performance bags are rectangular.

For the warmest and lightest sleep system, choose a mummy bag with narrower shoulder/hip specs, as long as you are going to be comfortable in the narrow space. If it feels too restrictive, you have a broad frame, or you are a restless sleeper, you might want a bag that's wider at the shoulder and hip. Keep in mind that larger bags are heavier.

CONSTRUCTION

Several techniques are used to make sleeping bags. All have the same goal: to maintain even distribution of the fill in order to prevent cold spots and drafts. Down bags generally use a baffle system, while synthetic bags use a shingle or layered system.

Down bags are sewn using two techniques:

1. The box technique is where each baffle is sewn like a three-dimensional rectangle before down is inserted. This allows room for the down without compressing it. This system is most often used on warmer sleeping bags.

Photos top and bottom left by Russ Sackson; top right courtesy Montbell

FOR BEST LOFT / INSULATION:
If you can, unpack your sleeping bag when you first stop for the night instead of waiting until getting ready to sleep. The bag has time to decompress, adding more loft. If it's nice out during the day, air out your sleeping bag during hiking breaks in the day. This will help keep it dry and lofty when you need it later. Some newer sleeping bags are also baffleless. This allows you to better "control" where the down is. After your bag "puffs up" for the night, you can shake more down into the top of the bag to provide extra warmth, since the bottom of the bag is getting compressed anyway.

Drying my gear and soaking up sun during a break after a couple of wet days

2. The sewn-through technique is often used in ultralight and warm-weather bags. It helps save weight because there isn't as much down in warmer bags and you don't need four sides on each baffle. There can be some cold spots at the sewn areas though, because there often isn't much room for down there.

Synthetic bags are usually sewn with one of two techniques:

1. The shingles technique uses sheets or pieces of fill overlapped like shingles on a roof. These are stitched to both the outside and lining of the bag.

2. The layered technique has two offset layers: one sewn to the outside shell and the other to the inner lining. With two offset layers of continuous insulation, it reduces cold spots at the seams.

Other sewing techniques used in sleeping bags include quilted-through sewing and welded seams. Quilted through is cheap and used on warm-weather bags, since all the layers are sewn into one seam. When everything is sewn into one seam, it's more susceptible to cold spots.

There are also a few bags on the market with welded seams. They're not sewn through at all, which helps reduce the potential for drafts and fill loss through the needle holes. Many have a laminated waterproof outer material. These bags can be very pricey.

SHELL AND LINING

The outer shell of most sleeping bags is made of ripstop nylon. Most high-quality bags also have an outer shell treated with a durable water repellent (DWR). DWR helps keep the insulation from getting wet. There is no DWR finish on the inner lining, because such a sleeping bag would get really clammy when you are inside of it.

DownTek and DriDown:

Some manufacturers are now purchasing hydrophobic down for their products. This down is treated with a water-repellent coating. The companies making the hydrophobic down are trademarked under DownTek and DriDown. These are relatively new products. If it is one of your concerns, they seemingly take some of the fear factor away from getting your down jacket or sleeping bag wet. The treated down will still lose some of its loft, but it will be similar to synthetic insulation, where it still retains some of its capabilities to insulate.

If these work like the advertising says, it ameliorates a major concern when using down. However, I am comfortable with my capabilities to not get my sleeping bag or down insulation layer wet. So from my perspective, this is not something I would specifically seek out. If it came with a product I wanted anyway, at a minimal increased cost, then I would use it. Also, being that the products are relatively new, I don't know how the added coating onto fairly fragile down filaments will affect their durability and the loft over the long term. Nor do we fully comprehend the environmental impacts of the nanoparticles, like many nanotechnologies becoming more prevalent inside and outside the outdoor industry.

WOMEN'S BAGS

These bags are cut to fit a woman's body shape. Here are the main differences:

- Shorter in length.
- Narrower at the shoulders.
- Wider proportionally at the hips.
- Some have extra insulation in the upper body and/or foot-box.
- Sleeping bag sizing.

Other Sleeping Bag Types

BOTTOMLESS: A full sleeping bag but has only fabric on the bottom. Instead of insulation in the bottom, many have a built-in sleeve to put your sleeping bad in, since the compressed insulation will not provide warmth anyway. Big Agnes has a number of models designed this way.

QUILTS: Quilts cut out even more material than the bottomless system mentioned above by having no material between you and the pad. Some quilts have a strap system to help keep the quilt tight around you in case the temperature is close to the quilt's cold temperature rating.

Bottomless bag pros:

✓ Quilts weigh less than regular sleeping bags.

✓ Big Agnes models have a sleeve on the bottom instead of insulation so your sleeping pad can slide right in and always be on the bottom.

Bottomless bag cons:

x They can be drafty or have cold spots, especially if it's windy.

x If you roll around while you sleep, you will feel those drafts.

ROOM FOR TWO: Many bags can be zipped together so couples can sleep together. This usually creates more airspace in a sleeping bag, so it isn't nearly as warm. You can also zip together bags of different temperature ratings if one person sleeps colder than the other. Bags can join together if:

- One bag has a right-hand zipper (bag opens on the right when lying on your back inside the bag) and the other a left-hand zipper.

- The zippers are the same size. Most sleeping bag makers use a number 5 or 8 zipper for sleeping bags.

- Zipper lengths are compatible (i.e., both are full-length or half-length zippers).

- If you want to zip bags together, it usually makes it easier if both bags are from the same manufacturer.

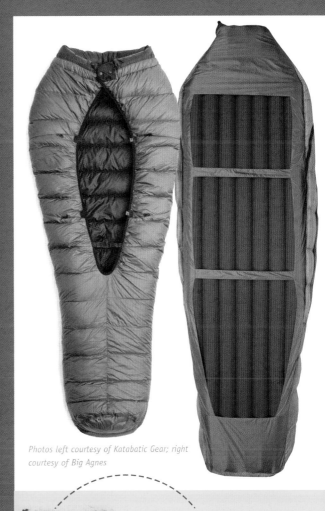

Photos left courtesy of Katabatic Gear; right courtesy of Big Agnes

TRAUMA TIP

TIPS TO STAY WARM: To stay warm at night, pee first. I am not sure why, but it helps. Maybe it's because you don't have to expend energy warming urine in your bladder through the night. It can also help to boil some water, put it in your water bottle, and put the warmed bottle between your legs in your sleeping bag. The warm bottle helps warm up blood headed to your feet. It can also help to eat something, like a couple spoonfuls of peanut butter, to give your body some calories to use to heat your body. Also make sure to use the drawstrings provided in the sleeping bag. Cinch the hood and draft collar up to prevent the cold air from getting in.

Sleeping Bag Features

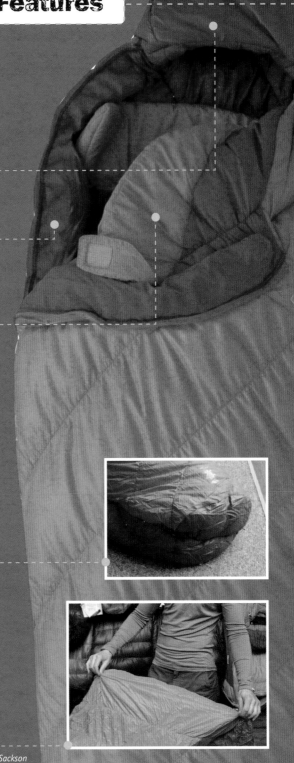

HOODS: A hood on a good mummy bag is integrated and essential. You will lose a lot of body heat without a hood. Only summer and warm-weather sleeping bags don't need a hood. All hoods should have drawstrings or a cinching system so you can tighten it down and have it snug around your head and face if it gets chilly.

DRAFT TUBE: This is crucial in any non-summer sleeping bag. This insulation-filled baffle runs along the inside of the zipper, covering it, to prevent drafts passing through zipper teeth or coils.

DRAFT COLLAR: This insulation-filled baffle forms a yoke around the collar of the bag. It sits atop the shoulders and neck to help prevent heat from escaping from the bag. It's usually on bags intended for below-freezing conditions.

STASH POCKET: Some sleeping bags may have a little pocket to keep a headlamp or glasses. They are great for utility, not so great if you roll around while you sleep.

PAD LOOPS: Some bags and quilts, like Big Agnes bags, have loops or a sleeve along the bottom to secure the sleeping pad to the bag so you won't roll off it.

TRAPEZOIDAL FOOT-BOX: If you sleep on your back, you might be interested in this. Most foot-boxes are shaped flatter. The trapezoidal foot-box is designed so that your feet can flop out anatomically while you're sleeping. It's not an issue if you sleep on your side or stomach.

SLEEPING BAG STRETCH: Montbell has historically used a patented stretch system in their sleeping bags. This is a nice feature that allows a bit more movement and is form fitting to your sleeping bag. Sierra Designs has licensed the first iteration of this stretch system, and Montbell uses a newer design.

BAFFLELESS SLEEPING BAG: Allows you to move the down around to provide more or less warmth and also prevents cold spots by reducing seams and pockets from stitching that didn't have down in them.

Photos by Russ Sackson

SLEEPING BAG LINERS

Sleeping bag liners have a few uses. First, they help keep your sleeping bag cleaner. You can wash bags less, which probably helps them last longer. Second, liners often add between 5 to 15 degrees of warmth to your sleeping system.

Some liners claim to add 25 degrees of warmth, but it depends on what they are made of. You can sleep in just a sleeping bag liner in hot weather, which gives your sleeping system more flexibility. Rectangular sleeping bag liners sometimes are called travel sheets.

Popular types of sleep liners:

SILK: This is the lightest-weight and most compact. Silk insulates in cold weather and breathes and absorbs moisture in warm weather. It's generally expensive.

COTTON: Cotton is durable and absorbs moisture well. It also takes longer to dry. It is not very lightweight or compact. It is reasonably priced.

FLEECE AND MICROFLEECE: Warmer option and moisture wicking. However, it's usually heavier and not very compact. Moderately priced.

SYNTHETICS (COOLMAX AND MTS): Moisture wicking and breathable. Moderately priced.

INSULATED (THERMOLITE REACTOR EXTREME): This liner can make your sleeping system 25 degrees warmer. Dries faster than cotton. Price ranges from moderate to expensive.

VAPOR BARRIER LINER: VBLs are used in the winter or extreme cold conditions. A vapor barrier liner adds some warmth to the sleeping system. Such liners prevent your sleeping bag from "wetting out." When camping in a cold climate, your body emits moisture and heat that will hit its dew point somewhere within the loft of your sleeping bag. If the weather is cold enough and you can't dry your sleeping bag during the day, use a VBL to prevent moisture from building up in your bag. It can

lose a little of its insulating ability every day—and get heavier. Sleeping in a VBL can get clammy, but it is sometimes a necessary evil.

POST-TRIP SLEEPING BAG CARE

STORAGE: Never store your sleeping bag in a compressed compression sack. Most high-quality sleeping bags come with a larger cotton bag for storage. Use that bag so the sleeping bag isn't compressed at all. Storing it compressed ruins the sleeping bag's loft and drastically reduces its lifespan.

When you return home from using your sleeping bag, lay it out or hang it up for a day or two. Flip it over, turn the foot-box inside out, and make sure it is completely dry before you pack it up and store it.

Use the included cotton stuff sack or a different large cotton sack, since it will breathe and allow your bag to stay lofted. Don't use any sort of waterproof or non-breathable sack, which can trap moisture or condensation and possibly lead to mildew.

CLEANING: Don't dry-clean a sleeping bag. This can damage the down or synthetic fill and ruin the loft.

When cleaning, use a down-cleaner soap (for example, Gear Aid's ReviveX Down Cleaner), available online or at a local gear shop. This is a very gentle, non-detergent soap that helps the down maintain the oils that help it keep its loft. It cleans well without damaging your sleeping bag.

Always use a front-loading washer when washing a sleeping bag. It helps to maintain the quality of the insulation without breaking it apart. NEVER use a top-loading washer or a washer with an agitator. Use the gentle cycle and cold water.

Some people prefer to hand-wash their sleeping bag in the bathtub. I have had good luck with front-loading washers. If you're a hand-washing aficionado, you should still use the down cleaner and cool water. Rinse the bag well to ensure all the soap is gone.

Air-dry your bag (which takes a long time), or use a front-loading dryer. If you use a dryer, use very low heat or no heat. You don't want to melt the nylon or get the insulation too warm. I have had good luck adding a tennis ball or two to the dryer while the bag is drying. This helps un-clump the insulation and re-loft the bag.

SLEEPING BAG MAINTENANCE

RESTORING DWR FINISH: The durable water repellent (DWR) finish on a sleeping bag will wear off over time. This is pretty easy to restore with a standard DWR treatment like ReviveX Down Cleaner by Gear Aid.

TREATING LEAKING DOWN: All bags will lose a few feathers here and there. Most manufacturers use a tightly woven material for the shell or a down-proof liner to help prevent this. But it is inevitable that a bag will lose a few feathers. Sometimes they're lost at the seams; other times the quills poke through the shell or liner. If this is happening, try to grab the feather through the opposite side of the sleeping bag and pull it back

TRAUMA TIP

If you need more space in your pack, keep your sleeping bag in a stuff sack or compression sack. Over time, this can reduce loft in a bag. I try to avoid using a sack for my bag when I can. I just push it down into my pack's garbage-bag lining, pushing it into the bottom, where it helps fill in all the bottom corners of the pack so there is no dead space.

Photo by Russ Sackson

in to the bag. The hole should be small and close up after the feather is pulled back through. If you can't do that, the feather is destined to come out. A few feathers won't affect the bag's performance. If you're losing feathers because of a rip in the shell material, you need to patch it.

TREATING FABRIC TEARS: If you are out camping or hiking, use a patch of nylon repair tape or some Tenacious Tape by Gear Aid. I carry a little bit of Tenacious Tape and duct tape. The Tenacious Tape works really well for gear repairs. It sticks amazingly well and comes off without leaving any residue, unlike duct tape.

BROKEN ZIPPER: It is easy to replace a slider. If the coil is damaged, the repair becomes more complicated. Getting it professionally done by a gear repair service or tailor is recommended, because the whole coil must be removed and replaced with another. It is hard to do unless you're a regular Betsy Ross.

TO REPLACE THE ZIPPER SLIDER: Get a slider that matches the one you are removing. Letters printed on the slider tell you the size you need. If the stop and end are sewn into the bag, use a seam ripper to carefully remove stitching around the lower ends of the zipper tabs. When the zipper's end is visible, pry off the metal stop at the bottom of the zipper. Take care not to tear the tape at the base of the zipper teeth, because it can unravel.

With the stop off, slide the old zipper slider off. Take the new zipper slider and guide it onto the track tape (the coils or teeth). Start on the side

the stop was on, if applicable. If there was a stop, replace it, then feed the opposite track tape in and test the zipper. If the stop was just sewn in, insert both track tapes into the top grooves of the slider, pushing them through to the slider's bottom. Use a pin if needed to work the track tapes through. Pull tapes gently to make sure the slider is sitting evenly on tracks. With both tapes threaded through the slider, gently pull it up until the locked track teeth appear at the bottom. Make sure they track evenly.

If the metal zipper ends were sewn into the bag itself, sew a new stop at the top of the tracks with needle and thread. Sew the zipper back into the sleeping bag, following the guidelines of needle holes left from where stitching was removed for repair.

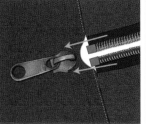
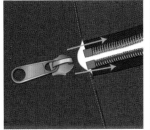
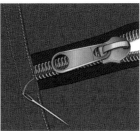

Illustrations courtesy of Gear Aid

Pepper eating dinner on an unnamed pass at the head of Moody Canyon, Utah, on the Hayduke Trail. What's the best thing about the end of a day of hiking? Eating dinner, getting in your sleeping bag, going to sleep, waking up, and eating again!

My sleep system

TRAUMA TIP

Pillows in the wild: Some companies make inflatable pillows. I believe this is a completely unnecessary purchase. It just adds extra weight and takes up space in your pack. Use your sleeping bag stuff sack or another sack as a pillow at night. Fill it with extra clothes. If you use a hydration bladder, you can add extra air and place it under your sleeping bag as another pillow option.

SLEEPING PADS

Sleeping pads are a critical component to most camping trips, except in the height of summer. They help with comfort, cushioning, and insulation. A sleeping pad keeps you from losing a lot of body heat to the ground. If you don't use one, you will get chilled, no matter how warm a sleeping bag you are using. The sleeping bag's loft will get compressed underneath you, reducing its ability to insulate you, and the ground will steal all your body heat.

R-VALUE

This is the measure of a pad's insulative properties. The higher the R-value number, the more insulating it is, and the warmer you will sleep.

SHAPE

Pads have different shapes. The most common shapes are mummy (contoured to your body's shape) or rectangular. The mummy pad shape helps cut down on extra material and saves weight. The type of sleeper you are (back, side, frequent roller, etc.) determines what shape and thickness of a pad you will want.

SLEEPING PAD CONSIDERATIONS

My friend Squeaky prefers a tent and full-length sleeping pad, despite the weight both add to his pack. He says the weight is worth it because the most important thing for him is getting a good night's sleep so he feels rested the next day.

Pepper doesn't like to go too short with a pad and prefers a three-quarter-length sleeping pad. I'll sleep anywhere. I use an extra small pad. Another buddy, Scott, uses a paper-thin foamie (foam mattress pad).

SLEEPING PAD TYPES

SELF-INFLATING PADS: These are pretty popular. They're usually made from open-cell foam that's sealed inside an airtight, waterproof nylon shell.

Self-inflating pad pros:
- ✓ Comfortable.
- ✓ Insulates you from the ground (good R-value).
- ✓ Adjustable firmness.
- ✓ Compact and very packable when not inflated.

Self-inflating pad cons:
- ✗ Typically heavier than foam pads of the same size.
- ✗ More expensive.
- ✗ Can puncture, but repairs aren't difficult.

BACKPACKING AIR PADS: Air pads use air for comfort and have to be blown up. Sometimes they have some foam or insulation incorporated into the pad for extra warmth.

Air pad pros:
- ✓ Comfortable.
- ✓ Compact when packed.

Air pad cons:
- ✗ Can puncture, but repairs aren't difficult.
- ✗ Can require a lot of air to blow them up.
- ✗ If uninsulated, they're not as warm as other pads.

FOAM PADS: Basic pads made of closed-cell foam.

Foam pad pros:
- ✓ Weight varies depending on size and thickness but can be very lightweight and the lightest pad system.
- ✓ Inexpensive.
- ✓ Durable.
- ✓ Good insulation.

Foam pad cons:
- ✗ Not as comfortable.
- ✗ Not as packable.

AIR MATTRESSES: These are way too big for backpacking. Air-filled mattresses are usually the size of a regular bed. They're mainly for car camping or visiting guests.

Air mattress pros:
- ✓ Very comfortable.

Air mattress cons:
- ✗ Heavy and bulky.
- ✗ Pump required to inflate.
- ✗ Can puncture or leak.
- ✗ No insulation in the mattress.

TRAUMA PICK

I like to use a small or extra-small inflatable sleeping pad, with an inch or so of inflation. This is enough to keep me comfortable without lifting my body too high off the ground. It packs down small and is lightweight. I like to fill my pack with my food and use that as the lower half of my sleeping pad. I sleep on my side most of the night so a relatively narrow pad works well for me.

RECOMMENDED PADS: Thermarest Pro-Lite XS or NeoAir UberLite for three-season use, Thermarest XTherm for winter use

Hiking above the clouds on Mount Kenya, Kenya

Cooking dinner and enjoying some downtime before bed. I love sandy campsites and decomposed granite. They offer great sleeping conditions and are gentle on the floor of your tent or groundsheet.

TENTS

TRAUMA TIP

FIRST-TIME SETUP: Whenever you get a new tent or shelter, take your shelter out of the stuff sack it is packaged in and check it out before you head out on a trip. Set it up at least once before you head out so you are familiar with the setup and can do it quickly if needed. If you don't, it's sure to be windy or raining and dark when you need to set it up the first time.

Also streamline what was packed in the stuff sack. There are usually some things in the stuff sack that you don't need to carry in your backpack. By setting up your tent, you can also check the seams to see if they are taped with waterproof tape. Sometimes I will seam seal a brand-new shelter before I head out on a trip. I also get my guylines ready and cut to size. This way I know my shelter is ready to roll and should hold up in any condition.

A dry run testing out a new tent   *Photo by Russ Sackson*

AND SHELTERS

Your choice of shelter is a personal preference more than any other gear. It will vary depending on where and when you are hiking.

CHOOSING A TENT OR SHELTER

Key factors to consider when buying a shelter are:

- The conditions and seasons when you plan to camp.
- The weight of the shelter. Tent weight varies by features. A typical one-person tent now weighs 2 to 3 pounds but can be lighter. A typical two-person tent can range from 3 to 4 pounds. Other shelter options are available and weigh anywhere from a few ounces to a couple pounds—in case you are interested in alternative ultralight shelters.
- The amount of usable space in the tent and the amount of space you need.
- Ease and speed of setup. When you want your shelter the most, you will often be wet and cold and may have lost some dexterity in your fingers. Can you still set up the shelter quickly so you don't get hypothermic—or eaten alive by mosquitoes?
- How many people will usually sleep in the tent? Are you hiking with other people? Do you want to share a shelter or have your own?

Most people will buy a three-season shelter, but four-season shelters are also available. The only major differences with a four-season shelter are:

- They are burlier and stand up to harsher conditions like heavy snow.
- They weigh more than a three-season tent.
- They usually have less ventilation, with a longer rainfly that extends closer to the ground to protect you from the elements. However, experienced thru-hikers will use most ultralight shelters for three seasons and maybe even the winter.

Choose a tent for the conditions you expect to encounter. For example, if you expect to hike in warm, humid weather where it could rain a lot, find a shelter with good ventilation to prevent condensation. A shelter with a lot of mesh panels or other ventilation options is better adapted for that climate. An open-air shelter would not be ideal in this climate, since you're likely to encounter mosquitoes, blackflies, or no-see-ums.

As you camp more, you may want different shelter systems for the different conditions and trips you take. For instance, I have an ultralight one-person tent and a tarp system. Depending on where I'm headed and when, I choose the best shelter for the trip. Before I hike, I research the temperatures and weather conditions I'm likely to encounter—including wind, rain, snow, humidity, bugs, shade, tree cover, where my route is going, and whether I'll be in alpine areas, in forest or open country, or meadows.

INTERIOR SPACE/TENT SIZE: Get a tent that fits you without sacrificing too much comfort. After all, you may be in there for hours—or even all day—if the weather is bad. Remember, the bigger the tent, the heavier it is. Balance comfort with weight, and only get what you need. Vestibule size is important too. It can accommodate wet stuff, shoes, maybe even your pack and a few other things. You don't need extra interior space for that stuff.

Consider how many people you're likely to camp with. If it's just you and your significant other, get a two-person or even a three-person tent. You can always split the weight by having one person carry poles and stakes and the other carry the tent. One person can carry the whole shelter system and the other the kitchen.

Tent sizes are not standardized in the industry. Like warmth ratings on sleeping bags, what each manufacturer calls a one-person or two-person tent is up to them. Most companies assume people want a smaller tent to minimize weight. Look for dimensions that fit you and your group's needs. If you're 6'6" and the tent is only 6 feet long, you'll want to consider other options. Most companies figure a two-person tent has to fit two sleeping pads side by side and more sleeping pads for larger tents.

Another consideration is being able to sit upright in your tent. You'll usually be lying down in your tent, but sometimes it's nice to sit up to change clothes. It is also beneficial if you get stuck in the tent all day or have to wait for your food to finish cooking in bad weather. Many tents shave some weight by slanting the roof from the tent's high point or by lowering the high point of the tent so more of it can be at the same height.

Getting organized at camp in the Himalayas. Don't be scared to camp on snow. It often offers comfortable, low-impact camping. If there's just a little snow on the ground, brush the area off before you set up your shelter. If there is snowpack, pack it down and set your tent up on top of it.

Manufacturers usually offer three dimensions to help people comparison shop: floor dimensions, floor area in square feet, and peak height. These help give you an idea of the space in the tent, but they don't really tell you much about its layout and design. A wedge-shaped tent has little space at the foot end of the tent. The dimensions won't detail how steep a tent's walls are either.

TENT DIMENSIONS: Tents usually aren't perfectly square or rectangular. This specification shows a tent's length and width measurements at their longest points. Tents are usually about 84 inches long. This is just enough for a 6'0" person. They might hit the foot and head of the tent a little because the walls slope in. Some companies offer longer and wider tents for taller people.

FLOOR AREA IN SQUARE FEET: Two tents can be said to have the same floor dimensions but still have different square footage, oddly enough. The tent with the smaller square footage usually tapers more toward the foot area. This is also true for the square footage of vestibules. This figure is a measure of the total footprint of the tent. It doesn't factor in the slope of the walls and actual usable area.

PEAK HEIGHT: Peak height is measured at the highest spot inside the tent. It usually considers that a person's head is round. Peak height is therefore measured around an 8-inch-diameter ball. This translates into the useful peak height, even though some tents may still have a higher point. Peak height does not factor in the slope of the walls or any other figures for the tent's size.

All of these numbers give you a good base for comparison. However, nothing is quite as good as seeing the tents in person. Look at how they're set up, and sit in them to truly gauge their comfort.

Shop around. Read user and online reviews. Do not rely on just magazine reviews. Get a good look at numerous designs, compare the weights, and test them out in person. All of this will ensure you've got the right tent for you.

MINIMUM WEIGHT: This is the total weight of the tent, the body, rainfly, and poles. This is the tent's essentials, minus stakes. This makes up the weight of what you will be carrying. When comparing tents, I'd recommend using this figure for comparison.

PACKED WEIGHT: This is the weight of everything packaged with the tent when you get it from the store. You can disregard this number, because chances are you're not carrying everything that comes with the tent on your hike. The package weight includes the instruction manual, a replacement pole segment, and other things you may not carry on your trek.

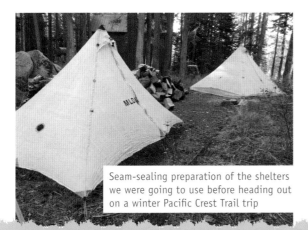
Seam-sealing preparation of the shelters we were going to use before heading out on a winter Pacific Crest Trail trip

PACKED SIZE: This is the manufacturer's figure for the amount of space the tent and components will take up in your pack. It's not important.

TENT FEATURES

Terms and information you should be familiar with to find the best tent or shelter for your needs:

STAKES: All tents come with stakes. These stakes are never the lightest-weight ones on the market. There are tons of different-shaped stakes. Most shelters take about six stakes. If you really want to set it up stout, bring and guy it out, you may need to bring a couple more. I usually carry six ultralight titanium stakes and then two others—regular stakes that came with my shelter that are shaped differently. If a certain stake shape isn't working with the ground, I have options and a few extras.

GEAR LOFT: A mesh "shelf" that attaches inside a tent's top. This is not mandatory, but it's helpful on certain trips. It's a great place to hang damp gear to dry at night. It could be helpful for winter camping and overnight ski touring trips.

POCKETS: Some tents have sleeves or interior stash pockets for glasses, headlamps, books, or other things. You can find things easily in the dark, and they won't clutter your tent. Ultralight tents don't have pockets in order to save weight. I don't think there is any need for pockets. I usually just put my hat or visor on the side of the tent and keep all of my things in the hat.

VENTILATION: Ventilation can be key to comfort depending on where and when you are hiking. On a humid or cold night, moisture can build up on the inside of the tent. If enough builds up, it can form drops big enough to fall on you—not ideal. In some conditions condensation is inevitable, but tents with good ventilation can help prevent it.

VENTED RAINFLIES: Some tents, mostly four-season tents, have some type of rainfly vent. This is

Photos by Russ Sackson

known as a chimney vent. It helps a little in rainy, humid weather and on cold winter nights. I think you will still get a lot of condensation with these.

VESTIBULE: The area the rainfly covers that isn't part of your sleeping area. Vestibules are handy for cooking, storing wet gear, shoes, or even your dog. It's nice to have at least some sort of vestibule on a tent.

MESH PANELS: Some tents have a lot of mesh panels; some don't. It's a personal preference. Mesh helps ventilate the tent so condensation collects on the fly instead of the interior. Mesh is also nice for stargazing if you don't set up the rainfly. The biggest benefit of mesh is keeping bugs out.

Remember that mesh weighs more than lightweight nylon and can actually increase tent weight over tents with less mesh. Mesh can also let in spindrift (blowing snow) or sand if you're in those conditions.

DOORS: Some tents have side doors; others, front doors. Some two-person tents have two doors, one on each side. This is a little more convenient, so you don't have to wake your partner if you have to go outside at night. Then again, who isn't going to wake up in a tent when someone gets up and unzips the door? Two doors also help with cross ventilation. In a tent you will get some airflow no matter what. That being said, if you are watching your pack weight, don't get a tent with two doors. It adds a fair amount of weight and isn't really necessary.

POLES: Most backpacking tent poles are made of aluminum. Aluminum poles are good because they are durable and have a high strength-to-weight ratio. All aluminum poles are anodized in order to resist corrosion and make them more durable. Aluminum poles are also made with various grades of aluminum, from 1000 series to 9000 series. The series depends on the alloys used in the aluminum. The alloy plays a key role in the strength and durability of the compound. The 6000 and 7000 series poles are standard. The 7000 series aluminum is the standard for high-end tents. The DAC Featherlite NSL poles use a very high-grade aluminum that is used in airplanes. It is strong, flexible, and lightweight.

POLE SLEEVES/POLE CLIPS: Most tents use a clip system to connect the poles to the tent body. It is much lighter than a fabric sleeve, which most tents used in the past. Some cheaper tents still use a sleeve, but in my opinion, sleeves are just a pain to deal with and add unnecessary weight. The clips create a larger airspace between the tent and the fly, increasing ventilation and minimizing condensation.

POLE HUBS: Pole hubs are a great addition to pole technology. The pole hub has led to many new developments in tents. It is a connector that allows one pole to do the work of multiple poles. It helps with organization, speeds and eases setup, and makes for a lighter-weight tent.

Setting up in a bitter, cold gale-force wind in the Indian Himalayas

Unexpected company at my campsite in the Indian Himalayas

Photo by Russ Sackson

GUY-OUT POINTS: Guy-out points are reinforced spots on a tent or tarp where you can attach a cord (guyline) to keep the tent taut. In tents with rain-flies, it keeps the fly from sagging into the interior, which helps prevent condensation by improving ventilation. Guylines also help keep a tent tight during wind and snow.

Some tents have guylines with reflective material. It's a little bonus so you don't kick or trip over the line at night.

FOOTPRINTS: A piece of material to protect the base of a tent. Most tent brands sell this as an accessory. You can make your own easily. Either way, make sure the footprint matches the exact dimensions of the tent floor—or is even smaller. Any bigger and it can draw water under the tent's floor when it's raining. One side is coated with a waterproof treatment. It's usually the shinier side of the material. Place that side up. It will make the footprint wear better and stay waterproof longer.

You don't need a footprint if you carefully choose your campsite and clean it before setting up your tent. A footprint just adds weight to your pack.

FLY/FOOTPRINT OPTION/QUICK SETUP: Some tents have a fast setup option. With these you use tent poles and the vestibule or rainfly to set it up first. This shelters you while you put the rest together underneath. I have tents with this feature but have never actually had to use it. The one advantage of doing this would be if it was raining. Then you could set it up quick and get under it easily. Once set up, you can hook up the interior of the tent from underneath the fly. You might be able to keep the interior of your tent from getting wet.

If it's a quick-setup rainfly, you can save weight by not carrying the tent interior. I think this feature is pointless. If you aren't going to set up the tent interior for bug protection, why not just use a tarp?

SHELTER COLOR: Color greatly affects the sales of a tent. If a company uses the right colors, a tent often sells well, despite if it's a good or bad shelter. But the shelter color can have a greater impact than most people think.

Lighter shelter colors allow morning sun to enter and light it up. Dark shelter colors block more sun, keeping the interior darker but heating it up. Dark colors fade faster and are more likely to suffer from ultraviolet damage, especially if a tent is often left up during the day.

Earth-toned tents blend into the landscape and aren't as intrusive to other people in the backcountry. Brightly colored tents can be an eyesore.

If camping in remote areas, though, they can help rescue crews find you.

My personal preference is a tent or shelter that isn't overly bright. I don't like obtrusive color. I would rather blend into the surroundings so that my tent doesn't affect other people's scenery or detract from the natural setting. Also, I often have to throw up my shelter in less than ideal places, called stealth camping. Whether it be near a road, dirt road, or near private property, I would rather be more inconspicuous. However, I will not choose my shelter based on the color. The most important things are the shelter design and functionality.

FREESTANDING: There are some technicalities, and people always argue about the definition of a freestanding tent. It is a tent that can stand on its own and doesn't necessarily need to be staked out. This is usually because the tent pole provides enough support. Just because a tent is freestanding doesn't mean you will not need to or want to stake or guy it out. It just means that if you are throwing it up really fast to get some peace of mind at lunch on a buggy day, you won't need to put the stakes in. A freestanding tent is very nice for some trips and conditions. If the soil is really rocky or you are camped on smooth rock, and it isn't bad

A freestanding tent *Photo courtesy of Montbell*

weather or windy, you might not have to deal with driving stakes in or piling rocks onto guylines.

ULTRALIGHT/MINIMALIST TENTS AND SHELTERS

Some people think ultralight or minimalist shelters are just for serious ounce and gram counters. I think the variety of minimal and ultralight shelters available these days meets almost everybody's needs and wants.

There aren't many reasons not to get an ultralight or lightweight shelter. Many tent designs are similar to mainstream tents, just lighter. Ultralight shelters typically save weight by using lightweight fabrics—usually a lower-denier nylon. The tent may be a little more expensive and slightly less durable, but if you take care of your equipment, it shouldn't make a difference.

When using an ultralight tent, try to choose a good campsite. I usually use an ultralight tent when I don't use a tarp. Typically I'll use a form of the Big Agnes Fly Creek 1. I never use a footprint, and I have never ripped the floor of the tent. If you choose a good campsite and clear rocks, pine needles and cones, and other sharp objects, you should have no problems.

SINGLE-WALL TENTS: Most tents are double-walled. They have an interior body and a separate rainfly. Single-wall tents consist of a waterproof main body, so you don't need a separate rainfly.

Single-wall tent pros:

✓ Often lighter than double-walled tents.

Single-wall tent cons:

x When not designed with adequate ventilation, condensation can be a problem, particularly in humidity or cold weather.

Using a Mountain Laurel Designs ultralight tepee tent in the Nepalese Himalayas—saving weight and staying dry in the biggest mountains in the world
Photo by Shawn Forry

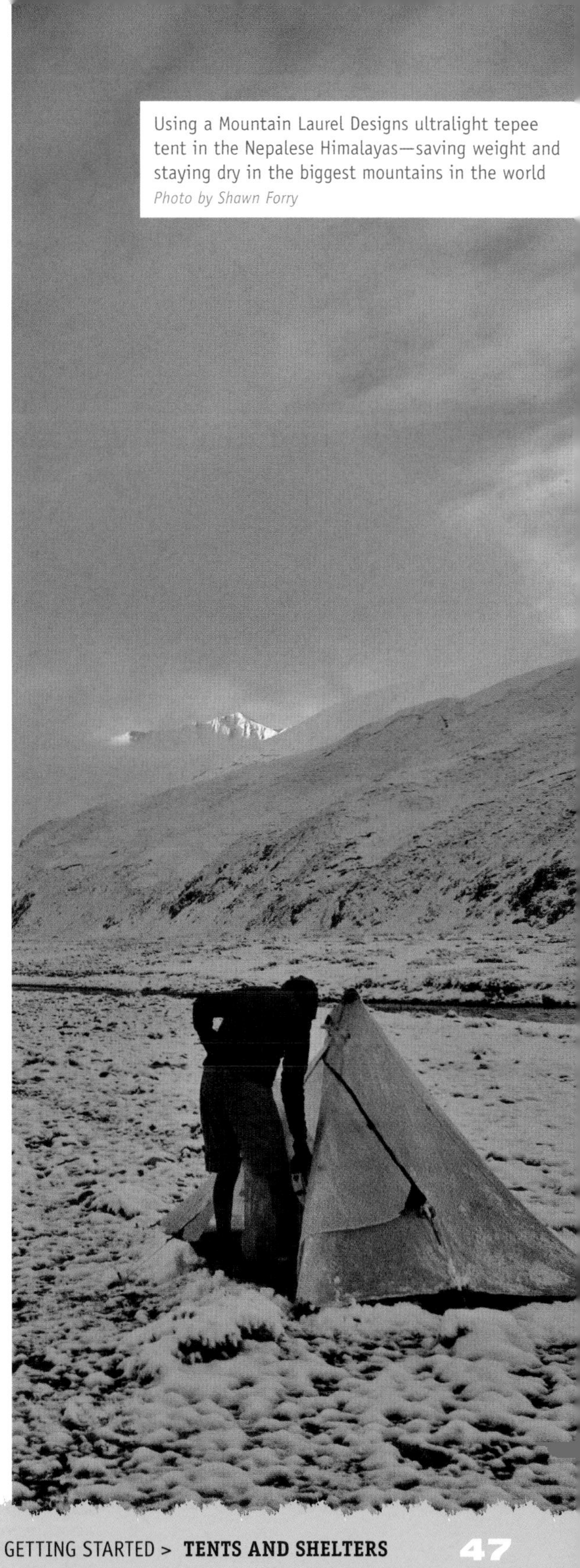

HYBRID TENTS: A cross between a single-wall and double-wall tent, a single-walled tent with double walls at the vestibule and foot ends with a mesh interior. It helps ventilate the tent and reduce condensation.

Hybrid pros:

✓ Can be lighter than a double-wall tent.

Hybrid cons:

x Likely to allow more condensation than a double-wall tent, an issue in humid climates.

TARPS, TARP SHELTERS, AND FLOORLESS TENTS: Tarps are basically a piece of fabric with stake-out points, allowing you to tie the tarp up between trees or trekking poles. Tarp shelters and floorless tents are usually single-walled shelters without a floor. None of these is like the heavy tarps at the hardware store you buy to cover up something at your house so it doesn't get wet. Most use lightweight, state-of-the-art fabric, usually either silnylon or DCF.

Setting up my tarp on the Benton MacKaye Trail, Georgia

These shelters don't have a floor, so they are usually lighter than tents and provide more covered space for less weight.

Tarp pros:

✓ These are the lightest shelters available.

✓ They are compact and packable.

Tarp cons:

x You may need to carry a separate groundsheet and bug protection—if the place and season require it.

x They're not for people who can't deal with bugs, or prefer to feel enclosed in a tent.

x They also don't provide as much coverage in stormy weather.

x Make sure to get comfortable with setting up well before using in the backcountry.

HAMMOCKS: Backpacking hammocks, like the Hennessy Hammock, are another lightweight shelter option. They have a rainfly and mesh bug netting to protect you from the elements—and bugs.

Hammock pros:

✓ Fairly lightweight, compact, and packable.

Hammock cons:

x Without trees or a strong sturdy connector point on both sides, you're out of luck.

x It takes a little while to get used to sleeping in a hammock.

x In cold or windy weather, hammocks can get cooler than tents because cold air can flow all around you.

x You may need a colder bag or longer sleeping pad. This will add more weight to your pack.

BUG SHELTERS: Usually just bug-proof mesh. Some have poles. Some you tie to a tree branch. Some have floors, but most just drape to the ground to prevent mosquitoes, blackflies, and no-see-ums from getting in.

Bug shelter pros:

✓ Usually fairly light, and there is nothing like keeping away from bugs when they're out with a vengeance.

Bug shelter cons:

✗ Another thing to carry. Unless you can integrate it with your primary shelter, it's only useful in good weather.

BIVVY SACKS (short for bivouac sack): A bivvy is a thin, waterproof cover for you and your sleeping bag. The top and bottom of bivvy sacks are usually made out of waterproof material. The top is a breathable fabric. Some models add extra headroom with a pole in the head area and mesh netting to keep the bugs out. Bivvy sacks can be confining. They are a good lightweight option if you're sleeping alone and expecting mild weather

These can also complement a tarp-sleeping system—if your tarp is small. When used with a tarp system, it will give you added protection against spindrift, raindrops, and windchills, and it can add about 10 degrees to your sleep system.

Bivvy pros:

✓ Packs well, saves space and weight.

Bivvy cons:

✗ Confining. Not for the claustrophobic.

✗ No room to sit up and change clothes.

✗ Bug exposure.

SEAMS AND SEAM SEALER

Shelters are made of waterproof materials—at least on the rainfly and floor. The needle puncture caused by sewing the different pieces of fabric of a shelter can lead to water seepage in rainy conditions. These seams need to be sealed with a waterproofing material.

Most brand-name tent makers use a waterproof tape to make sure the seams are watertight. They don't need to be seam-sealed—at least not at purchase. Some lightweight shelters, however, need seam-sealer to make them bomber (superwaterproof).

As a shelter gets older, waterproofing can fail. You may need to apply seam-sealer to keep it watertight. But don't worry, it's easy to use. Usually you just have to tape both sides of the area, push seam-sealer out of the tube (like toothpaste), apply it evenly with the brush, remove the tape, and let it dry—follow the directions. I'll usually seam-seal a tarp even before I use It.

TENT TIPS

QUALITY VS. DISCOUNT TENTS: Why buy a brand-name tent when you can get a cheaper tent at Walmart or another discount store? It's simple: You get what you pay for! If you're going backpacking, don't go cheap. For car-camping, cheap tents are fine, but for backpacking, they're not! You're out to have fun, and a low-quality tent might not withstand weather conditions. You could needlessly risk your life in a cheap tent. Brand-name tents are lighter. They have better materials and designs and are built to last longer.

EXTRA POLE PIECE: Most tents come with a short pole section in addition to the rest of the poles. This is a repair sleeve. You can use it as a splint on a pole that cracks or breaks. If that happens, you can slide the section over the damaged part of the pole and secure it in place with duct tape, providing support for the broken pole section. There is no need to carry that for a "just in case" situation. I have never carried this pole sleeve, nor have I ever broken a pole. However, if I did, I would likely duct-tape the damaged pole to give it support or tape a section of my trekking pole to the damaged section to brace it for the night.

PACKING THE POLES: Trying to put tent poles back into their bag can be frustrating. If there are two or more tent poles, put them in at the same time, or put one in, slide it back out a few inches, and then put the other(s) in. This helps keep the pole's bungee cord from catching on the bag and helps it slide in better.

DEALING WITH WET SHELTERS: Before packing up a wet tent or tarp, shake it out. This helps reduce the amount of water on the fabric, reducing its weight and lessening the chance of mustiness or mildew on your tent.

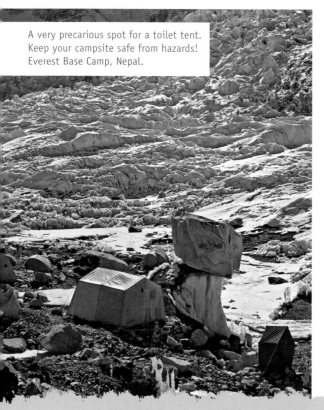

A very precarious spot for a toilet tent. Keep your campsite safe from hazards! Everest Base Camp, Nepal.

REMOVING STUCK STAKES: If you can't get a tent stake out by pulling on it directly, pull it from the webbing or cord on the tent for extra leverage. You can also loosen it by wiggling it side to side or knocking it back and forth with a rock.

STAKING A TENT ON LOOSE GROUND: If you are camping in sand, rocky terrain, or snow, there are specific stakes or methods you can use to stake out your tent. Try piling rocks on top of the stakes to make them hold, or fill a couple of stuff sacks with sand or snow, or bury them and tie them to the stake-out points of your tent to anchor it. You can tie cord to the stake-out loops on one end and to a rock a foot or two away on the other. Then pile a few rocks on the cord in between the tent and the rock it's tied to.

TENT CARE TIPS

There are a number of steps you can take to make your tent last longer on and off the trail.

On-trail tent care tips:

PACKING YOUR TENT: When packing your tent, stuff it into a stuff sack instead of folding it. It ensures you don't fold it the same way each time. Folding it the same way each time can create a crease that weakens the fabric and wears out the waterproofing.

POLE CARE: Be gentle with your tent poles when setting up and breaking down. Don't toss them out, trying to get all the sections to click into place when setting up. Do each section manually. It places less stress on the poles and shock cord. When breaking down the tent poles, break them in the center first. This helps reduce the stress on the shock cord in the pole when it's stretched out.

UV: If setting up camp early or leaving it up for a day or more, choose a shady spot. It minimizes ultraviolet exposure and helps keep your tent cooler.

Taking a break and waiting out a thunderstorm on the Continental Divide Trail in 2004. A lot of thunderstorms roll in during the afternoon in the Rockies. If you are headed above tree line, be prepared to wait them out.

If there are no shady spots available, put your rainfly on. It handles ultraviolet light better than the rest of the tent.

WIND DIRECTION: When setting a shelter up in the wind, figure out which direction the wind is blowing and set it up with the narrow end, usually the foot end, into the wind. Don't start attaching the poles until after the tent is entirely staked out. Setting up your tent this way uses the tent's aerodynamics so it doesn't get broadsided, doesn't put too much pressure on the poles, and keeps it quieter, since the material won't flap around as much.

SPINDRIFT: When camping in snow and wind, build a wall of snow on the windward side of the tent to break the wind. Position the tent so the door is opposite the wall. Pile snow up around the rainfly's bottom. This helps stop spindrift from blowing under the rainfly and vestibule.

CLEARING A SPOT: Choose good campsites to save the floor of the tent. Established campsites are good because you won't impact a new area. Usually they're already cleared, smooth, and level with no vegetation. Check and remove sharp objects or anything else that could hurt the fabric. Clear pinecones, pine needles, rocks and sticks, etc., from where you pitch your shelter. When you leave, spread around some duff (leaves and twigs) to make it look like the site was never used.

KEEP IT CLEAN: Keep shoes outside the tent in the vestibule when possible. It helps keep the shelter clean and prevents unnecessary wear.

TAKE DOWN: When breaking down a shelter, shake it out first. Remove any pine needles or other sharp debris from the inside. This helps prevent the chance of small punctures that can occur when such items are left in the tent. And you won't carry any extra weight.

AIR IT OUT: If your tent is wet, try to air it out, and shake it off before you leave for the day. If it's still wet, lay it in the sun during a break.

Off-trail tent care tips:

STORAGE: Never store a tent when it's wet or moist. The tent will get mildew, will smell horrible, and eventually be ruined. Make sure your gear is dry when stored. Store tents and other gear loosely and not in tight stuff sacks.

CLEANING: NEVER machine wash or machine dry a tent or shelter. It could ruin it. Use cold water, a nonabrasive sponge and a non-detergent soap, like Revivex or a Gear Aid product for tents. Gently wash the tent by hand. Don't use any household cleaners. Rinse the tent thoroughly and then set it up in a shady spot to air-dry.

Mildew in your tent:

Never let your tent get mildew! It's bad for the tent and smells horrible. If your tent gets mildew, try to get rid of it with the following:

1. Clean it as mentioned above, scrubbing the area lightly.

2. Use MiraZyme by Gear Aid diluted with water. If only a small area needs treatment, scrub it with a sponge soaked in the mix. If a larger area, mix the MiraZyme and water in a bathtub, and dip the whole tent in the tub.

3. Set the tent up to dry.

4. If it's still smelly, mix 1 gallon of hot water, 1 cup of salt, and 1 cup of lemon juice concentrate. Rub the mixture onto the areas with mildew.

5. Set the tent up again, allowing it to air-dry. This should take care of the smell. The stain will remain.

TRAUMA TIP

If you're a light sleeper and hiking a well-traveled trail or section and plan on sleeping in shelters with other hikers, make sure to bring some foam earplugs!

TRAUMA PICK

My shelter choice varies depending on the season and location of travel. During most three-season camping, I will use a DCF tarp because of its weight-to-space ratio. If the bugs are going to be miserable, I will also bring a bit of bug netting to drape inside the tarp or tie up to a tree. If the terrain is going to be mostly exposed, open, windy, and buggy, I will consider a one-person double-walled tent that weighs less than 2 pounds. If there are two people on the trip, I will take the two-person version that weighs less than 2.5 pounds. I have also used these tents and various tarps during the winter.

RECOMMENDED TENTS/TARPS: Big Agnes Fly Creek HV1 or Fly Creek HV 2 if you like a tent, Mountain Laurel Designs Patrol Shelter (in DCF), Mountain Laurel Designs Solomid or Duomid (in DCF), Mountain Laurel Designs Flat Tarp (in DCF). If you want a bug insert for certain seasons on your tarp, you can add that optionality through MLD.

Sleeping Well

Your sleep system should be flexible depending on the seasons. Here are some tips for making sure you've got the best gear for your trip.

NORMAL ULTRALIGHT SLEEP SYSTEM

A lightweight foam pad or short or half-length inflatable pad. Pack is used as the lower half of your sleeping pad. Sleeping bag for the low temperatures expected during the trip. Slightly warmer if using a tent, bivvy, or sleeping bag liner. Beanie, insulated jacket, socks for sleeping, and clothes to sleep in at night, increasing the warmth of your sleeping bag. Some people carry a small foamie, which they place under their inflatable pad for extra warmth when they're winter camping.

BEFORE YOU HEAD OUT CHECK THE WEATHER

If you're going for an extended period, look back at historical temperature data to get an idea of the weather patterns in the region during your time frame. Pay attention to the overnight lows. Bring gear designed for those conditions (e.g., a sleeping bag with the right temperature rating, a sleeping pad with the proper R-value, and clothes to bolster your sleep system).

Know how you sleep and the capabilities of your shelter and sleeping bag. Some ultralighters carry a small tarp and also carry a bivvy for a little more protection, which adds versatility to their sleep system.

IT ALL ADDS UP

Tents, bivvys, and sleeping bag liners can each increase the temperature of your sleep system by 10 degrees. If you're using any of these, adjust your sleep system accordingly.

TIPS FOR A LITTLE EXTRA WARMTH ON A COLD NIGHT:

- Find a campsite out of the wind.
- Urinate before going to sleep. This helps keep your body warm.
- Boil some water, put it in a water bottle, and place the water bottle between your legs in the sleeping bag (make sure the bottle won't leak and isn't hot enough to burn you).
- Cinch the hood on your sleeping bag up and cinch the draft collar. If it's really chilly, cinch it up until only your nose and mouth are exposed.
- Eat a snack.
- Sleep on your side.
- Do some push-ups and jumping jacks and then get into your sleeping bag.
- Pull your beanie down as far as it will go on your head or over your face.
- Usually your feet are the first part of your body to get cold. You can double up on sleep socks to keep your feet warmer or put on a second pair of pants but sag them low so they drape over your feet.
- If your feet are getting cold, it can also help to put the foot of your sleeping bag into your pack to add an extra layer of warmth.
- If you have any extra clothes, either put them on or stuff them in the dead spaces of your sleeping bag for insulation.
- Clear nights are the coldest. If you think it is going to be a clear, cold night, sleep under a tree with some low-lying branches. A good conifer works well. It helps trap and reflect some of the long-wave radiation back toward the earth. This will keep it a little warmer under the branches during the night.

Ascending Deerhorn Saddle along a variation of the Sierra High Route ski route in the High Sierra, CA

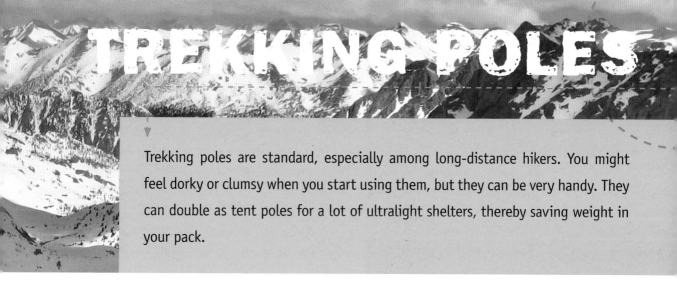

TREKKING POLES

Trekking poles are standard, especially among long-distance hikers. You might feel dorky or clumsy when you start using them, but they can be very handy. They can double as tent poles for a lot of ultralight shelters, thereby saving weight in your pack.

Carbon fiber is lighter and more expensive than aluminum. Most carbon fiber poles weigh between 13 and 18 ounces. They are strong but can snap under torque or during a fall. When they break they usually splinter and can be harder to repair than aluminum poles.

I've broken sections on both types of poles, and neither stands up to certain stresses. However, most companies will service a broken aluminum section under warranty without a problem. It can be a little hard to exercise a warranty claim on carbon fiber.

FIXED OR ADJUSTABLE

Some poles are fixed length with just one section. These need to be fitted when bought. Others are adjustable and made of up to three sections. Poles with multiple sections are adjustable to fit your needs. They collapse into a smaller pole for carrying, which is convenient, but they weigh slightly more. Adjustable poles, though slightly heavier, are usable for multiple purposes and allow you to customize them for different terrains.

PRICE

The material the poles are made out of determines the price. Carbon fiber is the most expensive.

TREKKING POLE FEATURES

LOCKING MECHANISMS: Some adjustable poles lock into place with a twisting mechanism. Turn the section to the right to lock it and left to unlock it. Overtightening can ruin the mechanism so that the pole is no longer adjustable. Other poles are locked into place with an external lever mechanism. There are also some poles that collapse like an accordion. This design was taken from avalanche probes and locks from the top. It is getting more popular from the manufacturers, but not my preference for hiking poles since they don't pack up as compactly when stashed.

They are all proprietary but similar in terms of keeping the pole locked in place. I think the twist-lock is lighter and sleeker than any of the external locking mechanisms, but the industry has trended more toward the external locking mechanisms. They're a little easier to adjust on the fly, less prone to breaking, and the locking mechanisms are more durable, so they're probably better when adjusting your poles daily for hiking and then setting up your shelter at night.

GRIPS: Shape and feel vary by brand. Some are designed specifically for the left or right hand. Cork, foam, or rubber are used for the grips. Cork

Using a trekking pole to measure a bear track

One way to get creative when trying to stake out your tent in rocky terrain
Photo by Shawn Forry

Pepper doing the limbo through a natural arch in Bryce Canyon

resists moisture, breaks in well, and conforms well to the hand. It also reduces vibration. Foam is very comfortable and soft, but it absorbs moisture. Rubber also absorbs vibration. It is mainly used for ski poles because it insulates in the winter but can create friction and blisters in warm weather.

Some poles have foam grips that extend below the main position. I had poles with this feature but never used it. If you're not sure you want it, I'd say pass on it. It adds weight to the pole.

WRIST STRAPS: Wrist straps on most poles are adjustable. After a while, they will customize to your wrist and hand. Choose a comfortable wrist strap that doesn't rub or chafe your hand or wrist.

BASKETS: Baskets are the circles above the pole tips. They keep the pole from sinking too far into wet ground. Trekking pole baskets are usually smaller than ski-pole baskets. They're removable and replaceable for different conditions. They are used in hiking or snowshoeing.

POLE TIPS: Most poles have carbide or steel tips, and they last a long, long time. They also come with rubber tips you can use if you're Nordic walking or using your poles on a road.

USING TREKKING POLES

Your elbow should be bent at a 90-degree angle when you plant the pole. You don't want to put all your weight on it but instead use it to offset some of your weight as you walk. With adjustable poles, try to make sure each section is at roughly the same length and none are extended near to their end or their maximum limit.

Some people shorten their poles when they go uphill and lengthen them when they are going downhill. This compensates for the change in distance your upper body has in relation to the ground when hiking on an incline.

USING WRIST STRAPS

Used correctly, the straps help bear the load and keep the pole in your hand. Most people use wrist straps incorrectly. If it's comfortable for them, then it works. Here's how to use them correctly:

1. Put your hand through the bottom of the strap—not the top.
2. Grip the pole.
3. Then tighten the strap.

Photos by Russ Sackson

POLING TECHNIQUE

It recently popped into my mind as I was out on my first cross-country ski of the year the other day. I am an avid skate skier and strider during the winter and have subconsciously crossed over much of my trekking pole technique from these sports. A lot of power is generated from poling in skiing, but I feel they could be used more efficiently in trekking. I haven't heard specifics of the topic discussed much in the hiking community, so I figured I would address this area.

I will also use a similar method of naming and association.

SINGLE STICKING: This would be typical walking where your left-hand pole is planted as your left foot lands and your right pole is planted as your right foot falls, or vice versa. This is the normal system. This adds slight efficiency to propel yourself forward—I'd say less than 15 percent, even with a good push-off—but does take some of the strain off your legs from the repetition of walking and on descents. It is especially valuable on steep descents (but I still find myself using the V2 Alternative more often on the steepest of descent).

V1 (YOUTUBE.COM/WATCH?V=J50I6STJYHO): In skating, this is where you make one double-pole push for each full stroke cycle of both leg pushes— with no distinct "glide" phase on the poling-side ski before the pole push starts. In skiing this is often used in high-resistance lower speed situations, and the poling takes place as your foot lands. See the video link above for details.

I often use this technique while grinding up hills or on steeper terrain. I will pole with both poles to carry me through a full stroke cycle of both leg pushes. It is a slow and steady motion that keeps a constant flow uphill.

I also sometimes use this technique on slow, technical downhills that require concentration on your foot and pole plants.

V2 (YOUTUBE.COM/WATCH?V=9PJZH_65-I4): In skiing, this is two double-pole pushes for each full stroke cycle of both leg pushes. So each single skate push is accompanied by a double-pole push. Used in a range of situations except high-resistance and very high-speed situations. Note that the initial pole plant happens just before the ski is set back down on the snow.

I mention this method because of the timing and pole plant timing. It is not used often. Mainly this will be used in trekking in slow downhill situations to brace yourself and prevent impact on your legs and knees as you step down steep steps or through steep, tricky terrain. It is hard to get two pole plants in per leg stroke cycle while trekking on normal ground.

V2 ALTERNATIVE (ALSO KNOWN AS V2 ALT.) (YOUTUBE.COM/WATCH?V=HXERUS42BBI): This differs from regular V2 because you are just poling on one side. Again the pole placement is right before your footfall.

I often use this technique on nontechnical terrain and well-graded trails, or while road walking. It works especially well on dirt or gravel roads when I am trying to get into the 3- to 4-mile-per-hour target speed and maintain that. The single push-off of the double pole at the time of your footfall propels you forward through your full stride cycle, while also giving you enough recovery time between pole strokes.

TRAUMA TIP

Never use just one trekking pole or hiking stick unless you have no choice because one broke. Not using both defeats the purpose. You're not lessening the stress on your joints as much. One pole will not help you balance as well as two can. If your shelter requires a trekking pole for setup, you'll want to have a second pole as a backup.

QUICKLY STASH YOUR POLES

There will be many times when you need to put your poles away in order to use your hands. It is a waste of energy to take your pack off to stash them. Here's how I do it:

1. Loosen a shoulder strap, and slide your poles between the strap and your body.

2. Thread the sternum strap through the wrist straps of the trekking poles.

3. Clip the sternum strap buckle and you are ready to go.

Photos by Russ Sackson

Pepper hating life and giving in to the Dirty Devil—quicksand in the Dirty Devil River, Utah.

POLE MAINTENANCE

The most common problem with adjustable trekking poles is slipping sections when a locking mechanism fails under pressure. This doesn't necessarily mean it's broken, but it likely needs some maintenance. Locking mechanisms on adjustable poles never need lubrication or WD-40.

For poles with an internal locking mechanism, preventive care can keep the problem from happening. It's simple: Clean your poles regularly and you will extend their life significantly. Manufacturers might recommend some different steps. Generally, loosen then separate each section; remove any dirt or moisture in the locking mechanism with a dry, soft nylon brush—an old toothbrush works nicely—then let them air-dry and put your poles back together.

If your pole has an external locking mechanism that is slipping, it can usually be tightened via a screw on the locking mechanism. Turning the screw to the right tightens it to reduce the chance of slippage. Tightened too much, however, the lever won't close easily. It should be firm to close but not overly tight.

Pole tips and grips can be replaced if necessary. Companies are usually very good about their warranties if you break a pole section or experience other problems.

OTHER HANDY USES FOR TREKKING POLES

- Balancing while river crossing or walking on narrow logs to keep your shoes dry.
- Scratching legs or swatting flies and mosquitoes off your legs while walking.
- Setting up your tarp.
- Makeshift tent stakes/deadman.
- Aerating soil.
- Scratching your back.
- Reduces swelling in hands while hiking.

TRAUMA TIP

I stash my poles on my pack and carry them when it is raining, snowing, or on a chilly morning. I can keep my hands warm in my pockets or in the sleeves of my rain jacket. I may also stash them when on a long road walk so I can read a book while walking. On talus or when rock hopping, it is easier to stash your poles in case you have to scramble. If you have them out, it's a classic time to wedge them between rocks and break a pole.

TIP

For a winter trip it can be helpful to add a slope angle gauge, like found at poleclinometer.com on to your pole. For basically no added weight this can give you an idea of the slope angle in avalanche terrain.

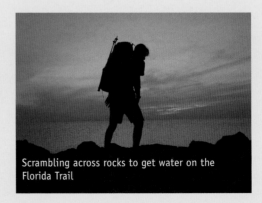

Scrambling across rocks to get water on the Florida Trail

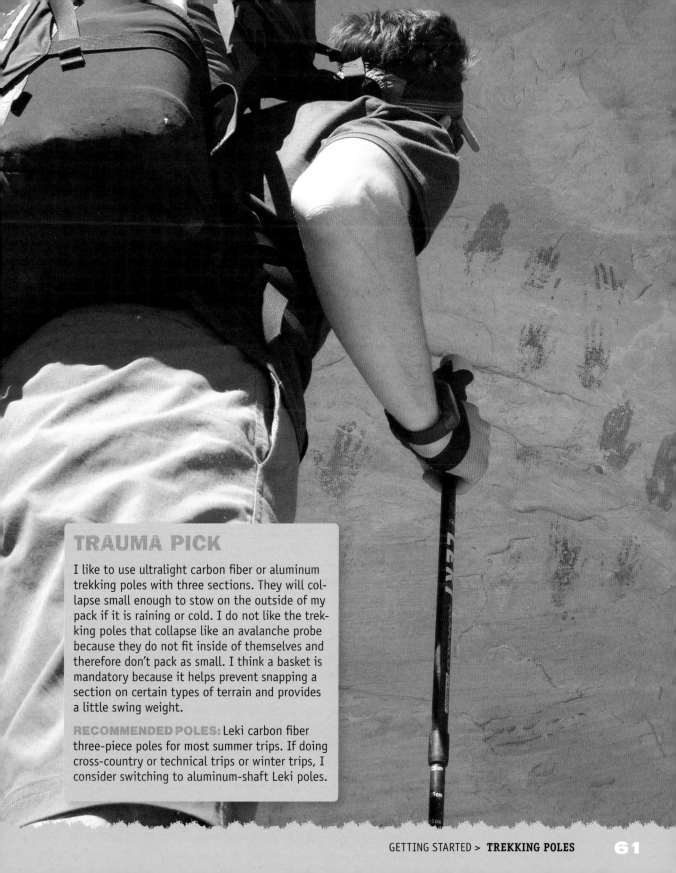

TRAUMA PICK

I like to use ultralight carbon fiber or aluminum trekking poles with three sections. They will collapse small enough to stow on the outside of my pack if it is raining or cold. I do not like the trekking poles that collapse like an avalanche probe because they do not fit inside of themselves and therefore don't pack as small. I think a basket is mandatory because it helps prevent snapping a section on certain types of terrain and provides a little swing weight.

RECOMMENDED POLES: Leki carbon fiber three-piece poles for most summer trips. If doing cross-country or technical trips or winter trips, I consider switching to aluminum-shaft Leki poles.

One way to break in shoes! Not really, but when you are long-distance hiking, get used to wet, dirty, stinky, and plain old nasty shoes.

TRAUMA PICK

During most conditions, I like to use a lightweight trail running shoe. I like trail runners because they minimize the break in time, dry faster, fit better, and are much lighter. I expect to have wet shoes at some point on a hike, and I'd much rather have wet trail runners than wet boots.

RECOMMENDED SHOES: Personal preference based on your foot specs. I have a narrow foot and have had good luck with Vasque trail runners, Salomon, and Garmont. Unfortunately, models seem to change every year, and from my experience often durability can be highly variable even within different production runs of the same shoes.

HIKING FOOTWEAR

Getting the right shoes for hiking is one of the most important things you can do. You want them to be comfortable right out of the box and durable. There are three main types of shoes for hiking: trail runners or running shoes, light hikers, and hiking boots. Depending on the amount of ankle support you need, shoes come in three heights: low-cut, mid-cut, and high-cut.

TYPES OF FOOTWEAR

TRAIL RUNNERS AND RUNNING SHOES: These are lightweight shoes designed for running or fast and light backpacking. They are the most breathable hiking shoes and dry faster than other shoes. They usually don't require any break-in time. They wear out and fall apart faster and offer less support than other hiking shoes. Their average life span is about 300 to 500 miles. It's a wide range because it depends on the shoe and conditions you'll encounter.

LIGHT HIKERS: These trail shoes are beefier than trail runners. They're still relatively lightweight and breathable, but are heavier and dry slower than trail runners. They are also more supportive and durable but less burlier than boots. Their average lifespan is between 500 and 1,000 miles.

HIKING BOOTS: These are sturdy, durable shoes heavier than other hiking shoes. They usually have Gore-Tex or other waterproof laminates that, while breathable, will probably also make your feet

hotter. If your feet do get wet in these boots, they will take longer to dry than in runners or light hikers. These boots often need breaking in before they feel comfortable. Their average life span is more than 1,000 miles.

LOW-CUT SHOES: These are often more comfortable and easier to break in. They provide the least amount of ankle support. If your ankles are bad or roll a lot, these aren't your best choice. Low-cut shoes are ideal for fast and light hiking with lightweight packs. If you like low-cut shoes, consider using lightweight gaiters with them in certain conditions to help keep out debris.

MID-CUT BOOTS: These are heavier than low-cut shoes and offer more ankle support. They usually take longer to dry and often require breaking in before hitting the trail.

HIGH-CUT BOOTS: These provide the most ankle support and are warmer for winter travel. I think they are too warm to use in summer months. These definitely need breaking in before heading out on a hike.

SHOE CONSTRUCTION

Shoes are made of three main parts: the upper or main body of the shoe, the midsole, and the tread or outsole.

UPPER: The fewer the seams in the upper, the less chance of failure. Seams can let water into the boot and, over time, lead to wear even if you can't see it. Such excess wear can lead to a blowout when you least expect it.

MIDSOLE: Midsoles are usually made of EVA, a thin layer of a rubbery, foamlike substance that helps with shock absorption and cushioning. However, some barefoot-style footwear doesn't have a mid-sole layer.

OUTSOLE: Shoes are often completed with a sole made by the shoe manufacturer. Other companies will use Vibram outsoles or soles made by a third-party manufacturer. Shoes with Vibram soles or soles from third parties usually cost more than those with generic soles because you are paying for the brand.

I have worn through a lot of Vibram and generic soles with all the miles I've hiked. Honestly, I can't tell any difference in how different soles wear. I don't recommend spending extra money just for the Vibram name. Make your choice based on the fit of the shoe, not the sole.

SHOE MATERIALS

The materials used on a shoe directly impact its weight, durability, breathability, and water resistance. Some materials break in faster than others.

FULL-GRAIN LEATHER: This upper material definitely requires breaking in. It's not nearly as lightweight or breathable as synthetic fabrics or other combinations. Still, it is the best choice for durability, abrasion resistance, and water resistance. Full-grain leather also is very easy to treat and care for.

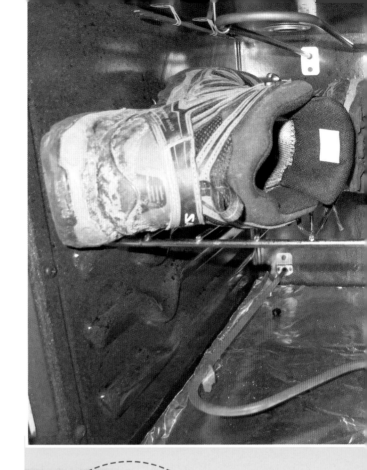

TRAUMA TIP

Toss those factory insoles. Most factory insoles with new shoes aren't good. They're typically a piece of foam that does not provide good arch support. I have packed out (flattened) some factory insoles in a day or two. I highly recommend replacing them with better insoles, like Superfeet or orthotics made for you by a professional.

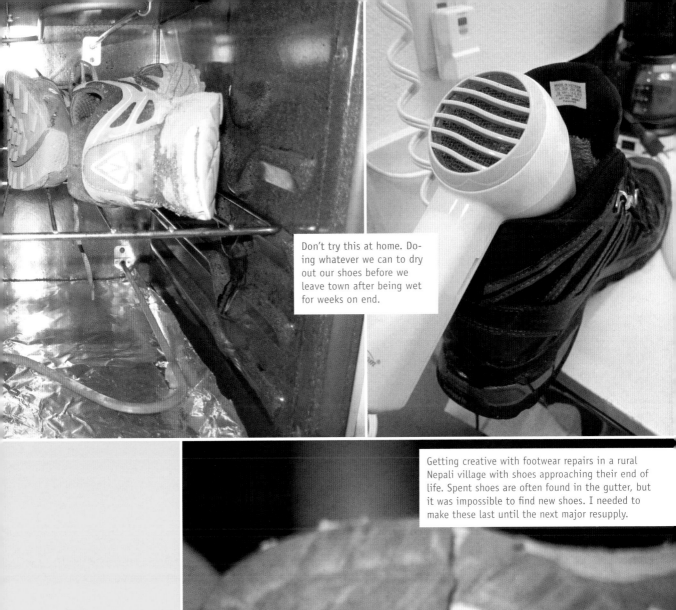

Don't try this at home. Doing whatever we can to dry out our shoes before we leave town after being wet for weeks on end.

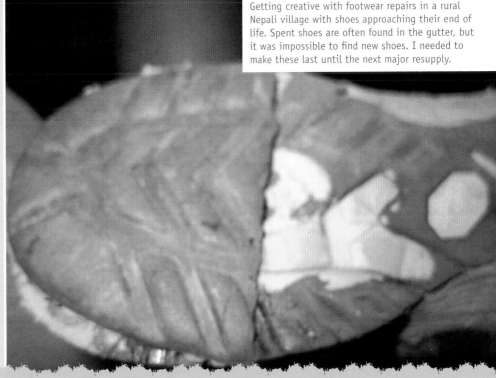

Getting creative with footwear repairs in a rural Nepali village with shoes approaching their end of life. Spent shoes are often found in the gutter, but it was impossible to find new shoes. I needed to make these last until the next major resupply.

NUBUCK LEATHER: Nubuck is buffed full-grain leather that resembles suede. It is durable and abrasion resistant but usually needs some breaking in.

SPLIT-GRAIN LEATHER: Split-grain leather is made by separating the inner part of cowhide from the exterior part. This makes it lighter and reduces break-in time. Split-grain leather is usually used with nylon panels. However, these boots have more seams than full-grain leather boots. They are usually offered in waterproofed and non-waterproofed varieties. Split-grain leather boots don't handle abrasion as well as full-grain leather and may not last as long as full-grain leather boots. They are, however, less expensive.

SYNTHETICS: Many shoes use synthetic materials, including polyester, nylon, and synthetic leather. They are lighter, break in faster, and cost less than real leather. They can wear faster.

REINFORCEMENTS

Boots and heavier shoes sometimes have a shank made of steel, plastic, or nylon in the midsole that provides stiffness and load-bearing support. Some shoes have plastic plates instead of shanks that provide a little stiffness to the forefoot and protect the foot from hard or sharp objects.

WATERPROOF LININGS

Many shoes today have waterproof laminates and/or membranes. Many laminates are designed to breathe more than leather. All sorts of shoes, from trail runners to boots, have waterproof linings like Gore-Tex or eVent fabrics.

Gore-Tex or eVent linings are pretty worthless in trail runners, in my opinion. You're just paying extra money for a shoe that will get wet when you cross a stream or creek.

GETTING A GOOD FIT

They say, "You can't judge a book by its cover." I say, "You can't judge a shoe by its box." It's imperative to try shoes on before you buy them. You can change your clothes, your socks, and maybe even your hat on the trail. You are stuck with your shoes until at least the next town. If you're in the wilderness for a week or more before hitting town, you could be really, really uncomfortable in a bad-fitting pair of shoes or boots.

Try them out in the store. Before trying them on, put on socks and any sock liners that match what you plan to wear while hiking. The thickness of the sock plays into the fit of the shoe. If you use a custom footbed orthotics or insoles like Superfeet, try the shoe on with them. They change the fit and volume of the shoe.

Walk around the store in the shoes. Go up and down steps, a handicap ramp, a fake rock if the store has one. Make sure your heel doesn't slide around in the heel cup and your toes aren't cramped or sliding into the front of the shoe. Try on a couple of different sizes and styles. Don't choose a shoe or boot in which the laces barely tie, or you have to tighten the laces up so much that they're cinched over the tongue. Most shoes stretch as they're worn and when wet. Either way, you won't have much additional room to tighten a loose shoe—or even tie it—if you get a shoe too big or small through the laces.

BREAKING IN FOOTWEAR

Get your boots or shoes well before you head out on a long trek so you can break them in. Remember, it takes more time to break in hiking boots than light hikers. Trail runners break in much faster. Boots should feel good when you first put them on. If they fit badly when you try them on, they won't feel good once they are broken in. If you notice

Footwear tips and tricks:

CAMPFIRE: Try not to sit at a campfire with your shoes toward the fire. Campfires can ruin shoes by melting the glues holding your shoes together and can even lead to delaminating. If you are comfortably warm while sitting, your shoes will be roasting.

BOOT-LACING: Relieve pressure and give your boots a custom fit with these lacing tricks: Skip-lacing can take pressure off sensitive areas. Skip-lacing means you skip a lace loop on your shoe where it feels too tight. Double-wrapping can create different levels of tightness on the upper and lower sections of the boot. The double wrap is crossing the laces like when tying your shoes, but not actually tying them. It's also called a surgeon's knot. It sometimes helps to tie this at the lace level before the ankle cuff.

TYING: If your shoelaces keep coming untied, you can double-knot them. Try tying them in the opposite way. You want the ears coming out horizontally. This helps keep your shoes tied. If one loop is cockeyed, the laces are more likely to untie.

STINKY FEET: If your feet stink like my friend Russ's do, pay attention! To de-funkify your shoes, use ReviveX Footwear Odor Eliminator. I've found it works really well. Make sure to spray it thoroughly on all surfaces of the shoe, especially the tongue.

If your sandals stink, as Chaco's often do, mix water and MiraZyme in a bucket or sink and scrub the footbed. Set the sandals out to air-dry. Don't hand dry them, since the MiraZyme literally eats the funk as they dry. When they are dry, put them in the freezer overnight to make sure no residual odors remain.

Minimize the time you wear your shoes without socks, even around camp. Bare feet inside your shoes will lead to stink.

SHOE-DRYING: If your shoes are wet, take the insoles out when you take your shoes off. Your shoes—and insoles—will dry faster and feel dry on your feet. If you're in town, you can also stuff newspaper inside your shoes to absorb moisture and help them dry quicker.

WET SHOES IN FREEZING CONDITIONS: If your shoes are wet at the end of the day and it will freeze overnight, open your shoes all the way, put them inside an inside-out pack liner or stuff sack, and sleep with them under your feet, or put them in your trash compactor bag and sleep with them. If they freeze solid—it can be like trying to put your feet into a block of wood. If you can't pry them back onto your feet in the morning, fire up your stove and carefully warm them up over the fire, or put them in your sleeping bag for a little while to thaw out.

RESOLE: If you love the boots you have and the uppers are in good shape but the soles are bare, remember that boots can be resoled. Just about any shoe-repair person or cobbler can do this. It's less expensive than buying a new pair of boots. You don't have to find and break in a new pair.

TREATING: Don't use oil-based treatments on leather hiking boots. This includes mink oil and any other oil-based product. Oil-based products make the leather softer and more supple, which can affect the amount of support the boot provides. Use only a wax- or silicone-based product.

GET CREATIVE ON THE TRAIL: Some shoes fit certain people's feet better, and sometimes they require adjustments. I have worn shoes that didn't fit right and blew them out in one day. One pair of shoes my friend Pepper wore had an ankle cut a little too high for him. As he was wearing them and packing out the midsole, it irritated the bottom of his ankle when he was walking on sidehills. He knew he had to raise his heel in the shoe. He ended up using leftover packaging from his lunch that day. He folded up the tuna packet and put it under the insole. It lifted his heel and ankle just enough to alleviate the problem.

I had a shoe that wasn't fitting right and the inside of the heel ripped. The hard plastic was rubbing my heel raw. I took out a knife and scissors when I got to town and turned them into clogs. I wore them for another couple hundred miles pain-free!

Remember: When you're out there hiking, you only have what's on your back. Keep an open mind, and get creative!

bad hot spots or discomfort from wearing the shoe around the house, you should return the shoe and try something else.

To break them in, wear them for a couple hours a day. Walk around in them and slowly work your way up to wearing them for a full day. Increase the distance you walk in them on a daily basis as well. This helps your feet adjust to the shoes as you break them in. It builds calluses so you won't get blisters in potential hot spots. Always wear the shoes with the socks you plan to wear while hiking.

When breaking in shoes and boots, make sure that the tongue is lined up straight. If they have a waterproof laminate, make sure the gussets attaching the tongue to the shoe lay flat. Creases created at the beginning of the break-in period will likely remain throughout the shoes' life span.

If your new boots are feeling pretty good but have a hot spot, you can try taking the boots to a cobbler, shoe repair store, or even some outdoor retailers with shoe repair services. They have a stretching device that can punch out the area that was causing the hot spot. However, if you do this, there is no way you'll be able to return the boot. Make sure these boots are going to work for you and fit well everywhere else before you do this.

Some people believe that getting your boots wet and wearing them for a long hike is the best way to break them in. It really doesn't speed up the break-in process, and it really isn't great for your boots or your feet.

SHOE CARE

This is most important for boots, since they cost the most and last the longest. With proper care they can last even longer. Most of this is irrelevant on the trail, but it is good practice between hikes.

Keep your shoes clean; always brush off dirt or mud, especially on the leather parts of your boots. Don't wash your shoes with detergent. Use a mild soap.

If your shoes are wet, when you get home let them dry slowly by leaving them in a warm place. You can also stuff them with newspaper to help dry the insides. Never dry them with a heater, by the fire, or with a hair dryer. Using excess heat can cause boots to shrink. Drying them slowly prevents shrinkage and keeps the leather from getting tight.

Leather boots need to be conditioned with the right treatment every once in a while. This keeps the leather healthy and moist. There are a lot of leather treating products on the market. Full-grain leather requires different treatment than nubuck or split leather.

A lot of people ask about choosing the right product to re-treat their shoes. Most lightweight hiking boots and light-hiking shoes are made with nubuck, suede, nylon, and Gore-Tex fabric. For these I use ReviveX Nubuck, Suede & Fabric Spray Water Repellent.

Midweight hiking and backpacking boots are usually made with full-grain leather. Most also have Gore-Tex fabric. For these I use ReviveX Leather Spray Water Repellent.

Mountaineering boots are usually made of full-grain leather and often include Gore-Tex fabric. ReviveX Leather Gel Water Repellent is good for the rougher conditions that mountaineering boots will encounter, such as kicking steps in snow, mixed conditions, and ice climbing. The leather gel will darken leather. Make sure you like the outcome by trying a small test area. If you don't like the darker color, you can use the ReviveX Leather Spray mentioned for the midweight boots.

If going on your first long-distance hike, I'd recommend getting a shoe a half-size larger. Many people's feet expand on the trail after hiking every day. Because most people's feet swell throughout the day, you'll get a better trail fit if you try shoes on at the end of the day.

(ABOVE) Getting creative to solve foot problems!
(BELOW) Embrace sand and sandy washes on the Hayduke Trail, or else you're in for your worst nightmare.

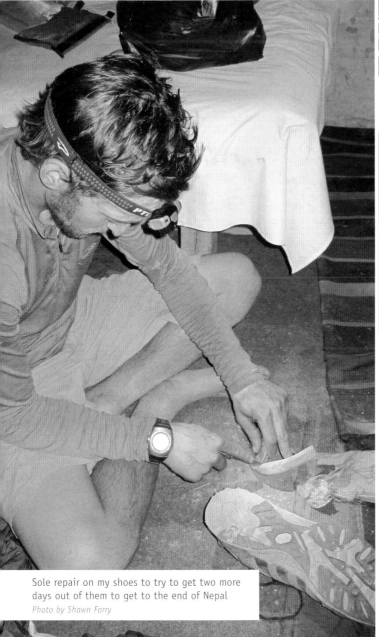

Sole repair on my shoes to try to get two more days out of them to get to the end of Nepal
Photo by Shawn Forry

Taking a break and letting my feet, shoes, and socks dry out

Taking a break and letting my feet, shoes, and socks dry out

TRAUMA TIP

Put socks and other damp materials in your sleeping bag at night to dry them. To prevent wet socks from freezing in cold weather, put them between your bag and your sleeping pad. However, on the PCT (Pacific Crest Trail) the air is so dry that you can leave things out overnight and they will usually dry. You can stab your trekking poles into the ground, put your socks over the handles, and by morning they will be dry.

Some ultralight hikers use lightweight dress socks as their hiking socks. They are inexpensive, and you can usually find them in any thrift store along the trail for a dollar or two. They don't last long, but are synthetic, thin, and dry fast.

A common seam that can blow out where the cuff rollover is sewn into the sock. Some socks do not have the seam in this location.
Photo by Russ Sackson

HIKING SOCKS

Socks are important to having a good hiking experience. Socks affect how your shoes fit. The wrong socks can cause blisters and/or rubbing. Choose your socks wisely.

The last thing you want are socks that blow out after a few days on the trail. Being limited to wearing a sock on one foot because of the blowout to prevent rubbing or wearing socks you intended to sleep in because you don't have any others can be a real problem.

Hiking socks are designed for durability, abrasion resistance, warmth, cushioning, weight, wicking, height (low, ankle, mid-calf, knee-high), quick-drying capabilities, and repelling odor. Get socks made for the conditions you'll encounter and footwear you plan to wear.

If you can, find a brand and style you like and stick with it. That way you'll know their size and how they work with your feet and shoes. You don't want a big sock or a sock that bunches up and slips around inside your shoes.

Depending on the season and where I am headed, I normally use lightweight hiking socks. I carry one or two pairs and a pair of midweight socks as my sleep socks. Using a heavier sock as a sleep sock helps keep me warm at night. If I blow out lightweight socks and have no other socks until the next time I get to town, I know the midweights should at least last longer. In winter I change out midweight sleep socks for heavyweight socks and also might hike in midweights.

SOCK CATEGORIES

There are distinct categories of socks. They range in thickness and purpose from liners, which are the thinnest, to heavy-duty socks for mountaineering, which are thick and heavy.

LINERS: Liners are lightweight, thin socks meant to be worn under other socks. They are moisture wicking and can help alleviate hot spots. They can help boots fit more comfortably while keeping your feet and socks from getting wet from sweaty feet. I have also worn liners as lightweight socks. They work but aren't as durable as other lightweight socks.

LIGHTWEIGHT HIKING/BACKPACKING SOCKS: These socks are made for warmer conditions and people who like less sock. They are good with trail-running shoes and light hiking shoes. Most ultralighters use this level of sock or even a sock designed for running. They usually are geared toward wicking more than warmth. They are a little thicker than sock liners and more durable. Some brands add a little cushioning and abrasion resistance in key areas and use a thinner weave in other areas to make the sock breathe more.

MIDWEIGHT HIKING/BACKPACKING SOCKS: These are heavier and have more cushioning than lightweight socks. Midweight socks are designed for use in average or cold temperatures, and for use with a heavier shoe, like a light hiker or a boot. You can wear these with liners, but it's just another thing to carry. If your feet are getting blisters or hot spots, try using these socks with liners. It can't hurt.

MOUNTAINEERING/HEAVY-DUTY SOCKS:

These are the thickest socks for hiking. I usually wear these for downhill skiing because they are the warmest and made for cold temperatures. They are not ideal for backpacking in summer because your feet will sweat a lot.

TYPES OF MATERIALS

What a sock is made of dramatically affects its performance. It's not just wool or cotton anymore. Many socks are made of a blend of materials for maximum performance.

WOOL: Wool is a popular sock material. If you think about Grandma's old wool sweater when you hear the word "wool," get the idea out of your head. Wool socks do not itch. Wool is comfortable, wicks, repels odor, and stays warm when wet. It can take a little longer than synthetic materials to dry and can be less durable. Some socks are made from a wool blend to compensate for these negatives.

SYNTHETIC: Many companies use synthetic materials for socks because they last longer and dry faster. Coolmax is the trade name of a synthetic commonly used in socks.

COTTON: Cotton is not an ideal hiking or backpacking sock material. It absorbs moisture, doesn't insulate well, gets dirty fast, and can lead to blisters.

CUSHIONING MATERIALS: Some manufacturers weave extra durable materials into cushioned spots. These socks usually look pretty slick with color changes and designs associated with the cushioned areas. They can be comfortable but are

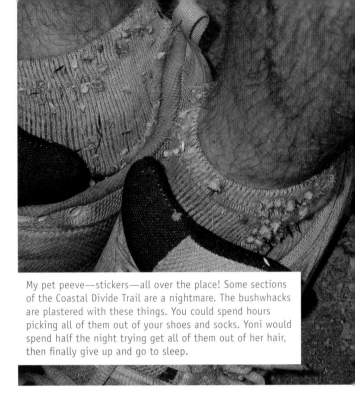

My pet peeve—stickers—all over the place! Some sections of the Coastal Divide Trail are a nightmare. The bushwhacks are plastered with these things. You could spend hours picking all of them out of your shoes and socks. Yoni would spend half the night trying get all of them out of her hair, then finally give up and go to sleep.

not a necessity. I think they are just a selling point for the sock. I've never noticed any significant level of cushioning in my socks—at least not in comparison to a nice cushy insole.

OTHER MATERIALS: Many socks also have other materials woven into them to increase certain properties. For example, most socks have nylon or Lycra woven in to increase stretch and shape retention.

TRAUMA PICK

I like a wool-blend sock. Wool doesn't get as smelly, and the nylon blend helps with the longevity of the sock. I usually prefer an ankle-high sock for hiking. I wear a calf- or knee-high sock for sleeping.

RECOMMENDED SOCKS: FITS Light Hiker Quarter, FITS Light Hiker Crew, Darn Tough, Icebreaker Hike+ Lite Crew

TRAUMA TRAIL STORY

It's important to know how to use your stove.

It's very important that you know how to use your stove correctly before setting out on the trail. On the IAT (International Appalachian Trail) I walked up to a wooden hut. These were like Hilton hotels to hikers on the IAT. The hut had decks, wood stoves, tables, and bunks.

A group of Québécois were attempting to cook dinner out on the deck with their stove. They were spraying white gas everywhere with a stove that was lit.

They kept turning the fuel bottle over, while the stove was lit. While they were doing this, the stove was swinging wildly, spewing fuel all over the place. The flames were starting to jump to that white gas that had been spilled all over the wooden deck.

I started stomping out the flames that were starting to spread around the deck. They joined in, and we got the fire under control before it caught the wood on fire.

I ran over and turned the knob on the fuel bottle to stop the flow of gas.

It was the first time they had ever used a backpacking stove. They said they thought the "On" and "Off" printed on the valve meant that when that print was facing up, the stove was either on or off. I showed them how to use their stove.

They finished cooking their dinner then sat down at the table to enjoy their cheese-and-cracker platter with a bottle of wine. They were extremely relieved, as I was, that a disaster had been averted.

A desolate landscape in the EPA Superfund site along the Pennsylvania stretch of the Appalachian Trail

BA

TRAUMA TIP

Finding denatured alcohol in the United States is not difficult. Look for HEET, gas-line antifreeze in the yellow bottle. It's methyl alcohol, burns cleanly, and is cheaper than denatured alcohol. HEET also comes in a red bottle. That's isopropyl alcohol, which doesn't burn as cleanly as the methyl alcohol, and will blacken your pot.

If you're desperate, you can use rubbing alcohol from a pharmacy. It blows out easily and blackens your pot, but it will eventually get the job done and boil water. Some alcohol stoves may be able to accommodate twig fires in a backup situation too.

Finding denatured alcohol internationally is not as hard as a lot of people think. I have found it in every country I've hiked. Keep an open mind, and remember that you're looking for methyl alcohol. In many countries it is used as a window-cleaning fluid. It may be dyed purple so people won't drink it, even though in reality it looks like Kool Aid.

Pepper cooking dinner in the Nepalese Himalayas

CKPACKING STOVES

Backpacking stoves are standard equipment. After all, campfires are not truly Leave No Trace–friendly. Cooking over a campfire is messy because you don't have a flat surface to cook on and you need to find dry wood every night. Campfires also attract animals to your camp and increase the possibility of starting a forest fire.

If you are cooking on your backpacking trip, get a stove for backpacking and not a car-camping stove. They are different. Backpacking stoves are lighter, smaller, and packable. They only have one burner.

There are three main types of stoves: canister, liquid-fuel, and alcohol. There are also some alternative-fuel stoves for backpackers. Each stove type has pros and cons. Most ultralighters use an alcohol stove for at least three seasons, if not year-round. I have used alcohol stoves in conditions as cold as negative 30°F and at 18,000 feet elevation and haven't had any problems.

Learn how to clean and maintain your stove properly. This is mostly a concern with liquid-fuel stoves. Bring a field maintenance kit if you're going out for more than a couple days.

Some ultralighters don't cook meals or boil water. They don't even bother carrying a stove. My friends Scott, Squeaky, and Pepper never cook and are perfectly happy eating cold meals at night. Some people just don't like cooking, don't want to take the time to cook, or don't want to carry the necessary supplies to cook a hot meal.

I like to cook one meal a day (dinner). It helps give me some variety in my diet and something to

look forward to at night, especially if it's been cold and wet. If you carry a stove, it's ideal that it and all its necessary components fit inside your pot.

ALCOHOL STOVES

These are simple, lightweight, quiet, and compact. There is nothing to go wrong, break, or clean. All you have to do is pour alcohol in the stove and light it. It burns slowly and will boil your water. You can also make your own alcohol stove out of soda, tuna, or cat food cans. You can't beat that price!

Alcohol stoves don't burn as hot as other types of stoves, so it can take longer to boil water, especially if it's windy. With alcohol stoves you definitely want a windscreen. Depending on the type

Photo by Russ Sackson

of alcohol stove you use, you may need a pot support or stand.

You can also make your own pot support by punching holes in your windscreen big enough to fit tent stakes through and use them to support your pot on a tripod.

Alcohol stove pros:

✓ Simple and easy to use.

✓ Compact and lightweight.

✓ Fuel is cheap and easy to find.

✓ Stove is cheaper than any other stove type, even if you buy the most expensive titanium alcohol stove.

✓ No parts to clean or break.

✓ Burns clean if you use the right fuel and leaves less soot on your pot.

✓ You can reuse any plastic bottle for a fuel bottle and refill it as much as you want.

Alcohol stove cons:

✕ Doesn't burn as hot as other stoves and takes longer to cook/boil water.

✕ Can be susceptible to windy conditions.

✕ Fuel efficiency and flame control are lower, especially in windy conditions. If you pour too much fuel in the stove, it can be dangerous to put out. It is difficult to pour leftover fuel back into your fuel bottle for later use. The Trangia alcohol stove is heavier but makes up for these drawbacks. You can snuff the fire out by putting the lid on and secure unused fuel. It has a separate simmer adapter also.

CANISTER STOVES

Canister stoves are fueled with a pressurized canister of isobutane or a butane-propane mix. You attach the stove to the canister by screwing it on. Then you open up the stove valve, light it with a

Photo by Russ Sackson

lighter or match, and you're ready to go. Some canister stoves even have a starter button. They sound like a jet engine and boil water really fast. The fuel canisters are self-sealing, so when you detach them from the stove, the gas won't leak out.

Canister stoves burn clean and are easy to use. They also have decent flame control, allowing you to simmer or boil water for different needs. Also, you never have to prime canister stoves as with liquid-fuel stoves.

While canister stoves heat your food quickly and are convenient in many ways, they have some issues other stoves don't have. For instance, you may need a little more than one canister's worth of fuel for your trip. You can't fill a canister partway. Unless you have one from an old trip, you have to carry two canisters. They don't get smaller when they are empty. Also, since you can't refill a canister, it creates extra waste that will end up in a landfill. Canisters are more expensive than other fuels. But most importantly, I have seen canisters depressurize in the cold—usually in below-freezing temperatures. Depressurized canisters can lead to a weak burn until the canister warms up.

Canister stove pros:

✓ Easy to use.

✓ Fairly compact and lightweight.

✓ Good flame control.

✓ No spilled fuel or direct fuel handling.

✓ Burns clean; leaves little soot on pots.

✓ Maximum heat output right away.

✓ No priming.

Canister stove cons:

✗ Fuel is more expensive.

✗ Poor cold-weather performance.

✗ Heat output reduces over time.

✗ As the fuel is used in the canister, the pressure decreases.

✗ Hard to tell how much fuel is remaining in a canister and how many uses are left in a canister.

✗ Hard to find canisters for resupply in some areas.

✗ Some models are unstable because their base is small. They are tall stoves with a high center of gravity, making them prone to tipping over.

ISS (INTEGRATED STOVE SYSTEM)

Some popular canister stove systems, like the Jetboil systems and MSR Reactor, include the stove and cooking pot or cup as an integrated system. Some stove kits come with other accessories. The Jetboil Flash includes a stabilizer system, a coffee press, and some other trinkets.

ISS pros:

✓ Have some of the fastest boil times.

✓ High fuel efficiency.

✓ All-in-one package means you don't need additional cookware.

PURCHASING CANISTER FUEL TIP

Most fuel canisters and stoves are interchangeable between brands. Most canisters use a Lindal valve and standardized threading so you can use them between brands even though the stove's manufacturer will recommend that you only use their brand of canister. You can use an MSR or Gigapower canister on a Jetboil stove.

ISS cons:

✗ Less versatility because the all-in-one package is designed to work as a system.

✗ More expensive.

✗ Not as lightweight as ultralight options.

CANISTER STOVE CONSIDERATIONS:

- NEVER use a windscreen on a canister stove where the stove attaches directly to the canister. This prohibits airflow and can cause overheating. The fuel can then explode. You can use a windscreen with canister stoves with the canister unattached to the stove. A remote canister can also be turned upside down to add pressure to the fuel as it becomes empty.

- Some models have internal pressure regulators to keep gas pressure consistent as the canister empties. It also helps cold-weather performance.

- Some canister stoves have stabilizers. With other stoves you have to buy them separately. Stabilizers are usually a piece of plastic that attaches to the fuel canister's bottom, creating a wider base to prevent the whole stove from tipping over.

MULTI-FUEL STOVES

Liquid-fueled stoves are common too. They're popular with outdoor groups and other backpackers. They are not favored by lightweight hikers. In the

United States these stoves use a refillable fuel bottle that's filled with white gas.

These stoves perform really well in extremely cold temperatures. They need to be manually pumped to pressurize them and primed to vaporize the fuel. Many of these liquid-fuel stoves can use multiple fuels. This is convenient because they can run on fuels like white gas, kerosene, unleaded gasoline, diesel, and even jet fuel. Check your manual to make sure the stove actually is a multi-fuel stove, and know which fuels it can burn.

Photo by Russ Sackson

Multi-fuel stove pros:

✓ The best option for cold-weather performance.

✓ Refillable fuel bottle.

✓ Can work with multiple fuels.

✓ Fuels are fairly inexpensive and can be found almost anywhere.

✓ Stable stovetops can handle large cookware.

Multi-fuel cons:

✗ Requires priming, which increases the likelihood of fuel spills.

✗ Expensive.

✗ Heavier than ultralight options.

✗ Components, including the fuel bottle, are usually bought separately.

MULTI-FUEL JETS: If you are using a multi-fuel stove, it's likely to have jets designed specifically for the different types of fuel it can burn. Make sure you use the right jet piece for the fuel you

A foggy, misty evening on the Washington section of the Pacific Crest Trail. Studying maps for the next day while cooking dinner.

plan to use. On your fuel bottle, write in a permanent marker which jet goes with what type of fuel in case you lose the instruction manual.

PRIMING: I've seen many people almost burn down AT shelters and cabins while trying to prime their liquid-fuel stoves. Priming a liquid-fuel stove is not difficult and doesn't have to create an eyebrow-singeing fireball. Read the instructions and practice in a safe environment. A cement patio or sidewalk will be a safe place to practice.

To prime a stove you let a little bit of liquid fuel into a dish on the stove and light it to preheat. That way, when you turn the stove on full blast, the gas vaporizes. Also, make sure you know how to turn the gas off quickly in case things get out of hand. Not knowing how to turn off the gas creates dangerous problems.

MULTI-FUEL STOVE FUEL CHOICE, PROS AND CONS: White gas is the cleanest fuel. If you burn other fuels beside white gas, you will need to clean the stove more often.

COOKING TIP: Soaking certain foods before you cook them helps them cook faster and conserves fuel—or, in some circumstances, uses no fuel at all. My friend Scott soaks and eats dehydrated beans every night without cooking them.

> **MULTI-FUEL TIP**
>
> If you plan to run your multi-fuel stove on unleaded gasoline, use the lowest octane fuel available. It burns more efficiently and cleaner than higher octane fuels. It will save you some money. However, you'll still have to clean it more often than you would running it on white gas.

White gas pros:
- ✓ The cleanest and most efficient liquid fuel choice.
- ✓ Evaporates quickly when spilled.

White gas cons:
- ✗ Spilled fuel is flammable and priming is required.

Gasoline and diesel pros:
- ✓ Common anywhere.

Gasoline and diesel cons:
- ✗ Spilled fuel is flammable and smells unpleasant.
- ✗ Need to prime the stove and clean it more often.

Kerosene pros:
- ✓ Spilled fuel is harder to ignite.
- ✓ Easy to find.

Kerosene cons:
- ✗ Spilled fuel evaporates slowly and smells unpleasant.
- ✗ Priming is required.

MAINTENANCE: If you plan on using a liquid-fuel stove, learn how to clean and maintain it. When you get it, read the instructions and play around with it. Learning how to maintain the stove while it's clean is much easier than learning on the trail when your stove won't work and you're hungry and cranky after a long day of hiking in the rain.

ALTERNATIVE-FUEL STOVES

There are some stove options that don't really fit neatly into other categories. Most of these alternative-fuel stoves are ultralight options that aren't as popular as an alcohol stove.

ESBIT TABLET STOVES: Fuel for these stoves are little white squares about the size of a shredded wheat. They light instantly when touched with flame and burn slowly. The stove consists of a little plate for the fuel tablet and a little titanium stand for your pot. The system is incredibly light. The main problem with the Esbit stove is that it is hard to find, as are the fuel tablets. It works well if you're doing mail drops (see "Thru-Hiking Tips"), because places that sell Esbit stoves are few and far between.

Esbit Tablet Stove

ZIPSTOVE/WOOD BURNING STOVE: This stove is similar to an alcohol stove but has a little fan that helps feed oxygen to the fire. You fuel the fire with little twigs, leaves, and other things you find that burn. The theory is you still have a stove but don't have to carry fuel with you.

It's an interesting concept, but it won't work in all hiking environments. On the AT there's enough wood, but it rains a lot. You may not always be able to find dry tinder. You may have to search for twigs at the end of a tiring day. I have seen some people use this system. They pick up dry tinder when they come across it on the trail and carry it with them to start their fire at night.

This method isn't my personal preference, as it seems like a hassle. Furthermore, natural fires don't burn clean, making pots sooty and black. The soot can get your hands and other gear inside your pack dirty.

STOVE DOS:

Make sure all fuel lines, valves, and any other connections are tight before turning on the fuel and lighting your stove.

- Try to cook on flat or semi-flat areas.
- Use a stabilizer with a canister stove. I've seen people with canister stoves spill dinners a few times by adding weight to the top of the stove; it doesn't make for happy campers. A stabilizer decreases the chance you'll knock over your stove and spill your dinner.
- Keep the lid on your pot while it's over the flame. This will heat your food or boil water a lot faster. It also uses less fuel and water.
- When possible, choose a pot that's wider than taller. It allows more contact area for the flame, increases efficiency, and helps lower the cook system's center of gravity.
- If you're trying to pump up a bottle for a liquid-fuel stove and not building any pressure, remove the bottle's top and flay out the rubber gasket that seals it to the bottle.
- If you're not planning to use your liquid-fuel stove for a while (several months or longer), empty the fuel bottle. Fuel can go bad over time.

- Consider using a heat exchanger with liquid-fuel stoves if you are headed out in the winter. It helps boil water faster, melts snow faster, and saves fuel.

- If you're camping in the cold with an alcohol stove and it won't light, hold the lighter to the alcohol for a longer period. Alternatively, light a piece of toilet paper and hold it above or drop it into the alcohol stove to act as a wick.

- In cold weather you can keep the canister warm by putting it in your sleeping bag at night (which works well for boiling water in the morning). And shortly before stopping for the evening, place it in a jacket pocket to warm the fuel up. You can also put your canister in water in your pot lid. If the water is above freezing, it will warm the canister just enough to get it out of that inefficient temperature range. Don't put it in hot water to warm it up it. The gas can expand too much.

STOVE DON'TS:

- Never cook inside your tent. You risk burning down your tent while you are inside it; you also risk carbon monoxide poisoning.

- Don't tip over a canister stove when the canister is full; it can cause a big flame-up. New fuel canisters may have a small air pocket at the top, which must flow out for a second or two before the stove will light.

- Don't fill the fuel bottle for a liquid-fuel stove above the bottle's fill line. If it's too full, you can't pressurize the fuel properly. Remember that fuel expands as it warms up. If the bottle gets hot from being near the stove or on a warm day, filling it below the fill line will prevent too much pressure from building up.

Staying warm in my tent while waiting for water to boil on a cold, windy evening in the Indian Himalayas

TRAUMA PICK

I use an alcohol stove under most circumstances. They are efficient and lightweight, even in cold conditions. They are tricky to use on windy days, but it is easy to devise ways to protect the stove. On some trips, like in the Himalayas, I have been forced to use a multi-fuel stove. These are fine also, but they need cleaning from time to time and have more parts to deal with. The beauty of the alcohol stove is in its simplicity and ultralight design.

RECOMMENDED STOVES: Trail Designs Sidewinder Ti Tri, homemade tuna can stove, Kovea Spider for winter use if you'll need to melt a lot of snow for water

COOKWARE

COOKWARE CONSIDERATIONS

- How many people are in the group you're cooking for?
- If you're with a group of people, figure out if everybody's cooking separately or as a group. If cooking for yourself with a group, you can save weight and space in your pack by eating out of your pot rather than a separate bowl or cup.
- Are you a backpack gourmet or just eating to keep going?
- Do you need a cookware set, or can you piece a good cookware system together with a pot and a spork? (Piecing your cooking system gives you more flexibility.)
- Weight.

HOW MUCH DO YOU EAT, DO YOU NEED TO COOK TO EAT, AND HOW LONG ARE YOU HIKING? FOR COOKING, EACH PERSON SHOULD CARRY:

1. A pot to cook with and eat out of. When I am hiking alone I like to carry a 0.9-liter pot. This size works perfectly for me, even when I have a ravenous appetite. If you're in a group cooking communally, each person needs a bowl or cup. You also need to determine how many people in the group need to carry stoves and pots. See the Trauma Tip chart for typical comparisons for people/cookware if you are cooking communally or alternating cooking.

2. A spork or spoon (use your pocket knife if you need to cut anything; don't bother carrying an extra knife for eating).

3. Pot handles for any pots that require an external handle.

OTHER CONSIDERATIONS

CAFFEINE: I am not a coffee or tea drinker, but if you need coffee or caffeine in the morning to get moving, try caffeinated bagged tea or instant coffee like Folgers or Nescafé. Starbucks also makes a higher quality instant coffee called Via. I've even seen some Vietnamese coffees and other specialty drinks in instant packages. These will be faster and save you effort and equipment to get your morning jolt. They're easier to make, lighter to carry, and create less waste. However, backpacking coffee presses and those types of things do exist. They just seem like extra things to carry. You can also make cowboy coffee, which is unstrained coffee, or carry some coffee filters or a bandana and strain your coffee when you pour it from your pot to your water bottle. I also know some hikers who substitute their coffee fix with a caffeine pill to avoid wasting time boiling water in the morning.

UTENSILS: There are tons of outdoor marketed utensils. I really like the versatility of a spork. A titanium spork is the only cooking utensil I carry.

COOKWARE MATERIALS

TITANIUM (ALSO KNOWN AS TI)

Titanium pros:

✓ Lightweight, so it's the top choice for ultra-lighters.

✓ Tough and durable. One Ti pot could last your whole life. I used the same Ti pot for more than 30,000 miles.

Titanium cons:

x More expensive.

x Conducts heat less than other materials.

ALUMINUM

Aluminum pros:

✓ Lightweight.

✓ Cheaper than Ti.

Aluminum cons:

x Dents and scratches easily.

x Breaks down slowly when used with acidic foods.

x Some people argue that cooking in aluminum is unhealthy.

x Cooking leafy greens and cauliflower in aluminum can change their taste and color (which is kind of scary).

STAINLESS STEEL

Stainless steel pros:

✓ Tough.

✓ Durable and more scratch resistant than aluminum.

Stainless steel cons:

x Heavy.

x Can heat unevenly, causing burned spots in the bottom of the pot.

PLASTIC

Plastic pros:

✓ Lightweight.

✓ Cheap.

✓ Durable and scratch resistant.

Plastic cons:

x Not as durable as metal products.

x Can melt.

x Some plastics are stained by foods like tomato sauce.

TRAUMA TIP Here are some typical comparisons for people/cookware if you are cooking communally or alternating cooking.

TO FIGURE NECESSARY TOTAL POT VOLUMES

Factor that 1 person will eat about 0.6 liter the first day or two and then up to 0.9 liter thereafter.

# of People	# of Stoves	# of Pots
1–3	1 stove	1 or 2 pots
3–5	1–2 stoves depending on what you are cooking	2–3 pots
	(if using an alcohol stove definitely 2 stoves)	
5+	2+ stoves (3+ if using an alcohol stove)	3+ pots

TRAUMA COOK SET

This is all I carry for a cook set on most trips.

- 0.9-liter Vargo or Evernew Ti pot
- Sidewinder Ti Tri and Caldera Cone
- Ti spork
- Mini Bic lighter
- 1- or 0.5-liter Platypus with HEET (clearly marked so nobody drinks from it)

TRAUMA PICK

All I use is a titanium spork and a 0.9- or 1.3-liter titanium pot. My fuel bottle typically is a 0.5- or 1-liter Platypus. It is the perfect size to fit about six to seven days' worth of fuel, depending on my menu. I use a small collapsible water bottle, like a Platypus (but make sure it is marked fuel so you never drink out of it). I use the collapsible bottle so it shrinks down as I use the fuel and packs smaller. If I have a longer stretch, I can just add another Platy or a small water bottle that crushes easy for that stretch.

RECOMMENDED COOKWARE: Vargo or Evernew Ti Ultralight pot (900- or 1,300-milliliter pot), Ti spork

Walking past a pristine alpine tarn in the High Sierras
Photo by Shawn Forry

Getting water from a great spring in Utah's canyon country. There's nothing like water that flows straight out of a rock!

TRAUMA TIP

If you're traveling where obtaining safe drinking water is an issue, you can get medication to treat potential illnesses. A doctor can prescribe medications like Metronidazole or Nitazoxanide to treat amoebic dysentery and giardia. If hiking internationally, I recommend carrying these as a precaution. You never know when you'll get sick, and it can be very helpful to have them on hand if something happens.

Pepper, floored on his second day in Nepal, after eating or drinking something bad

WATER TREATMENT

You never know the quality of water you'll find in the backcountry. You never know who or what's been there before you. It is important to carry some type of water treatment.

One of my friends doesn't carry any water treatment and ends up with giardia every time he hikes the PCT. Guess he doesn't mind waiting in town for a week or two until he feels better. He usually ends up in Mammoth, California. In fact, a number of stories I've heard lead me to believe that the South Fork of the Kern River is contaminated and makes people sick. It could be because of all the swallows that live in a bridge there and crap in the water. If you're hiking there, make sure you treat that water before drinking it.

I thoroughly believe that water treatment is often superfluous. Water in many places is clean. I think general perception is impacted by marketing and scare tactics. Many backcountry water sources and springs are safe to drink from. If a water source freezes solid in the winter and you're hiking early in the spring, it's probably safe.

That said, you're still better safe than sorry. You never know which sources are contaminated. Getting any waterborne illness isn't fun. Use water treatment properly. Most weigh 8 ounces—less than a can of soda—or less, so they don't add much weight to your pack.

Illnesses contracted in the backcountry are probably blamed on contaminated water. They're possibly caused by poor hygiene, improper handwashing, or cross-contamination from somebody else's hands. When most people say they had

giardia, it was probably a stomach "bug" caused by something in the water, but not giardia.

The main culprits that can be taken care of with the proper treatment options are:

PROTOZOAN CYSTS (*Cryptosporidium parvum, Giardia lamblia*). Small (1 to 300 microns; 1 micron = 1-millionth of a meter).

BACTERIA (*Escherichia coli,* or E. coli, salmonella, *Campylobacter jejuni, Yersinia enterocolitica, Leptospira interrogans,* and many others). Really small (0.1 to 10 microns).

VIRUSES (hepatitis A, rotavirus, enterovirus, norovirus). Super small (0.005 to 0.1 micron). Only purifiers, not filters, eliminate viruses because they are so small. Viruses aren't typically found in North American backcountry water sources.

WATER TREATMENT WORKS, AND HERE'S SOME FIRSTHAND PROOF

In the midst of a 30-mile waterless stretch on the CDT in New Mexico, I came across a stock reservoir. There was little shade that day, and the sun was relentless. I probably had enough water to make it the rest of the way, but I was getting uncomfortably parched. Because I underestimated the heat, I underestimated how much water I needed to be comfortable through the section. More water wouldn't hurt—and I hate carrying extra water.

A typical cloudy water source in the desert—yummy! Strain it with a bandana, let it sit overnight to settle out, or just add some Crystal Light and drink up— sometimes there's no choice! I'm used to it and don't even think twice anymore.

TRAUMA TIP

For really nasty water, treat it twice, or let your chemical treatment sit longer than recommended. After the cow reservoir ordeal, I told SteriPEN what happened and what I did to the water. They tested my theory in a lab and came to the same conclusion I did: After a double dose, the water was safe to drink. Products like Aquamira also work well; if you have a particularly nasty water source, you can just give the chemicals more time to treat the water.

Stock tanks and stock reservoirs are typical water sources on the CDT. You'll get some extra fiber and veggies drinking from this one! *Photo by Shawn Forry*

As I walked toward the stock reservoir, I saw a few blobs floating in thick, cloudy water. Two dead cows were stuck in mud at the edge of the reservoir. They'd been baking in the sun, causing their midsections to explode, exposing their bloated, rotting entrails. Apparently two mice eager for a meal had tried to swim out for a nibble but had drowned and were floating in the murky water.

Yoni, my furry companion, smelled the water and decided not to drink. She had "cameled up" at the last water source.

Depending on the trip, I usually use a SteriPEN to treat water instead of a filter. It uses ultraviolet light to purify water. I submerged my water bottle to fill it up. When I pulled it out of the water, I couldn't see my hand through the thin, clear bottle—it looked like a mud milkshake. I treated the water with my SteriPEN and couldn't see its light through the water. Just in case, I treated it twice.

I added a packet of Crystal Light Peach Iced Tea to help mask the taste. I mixed it up and chugged the liter down while attempting not to gag. It was a little gritty and almost the consistency of a milkshake. It quenched my thirst and kept me going. We hiked on and got to the next water source that evening. I never got sick, luckily!

You can usually avoid a situation like this by planning ahead. In the morning and whenever you stop throughout the day, consult your map or GPS device to locate water sources. If they are few and far between, you might want to either drink a lot of water when you stop or carry extra water throughout that day. It will add weight though.

WATER TREATMENT OPTIONS

In North America you'll usually only need to filter water, which rids most threats from water except for viruses. Purification, which includes pump- and gravity-based filters, boiling, ultraviolet light, mixed-oxidant solution pens, and chemical treatment, eliminates all biological hazards.

Purifiers have to meet EPA standards for getting rid of viruses, bacteria, and protozoa. Filters do not. For international travel, you might want a purifier or an alternative water treatment method. Some filter-based purifiers filter water and then add a chlorine solution to kill viruses.

Other treatment options include pump- and gravity-based filters and bottles with built-in filters. But remember, not all filters are purifiers. Some purification options like pumps cost more than filters without purification.

Key factors for evaluating water treatment methods are effectiveness, speed, weight, size, pore size (only relevant for filters), convenience and ease of use, maintenance, life span and durability, impact on taste, and cost.

WATER TREATMENT OPTIONS

Treatment/Evaluation	Speed	Weight	Size	Pore Size	Convenience	Ease of Use	Maintenance	Longevity	Durability	Quality of Taste	Cost
Filters/Purifiers*	2	2	2–3	4	2	2–3	3	3	3	5 (F), 3 (P)	$60–$220
Gravity filters	3	2	2–3	4	3	4	3	3	4	5	$65–$80
Squeeze bottles	3–4	3	3	3	4	4	2	3	3	5 (F), 3 (P)	$35–$50
UV light	5	4	4	NA	4	5	5	4	4	5	$79–$149
Mixed oxidant	4	3	4	NA	2–3	2–3	3	4	3	2–3	$140
Chemicals	1	5	5	NA	5	5	5	5	5	2–3	$6.50+

5 = Excellent, 4 = Very good, 3 = Good, 2 = Fair, 1 = Poor; NA = Not applicable.   *Some filters are not cleanable

Taking proper precautions and using the SteriPEN in the Indian Himalayas

TREATING WATER

Using chemicals to treat cold water takes longer than using them to treat warm water. It takes longer to treat viruses and cysts with chemicals because they have thick "shells." If you're at a nasty-looking water source—like a reservoir with cow carcasses floating in it—you might want to treat it twice or let chemicals sit longer than required.

Water treatment is a dicey subject to me. I have friends that don't treat water and don't get sick. Some don't treat water and get sick right away. A full third of people are giardia carriers and don't know it. That could be a reason some get sick and some don't. It's more likely that people get sick after a certain level of contamination.

Most people end up with a little bacteria or stomach bug and believe they have giardia. I personally think getting giardia is pretty rare.

There has to be a certain saturation in your body to make you sick. Since you're only drinking 1 liter from each water source it's unlikely, though possible, you'll hit that contamination level in one spot.

Some chemicals and other natural and unnatural things can make water taste bad. Tannin from trees, cow crap, and iodine are just a few examples. No matter your choice of water treatment, I recommend bringing a few packets of Crystal Light or some other single-serving instant drink mix. It's great to have some iced tea or lemonade when you really want to chug a liter.

With any water treatment you use, make sure all parts of your water treatment system dry completely between trips—especially if you are using a filter. Take things apart; air them out. If you don't, you could end up with mold on the filter and inside your water bottles.

FILTERS: If you're using a filter, another way to eliminate some of the bad taste is with a carbon component. Some filters come with it; others offer it as an add-on. The carbon component gets rid of the tastes. If you're using a purifying filter system, don't use the carbon component too soon. It can deactivate the chemical treatment before it has fully treated the water.

There are two main types of filters: pump and gravity. Pump filters are commonly used on the trail. Gravity filters are good for base camps, or if you're staying at a campground without running water. With the latter, you can just fill the bladder with water and hang it from a tree at night. You'll have fresh, filtered water to drink in the morning.

Always be proactive when using a water filter. When the flow becomes slow, clean the filter. Don't wait. It will just take longer and longer to fill your water bottles while hiking and it get more frustrating. Keeping the filter clean also will help it last longer.

The insides of a filter can be fragile. Handle it with care when you are cleaning or using it. Also, be extra careful in freezing temperatures. I don't recommend using a filter in cold conditions. If it is going to freeze at night, it's important to get rid of all of the water from the filter and the filtering medium. Water is left inside could freeze, expanding and cracking the filter cartridge.

Many hiking water filters are designed for field maintenance. This helps because you can clean the filter rather than replace it, but if you want to get the most out of your filter, consider cleaning it as soon as it gets harder to pump or the stream of pumped water lessens. If you're filtering silty water, you'll have to do this more often. It can be a pain.

To help reduce the amount of silt that hits the filter itself, many filters come with a pre-filter. Pre-filters can slow water intake, but if you're filtering silty water, use a pre-filter or cover the intake tube's open end with a bandana or coffee filter.

If your filter doesn't come with a pre-filter, don't spend extra money on an add-on. Use a coffee filter or bandana, and secure it around the end of the intake hose with a rubber band.

PRE-FILTER TIP: Even if you don't use a filter, placing a bandana at the bottom of your shirt or a coffee filter over the mouth of your water bottle when you fill it can prevent silt and floaty things from getting into your water.

CHEMICAL TREATMENT: Chemical treatments like Aquamira or iodine are a nice choice because they're lightweight and small. However, they can take a long time to fully treat water and can leave a residual taste. They can also take longer to treat very cold water, which is a little counterintuitive, since that's usually what you find In the mountains.

Some ultralighters use household bleach, which is basically chlorine, for water treatment. It is similar to Aquamira, which uses chlorine dioxide. It is not FDA approved. Chlorine, used improperly, is deadly. I don't recommend this method.

ULTRAVIOLET LIGHT: For a quick and effective water treatment option, check out ultraviolet light devices, like the SteriPEN. These are nice because all you have to do is dip your water bottle in water, dip the device into the water, and swirl the water around for a minute or so. You can treat water while walking if you need to. There's no sitting around pumping water while mosquitoes snack on you. There's nothing I hate more than feeling helpless, like a pincushion!

Since the SteriPEN treats water so fast, I often don't carry extra water. I know I can drink within a minute of getting to a water source, unlike a filter or chemical treatments, which can take a little longer to produce potable water.

If you use a SteriPEN, drink your water with a straw. Though the SteriPEN sterilizes all the

Please don't use normal soap in backcountry water sources. Most soap adds nutrients to water that can create algae blooms or encourage pathogen growth.

Rinsing off in an ice-cold shower near the end of the day; Yosemite National Park, California *Photo by Shawn Forry*

contaminants in your water, the rim of your water bottle could feasibly be contaminated. Using a straw makes sure you don't have to worry about it. Before you start using the SteriPEN—or any other water treatment options for that matter—read all instructions. I can't tell you how many times people have thought their SteriPEN was bad, but after I told them how to use it—wait for the green light to flash before you stick it in the water—voilà! The product was perfectly good after all.

If you know how to use your SteriPEN and are having problems with it, dry off its sensors a little or let it dry by leaving it out in the sun. Sometimes I stick it in my pocket for a while before or after use.

BATTERY OPERATED TREATMENT TIPS: When using a SteriPEN or other water treatment that uses a battery, and the user manual doesn't specify battery type, use lithium batteries. They are more expensive but last longer and are better in the cold.

If you're having trouble with batteries in cold temperatures, treat your water at night before you go to sleep. The batteries will be warmer from the day, and you'll have clean water in the morning. Another option is putting batteries or the water treatment device in your pocket for a little while before you need to use it to help warm it up.

BOILING WATER: Boiling all of your water is another option that kills everything, but I really don't recommend it. It is very time- and fuel-consuming. Also, you won't have cold refreshing water to drink immediately.

If you are hiking in the snow and want more water, it can help to add snow to the remaining water in your water bottle. This will help melt the snow faster. If you put snow into an empty water bottle, it will take longer to melt. An additional bonus of making this slurry is if you add some Crystal Light; then you can make a delicious and refreshing trail slushie.

CROSS-CONTAMINATION AND HYGIENE

I've already mentioned that I think most water is safe to drink. However, I am cautious and treat most of my water. I don't want to get a bug that makes me sick for even one day, let alone a whole week.

I think that most trail illnesses aren't caused by drinking water. For instance, on the well-travelled AT, I think a lot of people get sick from poor hygiene. Most of that can be easily prevented. For instance, don't let people dig into your bag of trail mix. Pour some into their hands. Simple things like that can help keep you healthy.

If you are really worried about water quality and want to take full precautions, you need to go the full 9 yards. Many people who treat water inadvertently do things that create potential cross-contamination from untreated water. It's best to assume that all untreated water from streams, lakes, etc., has something harmful in it.

If you use a filter, never allow the intake hose (the hose that goes into the water source) to touch the outflow (filtered water) hose, the inside of the filter, or your water bottle. Isolate the hoses in separate, marked Ziploc-type bags so that no untreated water from the intake hose touches any other part of the filter.

If you use a SteriPEN, technically you cannot clean the threads (screw-top) of your water bottle, and you don't want to put your mouth to the water bottle to drink. That's why, as I mentioned earlier, I'll keep a straw inside my water bottle and take it out when I fill and treat my water. You can also just

Jumping into ice-cold glacial runoff in the Canadian Rockies. There's nothing as refreshing as this "instant cooldown."
Photo by Shawn Forry

Bone-dry desert

make sure to wipe the threads of your water bottle off before you drink.

If you use chemicals to treat water, make sure to loosen the lid on your water bottle after 30 minutes or so and turn it upside down. Make sure the treated water wets the threads, and wait another 10 minutes or so before drinking. This disinfects where you are drinking from.

I may sound like a germaphobe, and probably am, but it's important to take full preventative measures. Treat your water to the fullest extent. After all, what's the point of taking all that time to pump water if what you end up drinking is partly contaminated?

AVOID CHEMICAL CONTAMINATION:
No water treatment option removes chemical contamination really well. It's best to avoid getting water from water sources near heavy agricultural runoff or current or abandoned mines.

Recommendation: SteriPEN Ultra or Ultralight (depending on trip details and resupply opportunities for recharging) or Aquamira.

THE TRAUMA WATER SYSTEM

I usually drink a liter or more of water when I stop at a water source and don't carry much water while hiking, since it's a lot of extra weight. I know that I won't get thirsty for a while, since I have just "cameled up." I also flavor it with Crystal Light, which helps me down a bunch of water quickly. Depending on the weather and distance between sources, I can get away with carrying no water on most of the Appalachian Trail. This system works extremely well with the SteriPEN, because my water is ready shortly after I get to a water source. Using this system, I have covered up to 30 miles of waterless stretches with only 1 liter of extra water.

The miles don't just take a toll on your body. After 1,200 hard miles, your equipment and clothes will start wearing out too.
Photo by Shawn Forry

TRAUMA TIP

I highly recommend spending the extra money for a wool base-layer shirt for hiking. I used to use synthetic clothes but now am a firm believer in merino wool. It doesn't hold odor like other base layers. If you get it wet in a creek or lake, it will smell like wet sheep while it is wet; but as soon as it dries, it's odor free, as if you just washed it. You just can't rid synthetic shirts of odor once it builds up. As salt deposits build up on synthetic base layers, they can feel like they are stabbing or scratching you. This can be a very unpleasant feeling.

Eating lunch on the first day of my hike across the Himalayas. I was a little disgruntled because I wasn't used to getting stared at by all the local kids yet.
Photo by Shawn Forry

Bundled and hiking across Iceland's windy, barren landscape

HIKING CLOTHES

Your clothes are one of your most important choices when hiking. They keep you warm in cold weather and cool in hot weather. An important thing to learn is how to layer clothes. Using a good layering system helps you carry less clothing while being prepared for more conditions. It also allows you to adjust on the go.

Each of the three primary layers has a specific function. The base layer provides moisture management, some warmth, and sun protection. The middle layers are insulating layers that protect you from the cold. The outer layer shields you from wind, rain, and snow.

BASE LAYER (MOISTURE MANAGEMENT)

The base layer is key to moving moisture (sweat) from your body. A good base layer is crucial to comfort in the outdoors. It helps prevent hypothermia in cold situations and overheating in warm conditions.

The amount of base-layer coverage is purely up to you. You might change your preferences based on where you're hiking. I usually use a lightweight quarter-sleeve shirt to a half-zip long-sleeve merino wool shirt. This keeps the sun off and is a little warmer. It also provides versatility for some extra ventilation.

When it comes to base layers, remember that "cotton kills." Cotton isn't good for hiking trips because it does not wick moisture or dry quickly. This makes you colder. A new type of cotton is supposed to dry faster. I have yet to try it.

Use a merino wool, silk (not very popular), or synthetic shirt (some trade names are Capilene, Coolmax, Zeoline, and PowerDry) as your base layer. A base layer isn't just a shirt; underwear (in all its forms) is also considered a base layer and is also available in a variety of synthetics.

SYNTHETICS

Synthetic pros:

✓ Very good moisture management.
✓ Best drying time.
✓ Cheaper than wool.
✓ Durable and available in various weights and thicknesses for different conditions.

Synthetic cons:

✗ They get stinky over time, and it's hard to get rid of the smell when you wash it.
✗ Petroleum-based materials.
✗ Can feel prickly when dirty.

MERINO WOOL

Merino pros:

- ✓ Offers good moisture management.
- ✓ Warm even when wet.
- ✓ Excellent odor resistance.
- ✓ Natural, soft on the skin.
- ✓ Comes in various weights and thicknesses.
- ✓ Can repel light rain.
- ✓ Stretches.
- ✓ Sustainable.
- ✓ Ultraviolet resistant.

Merino cons:

- x Pricey.
- x Slightly less durable than synthetic clothing.

SILK

Silk pros:

- ✓ Decent at wicking moisture.
- ✓ Good for cold-weather use.

Silk cons:

- x Pricey.
- x Not the most durable.
- x Not great for odor resistance.
- x Slow to dry and not usually machine washable.

MID LAYER (INSULATING LAYER)

The insulating layer, or mid layer, is a versatile layer that's key to the layering system. It can be a wool wicking layer or a down- or synthetic-filled jacket, depending on the conditions you will be facing. There are a number of options for mid layers from fleece, wool, or synthetic materials.

FLEECE: Fleece comes in many thicknesses (weights) and is now fairly inexpensive. It insulates when it is wet and is breathable. However, wind can whip through it, and it is bulky and not easily packable.

NATURAL FIBERS: Natural fibers include wool and down. Your mid layer can be a thicker wool shirt than your base layer. It can also be a down jacket. Down jackets come in various weights and thicknesses (like sleeping bags do).

Natural fibers allow you to match the thickness of your mid layer to the conditions, season, and temperatures. Down has the best warmth-to-weight ratio and compressibility. You don't want a down jacket to get wet, because it loses its insulative properties. Depending on your use and conditions, you may want a synthetic-fill jacket instead of down.

SYNTHETIC: Synthetic jackets also come in different fill weights for different conditions. They are usually slightly heavier than down jackets. They

TRAUMA TIP I usually like a down jacket or a synthetic jacket as a mid-layer because of its warmth-to-weight ratio and packability. The ideal loft and insulation weight varies. The choice depends on the climate I am headed into, how wet or cold it will be, and whether I plan to hike in the mid layer or just wear it at camp.

Making dinner during my winter hike, in one of the many three-sided shelters on the AT

Hiking through the snow in remote Dolpa, in the Nepalese Himalayas
Photo by Shawn Forry

insulate more when wet and stand up to wear underneath a backpack a bit better. A synthetic layer can be a great layer underneath your rain jacket and provide extra warmth on a cold, wet day.

FLEECE WIND STOPPER: They can be nice because they block the wind. They are usually warm. They're not great in a backpacking situation because they are bulky and not compressible.

OUTER LAYER (WIND AND WEATHER PROTECTION)

The shell or outer layer is crucial. It protects you from wind, rain, and snow. It keeps your inner layers from getting too wet and retains body heat. An improperly chosen shell layer that doesn't breathe could leave you just as wet on the inside because of condensation and sweat. The main considerations in a shell layer are weight, durability, waterproof laminate, DWR (durable water repellency), and breathability. Other basic features like pockets, pit zips, and hood should also be considered.

There are four main types of shell layers:

1. Waterproof/breathable shells: These are the typical hard shells and are the most functional for a long-distance hike. With a hard shell you are prepared for most bad weather conditions while still maintaining a fairly light weight. Most hard shells are laminated or coated with waterproofing like Gore-Tex, eVent, or Neoshell. Some hard shells are geared toward skiing and mountaineering. They can be more abrasion-resistant, are made of heavier materials, and have more features, but can be much heavier than a hard shell designed for hiking.

2. Water-resistant/breathable shells: These are known as soft shells or wind shells. They are best for mild weather, light precipitation, and high activity–level sports. Soft shells are breathable; wind shells aren't breathable. Neither handles precipitation as well as a hard shell. Most soft shells use some stretch material, which can make for a nice layer for skiing. But, except for cold winter conditions, they're not that good for backpacking because they don't pack very well.

3. Insulated shells: Some shells have a built-in insulation layer. These jackets are made more for resort skiing. I don't recommend these for backpacking, since they aren't as versatile as a good layering system. They don't pack as well. It's much nicer to have a separate insulation layer from your waterproof shell, because it keeps the insulation layer from getting wet.

Outer Layer Tips

TIP ON RAIN SHELLS: You can get a good lightweight rain shell for about $99. Remember that you get what you pay for. The major differences as price increases are quality, fabric, seam-taping, and attention to detail. There is no reason to buy the top-of-the-line rain jacket. No matter which brand you buy, they all wear out. A good rain jacket is nice to have in bad weather conditions.

ZIPPER PLACEMENT TIP: When trying on outer shells, pay attention to where the zippers (pockets and pit zips included) fall on your body. You don't want the slider under your hip belt; this can be uncomfortable.

TIP ON HOODS: I like using the hood on my rain jacket when it's raining. Hiking with a cold, wet head of hair in the rain, with water dripping down your neck, isn't fun. It makes you a lot colder and takes a long time to dry, especially if you have long hair.

TIP ON PUTTING ON RAIN GEAR: If you're below tree line and it starts to rain, find a good tree to stand under. Open up your pack and put your rain gear on. The tree will keep you and your gear from getting soaked while you are suiting up.

4. Waterproof/non-breathable shells: These are more economical but don't breathe at all. They are made for low activity levels like fishing. Don't skimp and buy this type of shell. If you hike in it, you are going to sweat a lot.

GAITERS

Gaiters are simple. They enclose the cuff of your shoes so that nothing can get in at the top. They are the only way waterproof shoes might actually stay dry after a day of hiking in the rain. Without them, water can drip down your legs and into your shoes.

Some people love gaiters; others hate them. I always think they're a good idea, but when it comes down to it, I rarely use them when I bring them. Some people consider them indispensable, and some people hate wet shoes. I don't mind getting some rain or pebbles in my shoes every now and again. Eventually you will hike in wet shoes. You get used to it.

After wearing wet shoes for days on end, it's nice to have dry shoes, but in my opinion there is no need to go the extra mile to try to have dry shoes all the time. For me, gaiters aren't really worth the hassle, nor are waterproofed shoes, unless you're hiking in a cold climate or in winter.

CHOOSING THE RIGHT GAITERS: There are different types of gaiters for different uses: heavy-duty and light. For hiking and backing I only recommend light gaiters. Other gaiters are for heavy-duty use like alpine expeditions or snow travel.

For hiking all you really need are gaiters that just go over the ankle and are made of Schoeller or some sort of DWR-treated stretch woven fabric. Since they stretch and are made of a softshell material, they are comfortable and low profile, which helps them last longer since they won't get snagged on things. The cord that runs underneath the sole of the shoe is the weakest part of the gaiter, but it's easy to change.

Gaiter Tips

IN THE RAIN: Wear your gaiters underneath your pants or rain pants. The pants provide an extra layer of rain protection with the gaiters underneath. This prevents water channeling into the gaiter, which will eventually soak the top of your shoes and socks.

SIZING: Gaiters come in different sizes. Make sure to get the right size, or you won't get the performance you were expecting. Gaiters should fit snugly around your leg and should fit well around whatever shoes you wear.

These gaiters provide basic protection against light rain, snow, grit, sand, and rocks. If you're going out in the winter, consider using a heavier duty nylon gaiter.

TRAUMA PICK

I like to wear a long-sleeve, half-zip merino wool shirt. This helps keep the sun off me because it has a higher collar and long sleeves. The sun can zap your energy at the end of the day, so it is important to keep it off your skin as much as possible. The weight of the shirt depends on where the trip is. I like to wear a 150g/m² or 200g/m² merino wool shirt. This wicks moisture well, dries fast, and prevents odors.

I also usually wear shorts. I like shorts with deeper pockets, or possible even a zippered pocket, so nothing falls out (my Chapstick); it is imperative that they dry fast.

I wear boxers and like merino wool 150g/m² boxers.

I also use a wind jacket and wind pants on most trips. They are the lightest weight for their warmth. Because they don't breathe very well, they help keep your body heat inside. At a few ounces per piece, they are amazingly versatile.

I also usually take a down jacket, parka, or synthetic jacket, depending on the location and season of the trip. If I think I am going to have to wear the insulation layer during the day or underneath my rain jacket for warmth, I will bring the synthetic jacket. If it is mainly for in camp and sleeping, I will bring the down jacket because there is less likelihood of it getting wet, and down is lighter than synthetic.

Finally, I also bring a merino wool beanie on most trips in case it gets chilly. Gloves and mittens vary by the location and season. I really like eVent mittens as overmitts. These are lightweight and help keep your hands warm in most conditions. They prevent your hands from getting wet and also help perspiration to escape. I usually wear a synthetic or merino wool glove liner underneath the overmitts.

RECOMMENDED CLOTHING: Icebreaker 150 or 200 g/m² long-sleeve half-zip shirt, Icebreaker boxers, Montbell Stretch Light Shorts, Montbell U.L. Down Parka or Montbell Thermawrap Pro Parka, Montbell Tachyon anorak or Dynamo Wind parka and Dynamo Wind pants, Icebreaker beanie

Besseggen Ridge, Jotunheimen
National Park, Norway

TRAUMA TIP Hiking in cold, wet weather: When it is raining or snowing and cold, stash your poles on your pack so you can put your hands inside your rain jacket. It will keep your hands a lot warmer! Also pack smartly and have layers and gloves conveniently packed in your pack so that you can reach them quickly if you are cold.

Fording the Rakaia River in New Zealand during a mix of cold rain and snow. This large, braided river was supposed to be one of the toughest fords on our hike through the South Island of New Zealand, but it turned out to be a walk in the park. *Photo by Shawn Forry*

RAIN GEAR

Rain gear is an important part of a hiker's clothing. It provides protection from the elements. Good rain gear for hiking must also be breathable, durable, and packable. With rain gear, little things can make a big difference.

FEATURES

The features you want in rain gear depend on how hot you get. If you get hot and sweat a lot, you'll want a rain jacket with more vents and pockets. Always get a rain jacket with a hood, unless you like water soaking through your layers of clothes from your neck down.

You really only need a front zipper to vent a rain jacket. Between that and pushing the sleeves up your arms, you should get decent ventilation. Pit zips seem like a great idea, but when you're hiking you usually keep your arms close to your body, reducing the effectiveness of pit zips.

One of my biggest pet peeves with rain gear is poorly designed wrist cuffs. Some cuffs absorb water, staying wet longer than the rest of the jacket. Wet wrist cuffs also make you colder, since they cool the blood flowing to your hands.

LAMINATES: The waterproof laminates and coatings on rain gear often wear out quicker than the fabrics and materials themselves. As soon as the materials start to get worn out, they can leak. The first places that get worn on rain gear are the areas in contact with your pack's shoulder straps and hip belt.

Rain jackets for backpacking have an inner waterproof layer. They are categorized by their layers as two-layer, two-and-a-half layer, and three-layer rain jackets.

Two-layer jackets are the most affordable. They're not the most practical for long trips. They're usually a little heavier and less breathable. They're designed more for lifestyle or day trips.

Two-and-a-half-layer jackets are the lightest weight full-featured waterproof, breathable jackets. They can be well priced and have either coatings or laminates.

Three-layer rain jackets are the most durable. These jackets have laminates. They're full-featured jackets that are highly breathable. They're usually more expensive.

There's not a good, universally accepted standard for fabric breathability that you will see on every product. Sometimes a tag might have a number in tens of thousands for waterproofness and breathability (30,000/30,000). Not all jackets will have the numbers though, and when they do, it is usually geared more toward skiing and snowboarding jackets.

A lot of people ask me about eVent versus Gore-Tex laminates. No waterproof jacket breathes as much as people want or desire. However, I think eVent breathes better than Gore-Tex, but I question its durability in rain gear. It lasts a long time in stuff sacks, but I have seen a lot of rain jackets with eVent leak when on-trail for extended periods of time. It happens with any jacket. It might happen a little quicker with eVent.

SEAM TAPE: Rain gear should be seam-taped. In the backcountry, anything less is unacceptable. It won't keep you dry, warm, or safe. Seam tape blocks puncture holes created by sewing needles when the jacket is made.

WEIGHT: Rain jackets vary in weight from about 5 to 6 ounces. Most 9- to 10-ounce shells are pretty solid, last a long time, and have enough features like pockets and vents.

Rain gear designed for mountaineering and hard off-trail travel usually weighs more than rain gear designed for hiking. Jackets with fewer features like pockets and zippers usually weigh less.

FIT: Keep in mind that many rain jackets have a trim, athletic cut. This can be because there isn't extra material to tuck away under your pack. Remember the trim fit when you try such jackets on. You'll likely want a little bit of room under the jacket for your mid layer on a cold rainy day.

RAIN GEAR ALTERNATIVES

UMBRELLAS: Some people love carrying an ultralight umbrella. It can be very useful on some trips. If you are under tree cover most of the time where you are protected from the wind, they can keep you from getting completely drenched. These conditions can be found on a lot of sections of the AT. In addition, they can be used as sunshades in the desert.

PONCHO: Some manufacturers make ultralight ponchos out of silnylon and other ultralight fabrics. These can be good on protected trails like the AT, as long as it isn't windy. If it is windy, they can blow around and won't provide effective weather protection. With a poncho you probably won't have to carry a rain jacket, rain pants, or a pack cover. Many ultralight ponchos are designed to go over your backpack also. Some ponchos are designed to be a tarp as well. In an area where it doesn't rain much, this can help save weight. Keep in mind that the tarp dimensions often are smaller, and you have to take off your rain gear in order to set up your shelter. This is not ideal in a rainy climate.

Not a happy camper—soaking wet, chilly, postholing in the sloppy snow, and about to blow off the ridge during a driving rain with low visibility and a gale-force wind on the Knife Edge Ridge during a winter PCT hike

TRAUMA PICK

I like a lightweight rain jacket (all seasons) and rain pants (except in the height of summer) for most trips. They can then be used as a layering tool. A hood is essential for the jacket.

RECOMMENDED RAIN GEAR: Montbell Versalite jacket and pants, Montbell Torrent shell and pants if bushwhacking and you need a little more durability

Photo courtesy of Montbell

Rain Gear Features

HOODS: Some jackets have hoods that stash in the collar or are detachable. I like the hood on my jacket, right behind my head. When it starts raining, snowing, or getting cold, I don't have to scramble to get it on.

Some hoods are made larger so the wearer can also wear a helmet under the hood. Either way, when trying on a rain jacket, make sure the hood cinches up around your head or helmet to keep water, wind, and cold air out. A little brim on the hood is nice because it keeps water from dripping into your face.

VENTS: The biggest and best vent on any coat is the front zipper. It lets the most air in. Some pockets double as vents because they have a mesh liner. Vents in the armpits are also a popular feature that let in more air. But remember, each vent, pocket, bell, and whistle can add ounces to the jacket's weight.

CHIN GUARDS: Some jackets have a chin guard, a piece of fabric or fleece on top of the zipper. It's a nice feature on a ski jacket, but it's not necessary on a rain jacket. On a wet rain jacket, fleece stays wet longer than the rest. It becomes a cold piece of fabric to rest your chin on, like a sponge. However, a flap that covers the zipper's top is crucial—you don't want to get your chin or facial hair caught in the top of the zipper. Been there, done that, and don't ever want to do it again!

STORM FLAP: Some rain jackets have a flap behind the main zipper to help keep wind and rain out. However, a jacket with a waterproof zipper doesn't need the flap and can save some weight.

POCKETS: More pockets equal a heavier jacket. When trying on rain gear, make sure the zipper sliders won't sit underneath your hip belt, climbing harness, or shoulder straps.

DROP-TAIL: Most hiking rain gear stops just below the hips. Snow gear and lifestyle gear usually have a drop tail that goes below your butt. Some rain gear might have a drop tail, but it's not really necessary, especially if you're wearing rain pants as well.

DRAWCORDS: Drawcords help cinch the rain jacket to the body to keep out more snow, wind, and rain. A drawcord at the hem allows the wearer to cinch the jacket at the bottom. Hiking rain gear doesn't need a powder or spray skirt. A drawcord on the hem is enough for almost all conditions and doesn't add the weight of a spray skirt. Drawcords on the hood are key to cinch it down for a good, tight fit.

Rain Gear Tips and Tricks

STAYING DRY

- If you're below tree line and it starts to rain, find a good tree to stand under before you open up your pack and throw your rain gear on. It'll keep you and your gear from getting soaked.

- While hiking in rain in humid climates: If it is raining on a hot and humid day, like midsummer on the AT, no rain gear will keep you dry. You'll be wet from sweating in the rain gear and from walking in the rain. In such situations, you might as well just get soaked in your clothes and change out of them when you stop. You can also try using an ultralight umbrella. You can slide it between your pack and shoulder straps so you don't have to hold it. This works well if it isn't windy during a storm. The umbrella can also work in the desert as a sunshade to block the sun during a break. I have seen people line the inside with Mylar to help reflect the sun.

MAINTAINING RAIN GEAR:

- Keep it out of the smoke: Over time, smoke affects the performance of rain gear. Unless it's raining and you're hanging out by a campfire for extra warmth, try to stay clear of smoke while wearing rain gear.

- Try to keep sunscreen and insect repellent (especially DEET!) off your rain gear. Wash your rain gear occasionally. For eVent gear, hang it to dry. For Gore-Tex, put it in a dryer at low or medium heat for 10 minutes. Washing and drying helps the gear last longer because it removes dirt and body oils that can diminish the performance of the waterproof breathable laminate or coating.

- If you do put your rain gear into a dryer, remove it promptly. Dryers remain hot after turning off. If your jacket settles on the wall and sits on a hot spot, it could melt.

- Keeping rain gear waterproof: First things first, I try not to wear my rain jacket as an extra layer unless I really have to. The less you wear it, especially with your backpack on, the better it will be when you do need it.

- After a lot of use: To stay dry you need to maintain the durable water repellent (DWR) treatment on the exterior of your rain gear. Over time, the materials lose their ability to repel water because of dirt, body oils, wear and tear, and washing. Washing your rain gear is the first step; treating it with DWR will help extend the life of your rain gear indefinitely.

- A machine washing can help bring rain gear back to life. But after a while you will notice that water droplets soak into the fabric, making it wet. That's when an aftermarket DWR revitalizer is needed. ReviveX and most companies make wash-in and spray-on DWR applications. With either you usually need a heat source like a dryer or iron to make sure the treatment adheres properly. Just read the instructions, and don't get out of control with the heat!

- I use spray-on DWR. It allows you to target the rain gear's exterior instead of a wash-in product that also coats the fabric on the inside, which may affect the breathability and wicking. A spray-on DWR also allows you to isolate areas for treatment, like the areas that come into contact with shoulder straps or hip belts. Those are most likely to lose waterproofing first.

Postholing on the descent from Nango La, Nepal

Jeff Knight and I figuring out how to traverse a burn area in the Boundary Waters, Minnesota. Burn areas can have tons of blowdowns, making it very tough to find, or stay on, the trail.

TRAUMA TIP

Prepare for bad reception areas: If you're going under heavy tree cover or into a canyon, try to fix and acquire satellite signals in an open area before you get into the thick of it.

Once the satellites are locked, the GPS will "hold" them for a longer period before losing them. If you don't acquire satellites before entering an area with spotty reception, the unit might not be able to locate enough satellites to fix a location.

Yoni and I hiking the canyon country of southern Utah
Photo by Russ Sackson

GPS UNITS

A lot of people use GPS units to navigate the backcountry. They are handy if navigation is going to be difficult. In a thick forest with few site references, a GPS can be useful (although if the forest is too thick, the unit will have trouble acquiring a signal). I'm old-school, so generally I prefer to use a map and compass. I find that a GPS adds more weight than it does navigation assistance.

GPS units range from super small (the size and weight of a cell phone) to larger, full-featured devices that weigh more than half a pound. The smallest, lightest models have fewer features and a smaller, less-effective antenna. There's a trade-off depending on which features are most important to you. Do your research, talk with other GPS users, and read reviews of different devices before making a purchase.

Some GPS units are waterproof and some float. If you think you'll use a GPS unit in a rainy climate or when crossing many rivers or streams, consider these factors before making a purchase.

The price of a GPS unit is affected by its screen type and size, memory capacity, internal maps, antenna type, and processor chip.

Real-world conditions for GPS units are rarely ideal. Thick tree cover, canyon walls, mountains—all can block signal reception. Therefore, a GPS does NOT replace a map and compass. You should always carry a detailed map of the area and a compass.

If you're interested in a GPS, there are a lot of options to consider. However, all GPS receivers for hiking are capable of performing four basic tasks: location, navigation, route plotting, and tracking.

LOCATION: The basic function of a GPS is to accurately give your location. It triangulates your position by receiving information from numerous satellites and reports it in UTM (Universal Transverse Mercator) coordinates or in terms of latitude and longitude.

NAVIGATION: GPS units use set waypoints—known points or destinations—to help the user navigate the route. The device shows the distance to the waypoints entered into the device. You can enter waypoints gleaned from guidebooks or other sources into the unit or use software that is preloaded with waypoints. Waypoints can include trailheads, campsites, water sources, and other landmarks.

ROUTE PLOTTING: You can enter all the navigation and trail information into a GPS before leaving home or use preprogrammed software to identify your route if you're hiking on known trails. If you input numerous waypoints into a GPS unit, it will create a route plotted by the coordinates entered. It will also show you the distances from point to point. However, it will plot the course with straight lines between each waypoint—and you usually won't be walking in a straight line for too long when hiking. That's where preprogrammed software can come in handy.

TRACKING: As long as a GPS unit is on, it tracks your hike, leaving "breadcrumbs" at set time or distance intervals so that you will have a track of your route. You can turn this feature off if you prefer, but it can be very helpful if you need to backtrack. You can also tag locations for geocaching or to remember a particular site.

SCREENS: Depending on the make and model, GPS units are equipped with black-and-white, color, or touch screens. The latter two are more expensive. Color screens are nice because they help the user differentiate between landforms and water. Backlit screens are nice if you're going to use the GPS at night or in low-light conditions. Touch screens often don't work with gloves, so they're not ideal for winter use. Also, touch screens, color screens, and backlit screens use more power than simpler screens.

ANTENNAS: There are two main types of antennas for GPS units: quadrifilar helix antennas and flat patch antennas.

The quadrifilar helix, or quad helix, antenna is the most common. It performs better under tree cover than flat patch antennas.

However, flat patch antenna–based GPS units are less expensive and a good option if you're hiking in open country.

The reception and accuracy of a GPS unit depends on its processor chip, like the SiRF Star III. Highly sensitive chips and antennas allow the device to quickly lock onto satellites and report location information.

INTERNAL MAPS: Some GPS units come preloaded with maps. Others use preloaded memory cards. The maps that come with a unit affect its price. The more-detailed maps cost more. Being able to load maps onto a unit is a beneficial feature to aid in navigation.

ALTIMETER: All GPS units provide elevation data. It's part of the information they receive from the satellites. Some also feature a barometric altimeter, which can help the GPS unit determine your location even if it can't triangulate your location—it happens. GPS units with barometric altimeters are great if you don't use an altimeter watch like I do. An altimeter helps me navigate by giving me an idea of what my elevation is. The barometer can also help you prepare for the weather.

BATTERIES: When choosing a GPS unit, consider what size batteries it uses. If multiple battery-operated devices can share batteries, you might reduce how many you need and also reduce the weight you carry. Lithium batteries work best and last the longest.

To preserve battery life in a GPS device, turn off its magnetic compass. It won't affect GPS

GPS Tips

Set a waypoint at the start of your hike. If you're using your GPS on a short hike, mark the location of your vehicle as a waypoint. It helps familiarize you with the device and can be useful if you get lost or get stuck in bad weather.

I think GPS devices are extraneous for most long-distance hikes—especially the AT. They are one of the more expensive pieces of equipment. Unless you're traveling on snow, in bad weather, or in an area that's hard to navigate, they're likely not necessary. Many people, like Guthook, have developed apps for smartphones that are tailored to specific hiking trails. Other apps like Gaia GPS are great for backcountry travel and more versatile for general hiking and other wilderness routes and travel not on mainstream trails. These apps can be downloaded relatively inexpensively and will help with location finding on a device that you'll likely be carrying anyway, so no added weight. The only issue is making sure to have enough charge and battery life in your phone for when you need it. I typically keep my phone off or in airplane mode so the battery doesn't drain. Also make sure to keep the battery warm on cold days by keeping your phone in your inside jacket pocket to preserve the battery life.

Many GPS units can now be satellite messengers too. If you need to contact friends and family and have emergency options while on the trail this is a handy product.

navigation information it collects from satellites. Turn off other nonessential features like backlighting and auto-routing when you aren't using them.

Most modern GPS receivers have built-in back-up batteries to keep your stored information safe when the main battery runs out. If this fails, it can be replaced by the manufacturer. They can save and reload your saved data also.

SPEED: When comparing GPS models, check the TTFF (Time To First Fix). This tells you how long it takes a unit to "lock on" to satellites and start reporting location information.

Personal Locator Beacons (PLBs) Satellite Phones

A personal locator beacon (PLB) is a portable beacon that sends distress signals via satellite to emergency responders and helps them locate you. Satellite phones connect to satellites rather than earthbound cell phone towers. Both work throughout most of the world.

PLBs may help ease friends' and family's worries while you're on a trip. PLBs are starting to offer other features as well. This is really nice, so they're no longer a "just in case" weight sitting in your pack.

The product line is now blending with satellite communicators. ZOLEO, Garmin inReach and SPOT's satellite messengers are PLBs that can also send messages and coordinates out. They link to cell phones, some more seamlessly than others. They have annual subscription fees, and some devices can partner as a GPS. This allows you to send text messages and update social media pages also. Some, like Zoleo and Garmin, can also get local forecasts texted to you. For inReach the instructions can be found at https://wx2inreach. weebly.com. It's nice that it's not just dead weight in your pack waiting for an emergency, though I still don't think it's necessary on most trips.

With a satellite phone you get more benefits. You can get and receive voicemail messages, make calls, and send and receive text messages. These texts often don't even count as using minutes. Sat phones are definitely more versatile at conveying a message but are more expensive.

If you're hiking the AT, a PLB is unnecessary. Plenty of people hike it, and throughout most of the trail you're close enough to roads and towns, making it easy to find help quickly and talk with your family and friends as often as you—or they—need to. I feel the same about satellite phones on the AT. You can get in touch anywhere on the trail with just a cell phone.

If you're hiking in remote locations, far from towns, then it is probably worth it to carry a PLB or sat phone. Before you choose to do so, check their coverage range. SPOT, for instance, runs off of Globalstar's satellite network and has some gray and low-service areas across the globe. Iridium's coverage is worldwide.

These satellite communicators can now also connect with Facebook, Google maps, text messaging, and other social media and online sources to tell people you're OK, put your location on a map and track your trip and coordinates, and even send custom messages up to a certain character length (usually 140 characters). These features can make the PLB much more useful than just an emergency beacon, and also a more cost-effective option than a satellite phone.

Wristwatches/Altimeters

A backpacking wristwatch with an altimeter helps you navigate and predict pending weather.

Most backpacking wristwatches have altimeters, thermometers, barometers, and compasses. The altimeter will show your elevation, giving you a better idea of your location when looking at a topographic map. However, it's important to learn how to use a wristwatch's features before coming to rely on it. It becomes even more useful as you use it more.

Tip: The altimeter measures barometric pressure. It is crucial to calibrate your elevation at known points a few times per week to keep the barometer and altimeter accurate.

Pepper and I camping in an alcove waiting while our dinner cooks. This is two days from the end of the Nepal section of our Himalaya hike and shortly after descending out of the high country for the last time and entering into hot, humid, low-elevation areas for the remaining miles.

AND HEADLAMPS

The only light system I recommend for hiking, backpacking, or any outdoor adventure is a headlamp. In fact a headlamp probably saved my life one night.

I'd been reading by headlamp in my tent for about an hour. It was time to sleep but I figured I'd take a last look around before crashing. It was another epic day of hiking. I'd already been chased by an angry elephant and, while running for my life, spooked a lion that was camouflaged and napping in the grass. Luckily, when the lion took off, the elephant went after it. This was about 1,500 miles into a solo southbound hike across Africa, in a wildlife preserve near the border of Kenya and Tanzania.

Ready for a nice, quiet evening I peered out of my tent. My battery-starved headlamp (I have a habit of waiting until my batteries are completely dead before changing them) barely sliced through the tall grass around me. It illuminated a large female lion sitting about 30 feet in front of me. I yelled, shined my light in her eyes, and yelled

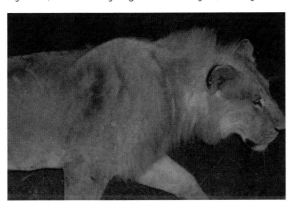

more—she wasn't budging. She just kept staring at me. Using the headlamp I looked around and spotted movement about 35 feet behind me—it was another female lion. She had been creeping up behind me in the grass, trying to flush me out of my spot so the other female could attack. This is exactly how female lions hunt prey.

I reached down, grabbed my trekking poles, and started screaming and banging my poles. I was trying to act as intimidating as possible. Nothing. The lion behind me crept closer, while her hunting buddy stared me down. I kept yelling, banging the poles and shaking the tent. Still, nothing. I quickly grabbed my camera. I was hoping the flash would scare the predators off. Nope. The lion from behind had crept around and was now only a few feet away on my left. She was walking toward me and gave me a mean, hard glare as she walked past. I used the camera and flashed her again. I inadvertently took some up-close photos of the lion just as she sauntered by, and she began to walk away. Her companion watched as she trod on and luckily got up to follow her hunting partner. Amazing!

I don't know why they spared me, but I'm not complaining. Not surprisingly, I didn't sleep at all that night. I decided to change my route and get out of the nature preserve as soon as possible. I sincerely believe that without a headlamp, I might not be writing this book today. If my hands were busy with a handheld flashlight, I would not have had the freedom to use the camera flash or make noise with my poles. I also had to keep my eyes on them at all times. So, when I say, "Nothing compares to hands-free lighting with a headlamp," I mean it. Here's what to shop for in a headlamp.

FEATURES: Headlamps should tell you their lumens (brightness), run-time, weight, and beam distance (see table). Compare the figures on a number of models. Try each one to find out which fits your head best. Choose the model that offers the best combination of comfort, features, and price.

Modern hiking headlamps use LEDs, which are very efficient and effective. Skip the headlamps with a separate battery pack. They're heavier and add weight and bulk to your hiking gear. That is, unless you plan on spelunking on the trail.

Some models have two types of LEDs in one headlamp. One is for hiking because it illuminates better. The other is for reading, cooking, and accomplishing tasks around camp.

Manufacturers also are including a red, green, or blue LED as the second option in the headlamp.

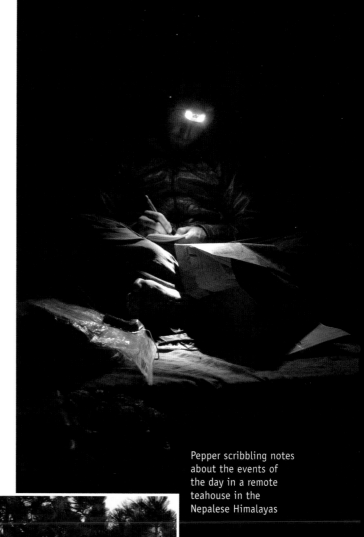

Pepper scribbling notes about the events of the day in a remote teahouse in the Nepalese Himalayas

Relaxing before bedtime in the Sierra Nevada Mountains, California

Headlamp Tips

Don't use lithium batteries in a headlamp unless the instructions specifically say to use them or the headlamp comes with lithium batteries in the box. Lithium batteries can burn out the circuitry. However, if the instructions say to use lithium batteries, follow the directions. They work better in cold conditions and last longer.

Some companies sell a lantern adaptor for headlamps. This is a reasonable idea, but it's overkill. Your headlamp illuminates everything that you look at, and the beam follows where you turn your head. If you need to flood a larger area, you can hang it in the tent's canopy.

These are designed to be easier on your eyes because they don't make your pupils contract as a white LED does. They're also not as bright. The light won't wake up your partner if you're reading late.

HEADLAMP MODES: Most headlamps have a few different modes, or brightness levels. This helps conserve the battery when you don't need it on full force. Some also have a strobe feature. That can serve as an emergency beacon in case something happens—or maybe it could scare off large animals.

BEAM: The beam on some headlamps is adjustable from a flood or wide light to a spot or focused light. Others use two LEDs to give you the same flexibility. Some have just one option.

REGULATED OUTPUT: Many new LED headlamps feature regulated output. Instead of losing light as the batteries drain, they sustain their brightness throughout the life of the batteries. This is a great feature, but when the batteries reach a low point, the power will fade quickly.

TILT: Most headlamps allow you to tilt the light various degrees to illuminate whatever you're doing: looking at the trail in front of you or the food you're cooking. It's an important feature. I don't recommend getting a lamp that doesn't tilt.

WATER RESISTANCE/DURABILITY: Most good headlamps are fairly tough and can handle some rain. You probably don't need one that is completely water- and submersion-proof. If it's pouring rain, you probably won't be hiking at night anyway. I'd much rather be curled up in my shelter and warm.

ON/OFF-MODE SWITCH: The headlamp's switch is pretty basic. You want to make sure it will operate easily in all the conditions you'll face. And you don't want the light to turn on so easily that it goes on in your pack, draining you batteries during the day. On the other hand, you don't want to struggle with turning it on when you need it most. Depending on when you're hiking, you may also be wearing gloves. This can affect your ability to turn the light on and off. Play around with different models in the shop.

Some headlamps now have a plug-in rechargeable battery. Depending on the type of hiking and backpacking and length between resupplies, this may be a good option. Personally, I'd rather use batteries; they are more easily found at resupplies and typically functional for multiple electronic items I may be carrying. It seems like every item has a different recharger, and I don't want to carry extra chargers or be tied to a bounce box at every resupply.

HEADLAMP FEATURES

Characteristic	Units of Measurement	Meaning
Light output/ brightness	Lumens	How bright the light is at its source. The higher the number, the brighter.
Beam distance	Meters	How far the unit's beam will illuminate a surface.
Run time/battery life	Hours	At its LOWEST setting, how long the unit should be able to produce usable light.
Weight	Ounces or grams	Most headlamps are between 3 and 6 ounces. Heavy-duty, high-intensity lights are heavier.
Size	Inches or centimeters	The dimensions of the headlamp itself. Headlamp straps are adjustable and should fit just about any head.

How do you think we trek big miles? Actually this is Pepper dividing up powdered milk for the Nepal section of the Himalaya hike. Save weight and space by repackaging items. Only take with you the amount you need until your next resupply.

TRAUMA TIP Just as baseball has dealt with steroid use, long-distance hiking has its own set of controversies. Some long-distance hikers take caffeine pills—purportedly, they help hikers trek through lulls and stay on schedule. Perhaps they help hikers keep their competitive edge on the trail. As for me, I'd rather just eat chocolate and more candy bars.

TRAIL FOOD

Food is one of the most important considerations when you are backpacking and hiking—especially on long-distance hikes.

Food will consume much of your thoughts while walking. People have different cravings, from chocolate to juicy cheeseburgers to Ben & Jerry's ice cream. When considering trail foods, there are many things to consider. You're hiking for extended periods of time, and your metabolic rate will increase substantially. I've witnessed people lose more than 100 pounds in two months of long-distance hiking.

Who needs Weight Watchers when you can go on the Trauma diet—eat anything and everything you see and still lose weight! Food is a personal preference, more so than any other item. Whatever your pleasure, you need nutrient-rich, calorie-rich, and good-tasting food.

Pepper loves salty trail food like tortilla chips and potato chips. My friend Nacho likes salami, pepperoni, peanut butter, and dried fruit tortillas (made with precision). Squeaky could eat Powerbars all day long. I love bagels (only Thomas' and Sara Lee, because they are moist and you don't need to toast them on the trail) and cream cheese, tortillas, cashews, and dried apricots. Another favorite is my Nutella and potato chip wrap. My all-out favorite, which I eat every night of a hike, is pasta. I'm more of a sweet-treat fan than a salty snack fan.

Food will be the majority of your pack weight. Food can be measured in calories per ounce. It's important to shop for densely caloric and nutrient-rich food when planning for a hiking trip—leave the Twinkies at home!

The more calories per ounce, the less food weight you have to carry. Many foods weigh in at 150 calories per ounce or higher. For instance, olive oil and ghee are closer to 250 calories per ounce. Carbohydrates and protein have about 100 calories per ounce, while fat has up to 250 calories per ounce.

Food that's under 110 calories per ounce isn't ideal for hiking, because you must carry extra food weight to meet your dietary needs while hiking. Anything under 110 calories per ounce has water weight. Water is heavy and has no calories, so it's a lose-lose choice for hiking food.

Foods with calories per ounce of 125 or greater are ideal for hiking. If you are trying to meet a 4,000-calorie-per-day diet—I can burn 8,000 calories per day on the trail—you'd only have to carry 2 pounds of food per day.

When hiking sunup to sundown on a strenuous trip, it's easy to blow past 4,000 calories in a day. It sustains my energy. When I get to town, I do a town binge—eating everything in sight to make up for the deficit.

Some people try to cut their pack weight by cutting the amount of food they carry. I met a guy attempting his second thru-hike on the Pacific Crest Trail. He had tried the trip the previous year but quit after about 800 miles. He said he got too weak to continue hiking. He was obsessed with cutting down his pack weight to make the hiking easier. He cut down on the amount of food he carried, and his strategy backfired. You need the calories for energy. Cutting weight is fine, but don't shortchange yourself on food. To combat weakness, add calories to your diet.

To cut weight, examine your cook system and other gear. Make lighter gear choices so you can carry more food on long trips. Your pack will be heavier after resupplying, but it gets progressively lighter every day.

I am a sugar junkie. After a full year of hiking, I was sick of so many of my typical hiking foods that I had to resort to whatever I could eat without gagging. This was my typical food for the last two days of my 10,000-mile trek. *Photo by Shawn Forry*

Enjoying fresh seafood on a beach walk during the New Zealand hike. Tastes like chicken!

FOOD BASICS

When hiking, most people need 2,500 to 4,500 calories per day. That's about 1.5 to 2.5 pounds of calorie-rich food per day. Each individual is different and has different caloric needs, but it's a good place to start. If you're unsure of how much food to take with you, err on the side of caution. Take extra meals or a few more packets of ramen. It's better to have more food than not enough.

When shopping for food during resupply or before starting a trip, be organized. The more long hikes you take, the better you'll become at estimating ten days' worth of food. When starting out, organize your shopping list and meal plans ahead of time. Think about what you are going to eat each day for breakfast, lunch, snacks, dinner, and dessert. This will help you get what you need without feeling overwhelmed.

Remember that weight, size, and packaging of the food matters. It determines how it will fit in your backpack. You don't want foods with a lot of space around them, like a box of crackers. Consider the ease of preparation also.

Taste is crucial. You don't want to eat food you don't like after a long day of hiking. I don't enjoy most backpacking- and hiking-specific foods. I like normal foods from the grocery store. I also rotate foods so I don't get tired of eating the same thing.

A lot of people think freeze-dried foods are their only option for eating in the backcountry. They're wrong. There are plenty of other easy-to-prepare meals available in the supermarket. Lipton Sides, pasta (ideally angel hair, because it cooks fastest), instant soup mixes, couscous, polenta, and quinoa are just a few examples. These options are a lot less expensive than freeze-dried meals.

Certain fresh foods will last for days in your backpack, depending on the weather. For instance, cheese can last for days in most weather conditions. Cream cheese usually lasts three to four days, unless it's really hot. Cheddar will last up to 6 days, unless it's really hot and dry. Jack and Parmesan last the longest. Capsicum peppers can last a day or two, and carrots can last a few days.

You don't need canned foods. Foods like tuna come in packets, which are handy for camping. Cans are heavy, and since you have to pack out empty cans, you never really get rid of the bulk. Canned food is usually packed in liquid, which adds a lot of extra water weight, not calories, to your food.

When possible, repack food in sealable zipper bags. Taking things out of their original packaging and putting them in bags gets rid of a lot of extra air and space in your pack. It makes the food more packable and easier to see what is what. And you will have a trash bag when you're done.

A lot of people ask me how I get my protein when I am hiking since I don't eat much meat on the trail (besides the occasional packet of tuna). I recommend nuts (and a whole lot of them), cheese (small amount of protein), jerky, salami, or tuna (occasionally), and of course Gummi Bears (they're not going to break the bank and have 1 gram of protein per serving!). Another trick is to prepackage your powdered milk, if you are going to be eating cereal for breakfast or making curries at night, and you can add whey protein to the powdered milk Ziploc. This also helps the powdered milk taste better.

FOOD OPTIONS

Here are some considerations for tasty and healthy trail food.

BREAKFAST: Cereal with powdered milk is my breakfast of choice. Other hikers like Pop-Tarts or breakfast or energy bars. All of these are easy to prepare and make it faster to pack up and move on quickly. Oatmeal, cream of wheat, and other hot cereals are good if you don't mind cooking in the morning.

LUNCH: Dried fruit, protein bars, bagels, nuts, pretzels, chips, jerky, tuna packets, tortillas, cheese, salami, pepperoni, chocolate, Nutella, peanut butter and jelly, and Pop-Tarts are all good options.

SNACKS: Eating snacks throughout the day while hiking is important to keeping you going. You might try protein/energy bars, gorp (aka trail mix), dried fruit, chips, pretzels, chocolate—and anything else that you might like. It can be easy to eat while hiking or go down fast to keep your energy level up if the weather is bad.

DINNER: If you want to go superlight and not carry a stove, a variety of lunch foods also work for dinner. If you carry a stove, you have a wide range of options. Get calorie-rich foods that have little to no water weight. You can cook angel hair pasta, instant rice, Tasty Bites, Lipton Sides, ramen noodles, instant soups, instant mashed potatoes, or freeze-dried prepared meals for camping. I find some of the latter can be tough on your stomach.

Food Tips:

When eating an energy bar, drink at least a swig of water with it. It helps your body digest the bar and absorb the nutrients.

Take multivitamins on a long-distance hike as a nutritional supplement. You won't be eating many nutrient-rich fresh greens or food while hiking.

Chia seeds are good trail food. If you soak them, they become like a pudding and can be a healthy snack.

You can grow sprouts while hiking. It's a great trick for any stretch over four days. Take an empty small plastic jar, like a peanut butter jar, and put some seeds in it. Soak the seeds overnight and empty the water in the morning, making sure the seeds don't come out. Rinse them a couple of times a day over the next few days. Dry out between rinses so they don't get moldy. In a few days you'll have fresh sprouts.

GETTING READY FOR
THE TRAIL

Approaching the Arrow Glacier while ascending the
Western Breach Route on Mount Kilimanjaro, Tanzania

GETTING IN SHAPE

It is very important to get yourself and your equipment ready before a long hike. Getting yourself in shape is easily overlooked by the logistics and planning for a long hike, but it is just as important. Your hike can easily be cut short if you don't physically prepare yourself. It is also crucial to use your gear and familiarize yourself with everything. This will give you the opportunity to tweak and adjust things to your preferences before you begin. It might save a few ounces in the process!

Looking at Mount Aspiring on the descent from Cascade Saddle, New Zealand

The amount of time you need to start conditioning and training for backpacking varies based on your fitness level and the amount of time you usually spend exercising. You always use slightly different muscles when hiking than cross-training.

The best way to train for backpacking is hiking. Start with an empty backpack and get used to a base mileage. Over time, add weight to the pack until you hit the weight you expect to carry. This will help you be more comfortable with your pack on the trail. Similarly, my friend, a polar adventurer, trains by pulling tires behind him across grass fields. He uses the same harness he uses to pull his pulk sled on the ice cap. This gets his body ready for the contact points and pressures. Training is very important before you set out on any trek of length.

The training time is a chance to build your base daily mileage. Increase your base mileage slowly—going farther one day then returning to your shorter base mileage for subsequent hikes before pushing farther again. This will keep your body from getting overwhelmed and tired. It reduces the chance for injury. Train on hikes that best mimic the terrain where you're planning to backpack. If you're climbing peaks on your trip, practice by hiking where there's significant elevation gains.

If it's winter and you can't be outside or can't get to a suitable hiking area, train in the gym. Do ellipticals, stair-climbing machines, bike, treadmill, and swim. Do all the exercises that focus on distance and endurance. Get practice wearing your weighted pack and breaking in your shoes.

ADJUSTING AND TWEAKING GEAR CAN REDUCE WEIGHT

Equipment is designed to fit a spectrum of people within a size range. As you get used to your equipment, you'll find you can make some small tweaks. Shortening adjustment straps can save a few ounces. Don't do this as soon as you get new gear; you may get rid of something that could have been useful. When you're familiar with your gear, adjust it to save a few ounces and reduce clutter from your backpack, tent, clothes, and stove.

Test your gear. Pay attention to what adjustments you make for different conditions. There's plenty of webbing on your backpack that can be eliminated. Some of the length around your hip belt can be removed. Consider marking your adjuster straps at points that show you where the straps need to be. Over time, see if that changes. Determine how much you can safely cut off, then cut it.

Never cut anything too close to the minimum. It will be hard to tighten and grip and can slide through the hardware. There's no going back once

it's gone. I had a friend who trimmed webbing on his sleeping bag's draft collar too much. He could no longer cinch the bag around his face at night for extra warmth. He hadn't anticipated how he would fill the extra volume. Once you're familiar with your backpack, shelter, or other gear, you can consider cutting some of the extra stuff.

On backpacks you can cut extra webbing from shoulder straps, load-lifters, and the hip belt. Make sure you leave at least 6 extra inches, and make sure you don't need that webbing for the pack to fit correctly. If you know how to sew, think about shortening the overflow collar if you don't need it.

On shelters and tents you can sometimes trim some cord from the stake guylines or other connector loops. Be sure before you do it that you don't need them and won't use them. You can also swap out guylines for lighter-weight cordelette.

A windy day on the AT, Franconia Ridge, New Hampshire

Cutting off excess webbing but leaving enough for minor adjustments

Singe the ends to prevent fraying.

A mountain goat licking a rock, presumably because someone sweaty sat on or peed on it, leaving salt deposits; Glacier National Park, Montana

A water cache on the PCT left through the winter

A backpack with "Leave No Trace" principles printed on it *Photo by Russ Sackson*

A trashy stream in the Indian Himalayas

The ridiculous amount of stonemen (aka ducks or cairns) don't make navigation any easier

MINIMIZING IMPACT

Minimizing your impact is key to everyone's enjoyment of the outdoors. It's also vital to the future of the outdoors. It's not hard to understand or do.

The tenet is simple: Try to leave everything either as you found it or better. Don't leave any signs that you have been there—cairns, campsites, fires, etchings in bark, etc. The backcountry should be respected for what it is: natural. The best way is to make as little impact as possible.

PACK IT IN, PACK IT OUT: Never leave any trash behind. Aluminum never burns completely in a campfire. Orange and banana peels take a long time to break down, so don't leave them in the backcountry. Pack all of it out. Take only pictures; leave only footprints.

TREAD LIGHTLY: Leave nothing behind, and don't disturb anything you don't need to. Don't trample or pick flowers. Don't break tree branches on living trees, and don't make a lot of noise. Campfires are heavy impact, even if there is an established firepit. I know campfires are part of many people's backcountry rituals, but don't make a campfire unless you need it. Definitely don't create a new fire ring unless absolutely necessary. If you have to establish a new fire ring, make sure the ashes are cool before you leave. Disperse or cover the ashes, and move the rocks elsewhere so no one else will use the same spot.

HIKE LIGHTLY: Always stay on established trails when they're available. Never cut switchbacks. When there aren't switchbacks on steep trails, you will wish there were. Don't ruin existing switchbacks and speed up trail erosion.

If there's no clear trail and you're facing multiple terrains, try to walk on rocks or snow instead of plant life and soil. If you are with a group hiking across meadows and there are no clear trails, it is better to spread out instead of hiking single file. It has less impact on plant life and is less likely to create a repeated-use trail. If the trail is muddy, walk through it, not around it. Don't complain—your shoes are going to get wet anyway.

DON'T TREAD ON CRYPTO: There is a black crust on desert sands that mounds up like a miniature termite hill. It's alive and it's known as cryptobiotic soil. It takes an extremely long time to grow. It helps prevent erosion. It is very fragile when stepped on, so avoid stepping on it whenever possible. If you're walking in a group, stay in single file and use the same footsteps.

USE ESTABLISHED CAMPSITES: Whenever possible, camp where others have camped. It helps prevent further damage on untouched land and prevents more campsites from being established.

DEALING WITH THE DOO-DOO: Always move human waste at least 200 feet from water and trails. Dig a cathole and bury it. Nothing's worse than seeing stray toilet paper float by on the wind in the wilderness or snared on a bush.

NEVER FEED WILDLIFE: Feeding Bambi isn't a favor to her. It's closer to a death sentence. Don't feed wildlife or try to draw them close to you. It changes animals' behavior and changes their diet.

TRAUMA TRAIL STORY

Like you, the trail can be fragile, and a simple mistake can have unexpected consequences. About a year before I hiked the PCT for the first time, a thru-hiker's bathroom foray started a wildfire that burned thousands of acres in the Southern California desert.

The hiker had abandoned the trail to take care of business. When he was finished, he broke out his lighter and lit his toilet paper on fire to "leave no trace." The breeze was blowing a little bit, and his TP fire got out of control. He did what he could to contain it. I'm sure he kicked dirt or sand on it, poured water he was carrying on the growing fire, perhaps tried to piss it out. No such luck. Between the breeze and dry tinder, SoCal was destined to burn.

That hiker's poop break caused thousands of acres on the PCT to burn before people could get it under control. Be careful on the trail, and pay attention to the conditions around you. It's better to pack out or bury a little TP and let it decompose than to start a forest fire and endanger lives.

Watching a fire burning in the San Gabriel Mountains on the southern section of the PCT and trying to figure out the best way around

FIRST AID

People generally pack more first-aid items than they need. I am a trained EMT and a ski patroller. I find it's very seldom that you need to perform first aid on the trail. There's only so much first aid you can do in the backcountry—even with a 10-pound first-aid kit. In a severe emergency, the main goal is do no more damage and get the person out of the backcountry and safely to higher medical care as quickly as possible.

A section of your trekking pole can help immobilize an injury, like a sprain—or even a fracture—if you're in the backcountry. Clothes can be used to apply direct pressure to an injury and to wrap it. Your water bottle or hydration bladder can double as an ice pack.

Get creative; you should have everything you need, even in a minimalist backpack.

First aid requires common sense. Remember RICE (rest, ice, compression, and elevation). This will help stop bleeding on fresh injuries and help injuries heal quicker.

The most important things you need are duct tape, a small knife, and ibuprofen. You can roll duct tape around your trekking poles or a fuel bottle. It can protect blisters and other foot issues. By placing a small piece of duct tape shiny side up against a larger piece's sticky side, the tape won't stick to the injury. By cutting out a small piece of fabric and placing it against the duct tape, you can create a bandage. Your small knife can be the knife you use for eating. Ibuprofen (Advil) is a nonsteroidal anti-inflammatory. Unlike acetaminophen (Tylenol), it won't just take care of the pain; ibuprofen also helps alleviate inflammation.

You can carry a topical antibiotic like Neosporin if you are worried about infections.

Remember to pack any prescription medications. Depending on the season and where you're hiking, also consider sunscreen, lip balm, and insect repellent.

SANITIZATION TIP: If you use a chemical water treatment, use it to sanitize your hands before dealing with broken skin if you think your hands are soiled. Just pour some Aquamira- or iodine-treated water over your hands. Or place a small dose of the chemical mix on your hands and rub them like you're applying hand sanitizer.

TRAIL SAFETY, HEALTH, AND WELL-BEING

Common outdoor issues and how to prevent or take care of them while in the backcountry:

SUNBURN: This is common on the trail despite dealing with it in everyday life. Elevation and snow increase the UV light that hits your exposed skin. In such conditions you should reapply sunscreen throughout the day.

A thru-hiker on the PCT needs to be very careful in the Sierras because snow reflects UV light and

My close call: On the next-to-last day of the Nepal traverse, I fell through a suspension bridge and was slammed in the face by a loose plank, leaving my eyebrow caught between the lens and frame of my sunglasses.

the sun is very strong. Many people get roasted. Don't forget your ears, the underside of your nose (if you are on snow), the back of your neck, and your calves and knees, if you are wearing shorts. Wear sunglasses at high elevations and when hiking on or through snow. Hike with your mouth closed—I have met people who got sunburned on the roof of their mouth.

Use aloe for sunburned skin. Try to keep that area from getting burned further by covering it or putting sunscreen on.

BLISTERS: Blisters are annoying, painful, and can ruin a trip. They are caused when friction rubs skin back and forth. It first causes hot spots then separating layers of skin, which fill with liquid. The best way to prevent blisters is to start all trips in old shoes that your feet are used to. Clean socks also help prevent blisters and rubbing.

If you feel a hot spot starting, try to address it immediately. Don't wait until it gets worse. If you take care of it early on, it can heal quickly without ever forming a blister. Put some duct tape or moleskin on the hot spot to reduce the friction. If you have a spot that often blisters, consider dressing it before you start hiking.

If a blister is painful, pop it by lancing the side of it with a needle at night, when it'll have time to start to heal and dry out before the next day. Make a duct tape patch to cover it by cutting out a piece of duct tape bigger than the blister. Place it shiny side up on the sticky side of a larger piece of duct tape. Then apply it to the affected area. When you remove the duct tape, you won't be pulling on a sore area or ripping the blister open. Take the bandage off every night when you are done hiking so the affected area can get air and heal quicker.

BLISTER TIP: Long-distance hikers feel strongly about their anti-blister techniques. I try to get the hot-spot calluses on my feet before a trip. I know that once I have calluses on my common hot spots, I am set. Some hikers apply antifungal cream on their feet twice a day for a month before a hike. They think it helps strengthen the skin on their feet. Still others apply Hydropel to their feet to prevent them from getting wet. Pruned skin is soft skin, which is more easily irritated.

CHAFING: Chafing is often a hiker's worst nightmare. It can be debilitating. It can make it almost too painful to walk. Common areas that chafe are the inner thighs, butt crack, feet, armpits, and back. Women may chafe under their bra line or bust. Moisture, friction, and the buildup of salt crystals from sweat are the root of the problem. The salt crystals combined with friction and moisture can make skin rough, irritated, and rubbed raw. If you're chafed, you may end up walking like John Wayne.

Treat chafing when you notice it. It can get worse and may even become infected. Wash chafed skin with fresh water, and let it dry completely. Promote airflow to the region to let it dry out. Make sure to keep it clean too.

If your feet or ankles are chafing, change or wash your socks. They may be gritty, causing the chafing.

Treat chafed skin with petroleum jelly like Vaseline, Sportslick, or other skin-lubricating products. The treatment will help prevent additional friction, giving the skin a chance to heal.

GENERAL ACHES AND PAINS: Most people have aches and pains when they begin a backpacking trip or a thru-hike. The best prevention is training. Get your body used to wearing a weighted backpack and hiking. Stretching in the morning, at breaks, and in the evening helps.

Don't push your body too hard before you're ready for it. Build your daily mileage slowly. As your body acclimates to a comfortable pace at the start, add a few more miles on some days. Other days, for about half a week, hike just the base mileage. Take a rest day. If you feel good, continue to up the mileage so the higher mileage becomes your base mileage. Repeat the whole process to reach a new level if you can. It takes a month to increase daily base mileage between 5 and 10 miles. Don't increase your mileage too much too fast. I have seen a lot of injuries result from increasing mileage too quickly.

For muscle aches, take vitamin I—ibuprofen; it helps with pain and inflammation. Massage your muscles, especially your iliotibial (IT) band. If it's too tight, your IT band can pull on your kneecap and create knee pain. This is a common source of knee pain, caused by the repetitive motion of walking and backpacking.

For joint pain, rest helps the most. Stop hiking a little earlier in the day to extend your rest time, or hike a few shorter days. You can also elevate the sore joints and ice them with cold water. Taking glucosamine and chondroitin pills during a long hike may also aid in the repair of cartilage.

Joint pain, particularly knee pain, will likely lessen as your weight goes down on the trail. A pound of weight loss equals 4 fewer pounds of pressure on your knees. "The accumulated reduction in knee load for a one-pound loss in weight would be more than 4,800 pounds per mile walked," wrote researcher Stephen P. Messier, PhD, of Wake Forest University in the July 2005 issue of *Arthritis & Rheumatism*. "For people losing 10 pounds, each knee would be subjected to 48,000 pounds less in compressive load per mile walked."

No studies have shown that weight loss can slow the progression of osteoarthritis of the knee. Researchers say a reduction of pressure on the joints of this magnitude would appear to have a major impact on the disease. Obesity is an important risk factor for osteoarthritis of the knee.

GENERAL ACHES AND PAINS TIPS:

> On hot days, dip your shirt or hat in water and put them back on for an "instant cool down." Getting in water can revitalize you on a hot day so you can keep hiking.

> I use my pack as the lower half of my sleeping pad. This saves weight and elevates my legs while I sleep. This helps prevent inflammation in my feet and legs. It keeps my shoes fitting properly.

> To reduce or prevent knee pain, massage the outside of your thigh with firm pressure from your knee to hip. Use a tennis ball, rock, or something firm to massage the area. It helps keep your IT band loose so your knee tracks correctly. You can also learn some stretches from a physical therapist to target this area.

FOOT CARE: It is important to look after your feet. Rest them whenever possible. Elevate your feet and legs to encourage good circulation and reduce swelling.

Ventilate and dry your feet out by removing your shoes and socks when you rest. At the same time, shake dirt and gravel out of them. Remove their insoles so they can dry out too. If it's hot out, get in a stream to soak your feet and legs.

When you put your socks on, make sure they're free of debris and wrinkles. Both can cause blisters. Keeping your socks clean and rinsing them out occasionally will help prevent them from getting gritty and can prevent rubbing and foot problems.

Be proactive with hot spots. Treat them with moleskin, bandages, and duct tape when they first start. At night, remove all foot bandages to help blisters, hot spots, or other foot injuries dry out and heal.

Cracked feet are due to dry conditions—often from hiking in sandals. If this is the case, wearing socks with your sandals will keep your feet from drying out. If necessary, clean the crack out and use superglue to help hold the crack together and help it heal.

Everybody has different routines for dealing with their feet. My friend Scott takes 40–45 minutes at night to take care of his feet and prevent foot problems. My dog, Yoni, also cleans her feet every night before she goes to sleep. All thru-hikers have their own routine, and they all know how important foot care is.

FOOT CARE TIPS:

> If it's convenient and you have time, soak your feet and legs in a creek or lake at the end of the day. It feels great and can help with injury recovery and prevention. It's like icing your legs. My friend Raina did this after a painful day. She didn't want to walk over to the nearby creek, but it really helped. When she came back she said it was well worth it. Bonus: It helps keep your sleeping bag clean!

> If you think you have an ingrown toenail, cut a V-shaped notch in the middle of the toenail. It can alleviate pressure on the side of the nail and help the ingrown part of the nail grow out as the toenail grows in.

POISON IVY, POISON OAK, POISON SUMAC, STINGING NETTLE: These plants are fairly common on parts of the AT, PCT, and hiking trails throughout the United States. Know what they look like, and do your best to avoid them. "Leaves of three, leave them be!" is a good rule of thumb for both poison ivy and poison oak. Poison sumac and stinging nettle are a little harder to discern. Until you wash these off, you can spread the oils or irritating hairs. Wash off as soon as possible if you think you have touched any of these plants.

If you aren't really sensitive to the plants—you don't have an immediate reaction—it's extra helpful to know what the plants look like. I have knowingly and unavoidably touched poison ivy and poison oak many times. I try to find a creek or water source to jump into and wash the affected area within 30 minutes. If I didn't know what the plant looked like, I could end up with a nasty rash. Washing soon after has avoided the itchy rash.

BITING INSECTS: A horde of biting insects sucks. Bugs are an unavoidable part of many backpacking trips. Try bug repellent, head nets, or insect-proof clothing to keep them away. In some really buggy places, only pure DEET works. Not even that is good enough to give you full peace of mind. Covering up can sometimes give you peace of mind when the bugs are really bad.

Some natural bug repellents work when the bugs aren't that bad. You need to reapply them more frequently than DEET. However, DEET has its own downsides. It will ruin anything plastic, synthetic fabric, watch crystals, and eyeglass frames.

I've seen what DEET can do. We had been hiking together off and on for a few weeks, thru-hiking the PCT. It was summer, and the bugs were out in full force. Mosquitoes were ravenous. We were killing five at a time with each swat on our shoulders and arms—even while we were walking. It was about 5 minutes from break time, and we were all ready to break and eat lunch.

One friend grabbed the bottle of 100 percent DEET from her pack and sprayed it on while she continued walking. She didn't want to give the little bloodsuckers any chance to attack when she stopped hiking. She spritzed on the DEET, and we walked for a few more minutes.

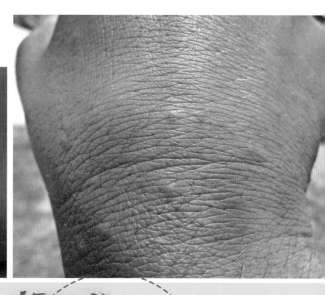

Earlier in the day I said, "I think I feel a little rubbing." Lesson: Stop when you first feel something.

A 15-minute pile of mosquitoes. Absolute misery turned into sheer joy and entertainment when we decided to see how many dead mosquitoes we could stack during a break. Poboktan Creek, Canadian Rockies.

TRAUMA TIP

When it's buggy out and you're on break, make sure your pants are covering your lower legs to keep the bugs off.

Eating dinner and covering up to keep sane and protect myself from a swarm of mosquitoes in the Canadian Rockies

We stopped in an open spot where a little breeze blew. The mosquitoes let up a little bit. I took my shoes and socks off, pulled out my bagels and cream cheese, and made my lunch. Everyone else did the same with their lunch.

The girl who applied DEET ate a burrito for lunch. She prepared and ate the burrito, using her tortilla bag as her plate. When she tried to take the plastic tortilla package off her leg, she couldn't. It had melted onto her skin.

She pried and scraped the package to get it off but was left with a Don Pablo's Tortilla tattoo on her leg. Name, logo, colors—all of it! She tried to pour water on it and scrub it off. No luck. The tattoo was on her leg for nearly three weeks before it disappeared!

Still, sometimes peace of mind is priceless. In the buggiest conditions, it's worth the weight to carry a head net and bug netting for your shelter or a bug-proof tent.

BITING BUG TIPS: When applying sunscreen and insect repellent, put the sunscreen on first and let it absorb into your skin for a few minutes. Then put the bug juice on.

> Natural insect repellents include tea tree oil (also an antibacterial), citronella, lemon eucalyptus, rose geranium, pennyroyal, patchouli, neem tree oil, and peppermint for ants. These are OK for certain situations. When bugs are really biting, DEET is the only repellent that really works.

STINGING INSECTS: You're not likely to encounter bees, wasps, hornets, or yellow jackets often. Stings are painful but relatively harmless for most people. If you are highly allergic, you should talk to your doctor and take appropriate precautions, like carrying an EpiPen. If you're stung, scrape the stinger out and ice the area. Benadryl can be helpful as an antihistamine.

TICKS: Ticks are common on the AT when it warms up. Do body checks, especially on the AT. Ticks can carry Lyme disease or Rocky Mountain spotted fever. I once pulled handfuls of ticks off Yoni near Waynesboro, Virginia, on the AT. There were hordes of them—I couldn't pull them off fast enough.

Not all ticks transmit Lyme disease, but the ones that do have nymphs that can be so small they can be hard to see.

Ticks are attracted to warm areas of the body. Check your head, nostrils, ears, armpits, and groin. If you find a tick, try to pull it out without squeezing the body. Pinch the tick near the head, and pull it out.

TICK REMOVAL TIP: If you're having trouble getting a tick out, there is a great trick. Put liquid soap on a cotton ball, cover the tick with the cotton ball, and swab it for 15 to 20 seconds. The tick will come out on its own and stick to the cotton ball.

SNAKEBITES: Many people are scared of snakes, particularly rattlesnakes. They're relatively easy to avoid. Pay attention in the day, particularly when you get to open rocky areas. Snakes love to sun themselves during the day on rocks. That's also when they have the energy to strike.

If you hear a rattle or see a snake, don't keep moving toward the snake or antagonize it. Most snakebites are on people's hands and wrists. People usually get bit because they antagonized the snakes. Give the snake some berth and walk around it.

Most rattlesnake bites are dry bites—bites that don't envenomate. Even rattlesnake bites with venom are rarely deadly except for children and elderly people.

A rattlesnake near Deep Creek, California, on the PCT

If you do get a bite, stay calm. Rinse the wound. Immobilize the extremity. Keep the wound at or below the level of your heart to slow the spread of potential venom. Apply antiseptic and antibiotic ointment, and hike out to find medical attention as soon as possible. DO NOT apply a tourniquet!

Use a marker to make a circle around the bite on the skin. If it starts swelling, mark additional circles with time notes so that you can monitor the progress of any swelling. It helps doctors understand the severity of the bite. It also helps if you can identify the type and size of snake that bit you.

ANIMAL AVOIDANCE TIP: On the AT, never leave your shoes or salty things in front of your shelter. This is asking for porcupine trouble. They'll eat anything that is salty from sweat. Many shelters on the AT have a "Deacon's Seat." This is a wood pole in front of the shelter that prevents porcupines from eating other wood on the shelter and salty things.

HANTAVIRUS: Hantavirus is usually spread by rodent droppings, saliva, and urine. Breathing fumes or dust tainted by rodents is the most likely way to contract the virus.

It's not common to get the disease. But AT shelters and other places on the trail can house rodents.

Hantavirus has an incubation period of one to five weeks. Initial symptoms can include fever, headaches, muscle aches, coughing, nausea, and vomiting. That's followed by difficulty breathing, shock, discolored skin, bleeding, and, in severe cases, death. If you suspect you've been exposed to or contracted hantavirus, seek medical attention immediately.

ALTITUDE SICKNESS (AMS): Altitude sickness is the illness people get when they travel to high altitudes. Some people start feeling it around 6,000 feet; others don't feel it until around 10,000 feet above sea level. Your reaction largely depends on the elevation where you live and your fitness level.

Initial symptoms of AMS are sluggishness and headaches. If it progresses, it can be debilitating and even deadly.

Controlled acclimatization is the best prevention for AMS. People generally try to ascend about 1,000 meters (3,000 feet) per day. Camp at the new level, and try to acclimatize.

When summiting high peaks like Mount Everest, people acclimatize by spending one night at a higher elevation then descending and camping at a lower level before ascending higher. That strategy helps their body adjust to the oxygen-starved environs.

At lower elevations, AMS can largely be prevented by staying hydrated, avoiding severe elevation changes in a short amount of time, and acclimatizing. If you are suffering from altitude sickness, the best thing to do is descend to a lower elevation.

Dusk was turning into complete darkness.

Clouds on the horizon were like flashbulbs popping at an old press conference. A thunderstorm was moving into the New Mexican desert. I came upon a USDA Forest Service campsite with a privy. I picked a decent camp spot, set up my tarp, and went to sleep. Nobody was in this remote camping area. It was October, and only hunters were around. Maybe everybody else had seen the weather forecast.

It poured all night long. After an hour, the crappy clay soil couldn't absorb any more water. Rain ran under my tarp like I had pitched it in the middle of a stream. Because of the rain, my tarp was sagging; the stakes couldn't take the pressure and were all bending in or pulling out of the ground. I piled rocks on them, but nothing held in the oversaturated soil. I was getting wet. My sleeping bag and pad

Hiking up the amazing Paria Canyon on the way to Las Vegas

TRAUMA TRAIL STORY

were accumulating water; my pack was also taking on water. At 2 in the morning I made the decision to abandon ship. I threw my stuff in my pack and ran to the covered entrance-way of the pit toilet. I slept there the rest of the night.

It was still raining and thundering all around when I woke up in the morning. It was like the thunderstorm wasn't moving. The ground looked like a hurricane had hit, with downed tree branches, leaves everywhere, and water flowing inches deep on all slopes and pooling in every depression.

I looked at the sad state of my tarp. It was a soaked, mangled mess that looked more like a bedsheet on a clothesline fresh from a washer without a spin cycle. It was a rough night and a humbling experience.

I later learned the same thing had happened to Pepper that night. He was about 100 miles ahead of me on the Continental Divide Trail (CDT). He too fought a losing battle all night but didn't have anywhere to run. He woke up soaked, his drenched tarp on top of him.

Both our adventures show how important it is to have the right shelter for the trip. I knew mine was getting old and the waterproof coating had worn off, but I was just trying to push it a few more weeks until the end of the hike.

Pepper's tarp after the deluge
Photo by Shawn Forry

the deluge

It was still raining and thundering all around when I woke up in the morning.

Indian Himalayas

Raina getting Yoni's food ready before the rain moves
in; Pasayten Wilderness, Cascades, Washington

CAMPSITE SELECTION

Depending on where you're hiking, you may have to camp in a certain location because of local rules. On other trails you can choose to camp wherever you want. Here's what you should look for in a campsite.

THREE-SEASON CAMPING

Many impacted campsites are along rivers, lakes, saddles, and other flat areas. These are often great places to camp, since you won't be impacting a new site. I often seek these out. They're flat and used, making them easy to set up on.

Try not to set up camp in fragile areas—in meadows, on fragile vegetation, or near a water source if there aren't many sources (desert). You can negatively impact wildlife habitats.

Camping near water is nice because you don't need to carry water to cook with. However, cold air settles around lakes and low points, which can make it colder than camping in a forest. Air near a water source is moist. You're likely to have more condensation form on your shelter or sleeping bag when camping near water, and dew is usually heavier. You'll be more likely to pack up a wet shelter in the morning.

If the bugs are out, they're more likely to be around water. If bugs are an issue, camp out in the open and away from water. On a ridgeline or in a saddle, there might be a breeze. This helps a little with the bugs. You can also—if it's safe—start a small smoke fire to try to get rid of them.

When you know you're sleeping in or setting up a multiday base camp, try to set up in a shady spot. It keeps your tent cooler and, by avoiding UV radiation, helps the fabrics last longer.

Try to find a spot that is sheltered from the wind. When that's not an option, face the narrow part of your tent or shelter into the wind. It reduces wind noise and the chance that the shelter will be broadsided by wind, which can keep you up all night.

Try not to set up camp in low spots in the landscape, places where water might run off and pool under your shelter if it rains overnight. This is even more important when sleeping in a canyon—make sure you're not pitched in a spot where flash flooding occurs. If you think it may rain or flash flood, make sure you have an exit route in mind.

When camping on a beach like in the Olympic National Park on the PCT, camp well above the high-tide line.

When camping on a previously undisturbed spot, try to minimize your impact by putting things (rocks, branches, pine needles, etc.) back where you found them. Try to make it look like no one has camped there. That minimizes the chance that someone else will use the spot as a campsite, preventing it from becoming another impacted area.

I like to sleep under the stars (cowboy camp) when I think it won't rain. I just throw out my groundsheet, sleeping pad, and sleeping bag and fall asleep under the starry canopy. It's easier and faster to pack up in the morning. My shelter makes a nice pillow, and I drift off under the stars. If it's cold and pushing the temperature range of my sleeping bag, I'll set up my shelter, since it adds 5 to 10 degrees to my sleep system.

Getting set up for a night of cowboy camping in a comfortable, sandy wash. I even had stone shelves to replicate a nightstand.

I like camping in sandy washes when I know it isn't going to rain. They drain well and are really comfortable. They are very low impact spots because nothing grows in the wash and your tracks disappear quickly.

WINTER OR COLD WEATHER

In winter or cold weather, you can camp on snow or cold, frozen ground. Don't be hesitant or scared to camp on snow, particularly if you know it won't get above freezing while you're camping. Camping on snow is zero impact! A bare rock, an un-vegetated area, or an exposed ridgeline where wind has blown the snow away are good spots to camp on if the weather is not going to blast you. These sites can be hard to find.

Cold air sinks at night. To stay warmer, try not to camp in open valley floors and low spots. Cold air accumulates in these areas.

When camping in winter, try to camp in a spot that gets the sun's first light in the morning. Try not to camp behind a peak or a spot that will be in the shadows. It's really nice to get hit by early sun when it is cold out.

Find shelter from the wind. Snowbanks, trees, windrows formed by wind on snow—all serve as wind protection. You can also make a wall out of the snow to the windward side of your tent. It helps break the wind and prevents your tent from getting buried if it is snowing or when snow is drifting in the wind. If you're using a tent or tarp, dig out a spot that's a few feet lower so your tent's below the rest of the snow. Pack down the snow where you plan to set up your tent. It will make it more comfortable and less likely to melt.

If it is very windy, I will sometimes build a rock wall at my campsite. Most of the time it is just a few rocks piled up to stop the wind from blowing on my stove, to improve its efficiency. Sometimes the little aluminum windscreen that I am carrying just needs another buffer. Other times the rock wall can be a little bigger so it stops the wind from blowing on me when I am sleeping or from funneling in under my tarp. This helps me maintain my body heat if it is a chilly and windy night. If it is windy and rainy, it will prevent splatter from entering underneath the tarp. Keep in mind that you should disperse the rocks in the morning so that you don't leave any impact when you leave.

When using a shelter in a downpour, sometimes you might have to excavate and dig a small drainage channel and add soil to bolster the inside wall. If the rain is really piling up, it can be beneficial to help it drain around your shelter, especially if it begins to flow into your tarp or underneath your tent. A few minutes' work with a sharp rock can save you a lot of headaches.

Make sure you're safe from avalanches. Check trees for flagging (broken branches on their uphill side show evidence of past avalanches), prior avalanche debris in snow, and the terrain around you.

Worst-case scenario: Make a snow cave to stay warm. Dig into snow on a hillside. Shovel out an area to sleep in the snow, making it high enough so you can sit up. Place a probe or something else tall at the opening so you can get out in the morning or mark your spot if it has snowed.

It's an example of piss-poor campsite selection when you wake up with a puddle on top of your groundsheet.

Finding the route through fresh snow during my first hike of the Great Divide Trail in the Canadian Rockies

TRAUMA TIP

Always leave an itinerary and trip details with a person or people you trust—ideally make sure they're in touch with one another as well. When on a long hike, I always give somebody my planned itinerary and resupply spots. I call or e-mail from each stop to let them know where I am and roughly when they should hear from me next. If they don't hear from me and it's more than a day late, they can initiate the search-and-rescue system, giving them an idea of where I should be.

Making sure we head up the right side canyon. In tight canyons it can be very difficult to figure out exactly where you are.

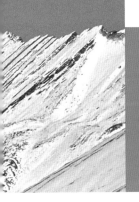

NAVIGATION

On most hikes and backcountry trips, people don't need to navigate because they're just following trails. It's usually enough to follow the trail. Check the map occasionally to make sure you know where you are and know what's coming up. For trips in more wild places and off-trail, knowing how to navigate is imperative.

NAVIGATION BASICS

Although you can hike popular trails like the Long Trail or the AT without knowing how to read a map or compass, knowing how to use your map and compass is an important hiking skill. Being able to read a map and compass can help you find your way back to the trail in case you get lost. You really should learn and practice using them, even if you use a GPS. After all, batteries fail. Maps and compasses are always reliable.

MAPS

There are many different styles of maps. Some are good for backpacking; some aren't. Many guidebooks have decent topo (topographic) maps. Some maps just have a line drawn on a shaded gray map. These are primarily for trip planning. Don't expect to navigate terrain with a bad map. It's just asking for trouble. Get appropriately scaled topographic maps for the terrain you are planning to hike.

On some well-signed trails, like the AT or Long Trail, you don't really need maps. You can get away with a good data book or trail log. Some people try to use a data book on the PCT, but I highly recommend carrying maps, whether they be those in the standard guidebook or other map sets, especially in and north of Kennedy Meadows, where snow can cover up the trail.

Hiking map options include US Geological Survey (USGS) quad maps or commercial maps like National Geographic's Trails Illustrated maps and mapping software that allows you to custom-make maps.

USGS QUAD MAPS

USGS quad pros:

✓ Easy to find your place on the map. They line up well, so there aren't any "dead spots."

USGS quad cons:

✗ They don't cover much terrain. If you are covering a decent amount of distance, getting all the quads can get expensive—and heavy.

✗ They aren't updated often, so trail locations, conditions, shorelines, bridges, rivers, and other things may have changed since the map was printed.

COMMERCIAL HIKING MAPS

Commercial map pros:

✓ These can be very well done and are easy to read.

✓ Some have extra features like trail distances.

✓ They can be printed on durable waterproof material that is tear-resistant.

Commercial maps cons:

✗ Only cover high-use and popular areas.

MAPPING SOFTWARE

Mapping software pros:

✓ You can customize maps, get distances, make notations (including GPS waypoints and coordinates), get multiple scales to meet your needs, print them at home at your convenience and on waterproof paper.

✓ You can buy an entire state or country. Once you buy the software, you can plan tons of different routes/trips from one purchase.

Mapping software cons:

✗ More expensive initially. Some software packages start at about $50.

✗ Getting used to using all the features can take practice.

TOPO MAPS: Topo maps are the best thing for hikers since sliced bread—better actually, because bread doesn't make for the best trail food. They help you better understand the terrain in an area so that you can choose the best routes. Two things are important in determining which topo map you need: the map's scale and its content.

CONTOUR LINES: Topo maps use contour lines to connect points of the same elevation. These lines can give you a three-dimensional perspective on the landscape. Tight bands of contour lines mean steeper terrain; areas with wide spaces are gentler. Depending on the map's scale and purpose, contour lines can demarcate elevation intervals between 10 feet and 200 feet. You can determine the contour interval by finding the elevations marked on two lines and subtracting the difference—giving you the distance between the two heights—then dividing that by the number of lines between the two numbered lines.

SCALE: Scale is another very important aspect of a map. The scale of a map is how much distance on the map represents the actual distance of the terrain. For example, if 1 inch on a map represents 1 mile of terrain, its scale would be written: "1 inch to 1 mile" or "1":1 mile."

A popular scale for USGS quad maps is 1:24,000, which means that 1 inch on the map represents 24,000 inches—0.38 mile—on the ground.

The larger the scale ratio, the less area the map covers but the more detail it can provide. A smaller-scale map like a 1:250,000 ratio map won't show as many details as a 1:50,000 ratio map. However, the smaller-scale map will cover a larger area. With smaller-scale maps, topo lines may run together on steep cliffs and terrain.

You can also use topo software that allows you to zoom in and out as needed and to print the scale of the map you need.

Tip: If you can't find a map with distances between trail junctions or the key distances you want to know, hold a string to the map's scale and mark it to match miles, half miles, and more if you need to. You can then use the string to measure distances on the trail, which will give you a fairly accurate measure of the trail's distance.

COLORS AND SHADING: The colors on a map are important when traveling cross-country. Dark shades of gray or green mean denser vegetation. Lighter greens and grays are areas with less-dense vegetation. White, beige, or no color usually mean alpine zones or other areas with little vegetation. White with blue lines usually signify glaciers or permanent snowfields. For symbols and shades you're not familiar with, check the map's legend for an explanation.

MAP GRIDS: Numbers around the edge of the map on the grid lines are used to determine your location. They show your latitude, longitude, and UTM coordinates. With the grid and a GPS, you can figure out your exact coordinates on a map.

EXTRA CONTENT: Some maps have other features that show distances between trail junctions; different types of lines that represent good trails and primitive trails (unmaintained trails); different

TRAUMA TIP

Sometimes the line intervals can't do the terrain justice. For example, if you have contour lines with 100-meter (300-foot) intervals, you could have a "hidden" 50-meter cliff that won't show up well on the map.

Navigating in Ethiopia near the huge escarpment of the Simien Mountains

types of blue lines for seasonal creeks, year-round streams, and springs; borders demarcating public lands and private lands; and boundaries for camping permits and regulations specific to the region. Look for features on the maps that you think are going to be helpful. With mapping software, you can also add your own information, like waypoints and notes.

Three blows on a whistle is a universal signal for help.

COMPASS

Everyone should carry a compass. While there's a wide variety of compasses available, you generally don't need a fancy one with a sighting mirror. You just need something to orient your map properly. Depending on where you're going, you can probably get away with just a watch that has a compass or a GPS with a compass option—especially if you are mindful of the GPS's batteries.

A compass has the four cardinal directions: north, east, south, and west. When I was young I remembered compass directions because they spelled "WE"; with west on my left and east on my right, I knew north was in front of me and south behind.

The basic purpose of a compass is to tell you where magnetic north is. Once you find that, you can find the other directions. This helps you align your map to the surroundings. Even if the weather is bad and you can't see anything, the compass and the map will help keep you on course.

A compass also tells you your bearing. This is the direction you're facing or heading in relation to magnetic north. It's the single most important tool for navigation available. Once you've oriented your map to the surroundings, you can use it to

Pepper feeling the altitude at over 17,000 feet near Jungben La, Dolpa, Nepal

plot a course. If you want to head over a saddle on the map that is 45 degrees to the right of magnetic north, with your compass calibrated to the map, you can refer to the compass to keep on course even if you can't see the pass because of weather, vegetation, or other geologic features in front of you. If, however, you just headed off in a north-easterly direction, you could easily miss the feature you're looking for. If you were 1 degree off in the direction you were headed, in 1 mile you would be 100 feet away from where you wanted to be. If you did that for 10 miles, you'd be 1,000 feet off, almost 0.2 mile. If you were looking for a water source or trying to avoid a cliff, you might miss your entire destination completely. You would have to look at the map and try to find where you are located.

MAGNETIC DECLINATION: Most maps with a legend have a little diagram with an acute angle. This is an angle of magnetic declination, the difference between the magnetic north pole (MN symbol) and the true north pole (star symbol).

The reason for both is that a compass points toward magnetic north but most maps are oriented to true north. The angle of declination varies by location and can be up to 20 degrees off. For navigational purposes, you want to align the compass to true north so that it matches with what the map is reading.

As you navigate with a map, make sure your compass is pointing toward true north, not magnetic north, and factor in the angle of declination appropriately.

Declination changes over time based on the magnetic properties of the Earth. Changes aren't too substantial. If you want to recheck the declination where you're going, you can look up current declination angles on the internet.

TIMEKEEPING AND NAVIGATION

One of the biggest tenets of good navigation is checking your location on the map at random intervals and matching your location with the time. It gives you an idea of both your pace and location. Then, if you get off course you can refer back to the last time you were still on course. You will have a better idea of where you are because you know where and when you were last on course. You can make plans to either double back or adjust your route to get on course.

Wear a watch, and know when sunset will occur. If your watch fails for any reason, knowing when sunset will happen can still help you figure out what time it is. Cover the sun with your thumb, palm facing you. Each finger above the horizon represents 10 to 15 minutes before sunset.

You can use the sun to tell direction using two methods. An analog watch hour hand can help you determine direction, or you can use a stick in the ground.

In the Northern Hemisphere the sun is due south at noon (it's easier to tell before and after summer, when the sun travels lower in the sky).

In the Southern Hemisphere the sun is due north at noon (it's easier to tell when the sun's lower in the sky).

When using an analog watch in the Northern Hemisphere to determine direction, point the hour hand in the direction of the sun, keeping the watch face flat. Halfway between the hour hand and the 12 is south. So if it's 5 p.m. in the Northern Hemisphere, south would be between 8 and 9. North is opposite of that. In the Southern Hemisphere, point the 12 on the watch face towards the sun. Halfway between the 12 and the hour hand is north.

Another method to determine direction is by using a stick in the ground. You can place a 3-foot-tall stick, your trekking pole, or something else upright in the ground. Mark the location at the end of the shadow. Wait about 20 minutes, and mark the tip of the shadow again. Draw a line connecting the two marks. This shows you an approximate east to west direction. You can calculate north and south by drawing a perpendicular line.

Navigating the Te Araroa Trail in New Zealand

TRIANGULATION

Triangulation is a great trick to figure out exactly where you are. All you need is your map, a compass, and two landmarks. A sheer cliff face, a body of water, or a nearby mountain are easy to find on the map. Here's how:

- Pick two landmarks; it's easier to triangulate if they are more than 60 degrees apart.
- Take a bearing of each one with your compass.
- Find the landmarks on the map, then transfer the bearings you just took to the map.
- Make or visualize a line that each bearing formed in relation to you. You are exactly where the lines cross!

DIRECTIONALLY CHALLENGED MOMENTS (AKA LOST, OR "WHERE THE HECK AM I?")

It is fairly common to become a little lost, directionally challenged, or not quite sure where you are. Over time, it's bound to happen, particularly if you're traveling cross-country.

When it happens, remember: Don't panic! Stay calm, stop, and look at the map. Use your last known point as a reference. People often consider just one possibility and attempt to make the terrain fit their assumption. They're usually in a different spot than they think they are.

Consider all the possible places you could be on the map. Narrow it down to what fits using landmarks to triangulate your location on the topo map.

You can always retrace your steps to get back on track. If you can determine your location without a doubt, you may be able to figure out a different route to intersect your planned route.

If you're totally lost, stop, remain calm, and evaluate the situation. Try to remember any landmarks you passed or how long ago you made a turn that changed your course. Can you triangulate from any obvious things (trails, roads, bodies of water, cliffs, changes in vegetation, etc.) that you recently passed? Think about how long you have until dark. If it's going to get dark before you can return to any known points, stay put and set up camp. It's better to set up at a place when you know you're lost than to continue hiking in the dark and get more confused.

If you're hiking with a group of people, talk things over. Figure out a reasonable plan of action for finding your location and how to get back on track. Don't act rashly! If you head out in one direction on a whim and have to backtrack, you'll end up wasting a lot of time and energy. Your fear will probably increase.

Getting rescued when you're lost can take hours or even days. Help rescuers find you by making a small smoke fire, or, if it's not too much effort, find an open area and lay rocks out in an "X" formation. Lay out some brightly colored clothes or your pack. Use something that will reflect sunlight onto planes flying overhead. If you're lost at night, don't camp near running water. It will make it harder for you to hear voices of people nearby.

If you've called for a heli rescue or used a PLB, be ready to give details about your condition, or a patient's condition. Details should include urgency, name, age, and sex. If calling, give your best estimate of location, whether you intend to move, and, if so, where to. When a helicopter or plane flies over, stand toward it with your arms in a "V" if you need help. If your arms are in a straight diagonal line, like a slash, it means "All OK." If for any reason you've found your way before a rescue team arrives, change your PLB signal or call them back to cancel rescue. It costs a lot of money to organize and deploy rescue services. You can be held liable for them.

Taking a break and cooking dinner in grizzly country. When in bear country, never cook where you camp. On the Rockwall Trail, part of the Great Divide Trail in the Canadian Rockies.

TRAUMA TIP

When your dog is first starting to wear his dog pack, make sure the strap behind the dog's front legs doesn't rub the back of his legs. It's a common issue that occurs when people overtighten the chest strap on the dog's pack. It causes the dog discomfort and can rub your pet's skin raw.

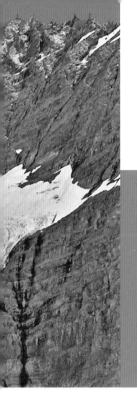

HIKING WITH YOUR DOG

When you are hiking/backpacking in the wilderness with your dog, you have the additional responsibility of caring for your pet. I've hiked thousands of wonderful miles with my dog, Yoni. What has worked well for Yoni and me may not work as well for you and your dog. Test things out and see how the two of you interact before going on a big hike. It's important to know your pet's limits and to read the signs of fatigue and pain, because your dog can't tell you what's wrong.

While it's great to experience the outdoors with your dog, not everyone likes pets. Some areas already restrict dogs because some unruly dog owners screwed it up for the rest of us. Be a responsible pet owner. Follow the rules and help keep dogs from being banned in any more places.

The size of the dog doesn't matter as much as its health and enthusiasm. The smaller a dog is, the more steps it needs to take. It's probably exerting more calories per pound than a larger dog. Smaller dogs may need more help getting up larger ledges and on river crossings. Larger dogs are heavier, and if you're going to do technical moves where you need to carry them or pick them up, it's going to put more strain on you.

PLANNING A TRIP WITH YOUR DOG

Planning a trip well is even more important if you are hiking with your dog. Make sure that all the areas where you're going allow pets. For instance, most US national parks don't allow pets on their trail systems. There are exceptions, so check the rules.

The main thing to remember when hiking with a dog is to maintain control of your dog at all times. If your dog is not well behaved around people, other dogs, horses, mountain bikes, or wildlife, please be respectful. Only bring your pet on trails in the off-season to avoid any problems with others.

LEASHES

Even if your dog is good off-leash, keep him or her on a leash. This is a rule in most areas for good reasons. It's safer for your dog, safer for wildlife, reduces the impact on wildlife and plant life, and is more respectful to other visitors.

It also prevents the "dog syndrome," where the dog actually walks at least twice the distance you walk because he wanders around and checks everything out. If both of you are putting in distance on a regular basis, you want to prevent your dog from getting burned out from the trek quickly. This will slow you down considerably.

A leash is also important so that your dog paces himself. Dogs get excited when they go outside and go hiking, but no matter how many times you tell them, "We are hiking 2,175 miles from Georgia to Maine, and you'll have plenty of time outside, so better chill out now and take it easy," they just won't listen when you first hit the trail. If you want them to last for the whole hike, you need to limit the extra miles, and the only way to do this is by keeping them on a leash. This will also help you know exactly how many miles you and your dog have done that day. This is very important, because you want to break your pet in slowly with distance and weight in his pack, just as you do with yourself. Depending on how much you have been walking or hiking with your dog, training will dictate reasonable mileages.

For example, when I first started long-distance hiking with Yoni, she was 1 year old. I had been day hiking with her previously, but nothing over 5 or 6 miles and nothing with a pack. When we started the AT, it was new to us. Three to 10 miles was a routine day for the first couple of weeks, with a rest day sporadically mixed in. Over the next couple of

Common "wildlife" sighting in New Mexico along the Continental Divide Trail.

TIP: I keep a 3-foot section of webbing in Yoni's pack. When we stop for the day or for a break, I can tie her to a tree or something else sturdy; this gives her some more distance to play with, but not too much. She knows when I do this that it's rest time and she can relax or sleep, and I don't have to keep holding the leash.

This also works really well on the AT if you're staying in shelters. You can tie your dog up in a corner of the shelter and he won't bother people who don't like dogs.

Some people on the AT don't think dogs belong on the trail or in shelters—at all. Be prepared for some antagonism from them. The best remedy is being respectful so they hardly even notice your dog in the shelter. Yoni knows it's bedtime when she's tied up, and she knows that's her space. When you're moving all of the time, tying your dog up can reassure him. And if something comes near camp at night, I know she's tied up and can't take off after it.

Other reasons to keep your dog on a leash: When he is wearing a dog pack, the leash loop on the back keeps the pack centered on his back so it doesn't slide down toward or even over his head on downhill walks, nor will it rub the back of his front legs. Also, if your dog runs through woods unleashed, there's a decent chance he could lose his pack and all his food. Then you have to hope you can find the pack. If you can't, you're up a creek for the remainder of the section or have to cut the trip short.

One of my usual methods of keeping Yoni corralled during break time *Photo by Russ Sackson*

weeks, we slowly upped it to 15 miles as our largest day, but still alternating between bigger and shorter days so we would have recovery days and not be pushing it too much. Continuing the next year on the PCT, we regressed from the 30 miles per day we had built up to and started the hike averaging 15–20 miles per day. It was easier to cover that distance, since our bodies were already used to it. We then increased on the PCT all the way up to 35-mile and 40-mile days until we could hike those distances day after day without feeling any strain. Each year we would start a new hike, we would only have to regress to 20–25 miles as our base distance, since our pack weights were lower and we were used to the motions of hiking. I cannot stress enough the importance of breaking in before increasing mileage, for both you and your dog.

Walking with a leash and trekking poles can be hard at first. With a little practice, though, both you and your dog can get used to it. Play around with different leash lengths to give more room or less room. Remember, because of restrictions, leashes in most places can be no longer than 6 feet.

Another option: Some people rig their dog leash with a carabiner and attach it to their waist belt. That way they don't have to hold the leash all day and can use their trekking poles freely. Some leashes, usually designed for running but certainly suitable for hiking, wrap around your waist, also keeping your hands free.

CONDITIONING AND TRAIL-TRAINING YOUR DOG

Is your dog ready to set out on a big trip? While you have an idea of what you're getting into and training for, your dog doesn't. So, get him ready. Get him into the routine of hiking with you so he's used to your days and distance.

Get him used to the lifestyle and slowly increase the mileage, mixing in rest days and shorter days. While hiking with you, dogs have to do a lot of what they'd do in the wild anyway. They'll adapt quickly. I find they're often better off because they have four legs and have a lower center of gravity.

Yoni has learned the lifestyle. She knows that if I stop to talk to anyone or stop to look at the map for a bit, she should take the opportunity to get off her feet and rest.

Yoni and I began hiking together on the Appalachian Trail when she was 1 year old after several day hikes and gradually longer treks. I would recommend not overdoing it when your dog is young. Wait until he is at least 1 year old to start racking up the miles, because his muscles and bones are still developing. I was also told not to run down hills because it is harder on the dog's joints. Talk to your vet for advice tailored to your dog's breed, age, and condition.

DOG PACKS (SADDLEBAGS)

If your dog is going to carry a pack with food and other things, get him used to that. Start off by letting him wear the empty pack around the house, then on short walks, and then on longer walks. Add weight slowly as he gets used to it.

The most any dog should carry is one-third of his body weight—if he is in top shape. Don't overdo it. On long-distance hikes you may want to reduce the weight so your dog will be happy and healthy for the long haul. One-quarter the dog's weight or less is much more comfortable for the dog and a more sustainable weight ratio.

You're certainly trying to carry much less than one-quarter your weight. For instance, if you're 160 pounds, one-third your weight is 53 pounds and one-quarter your weight is 40 pounds. Yet you usually want to get your pack weight below one-quarter your weight when possible (in winter and cold conditions, you may

have to carry more weight). Have the same consideration for your dog.

DOGS AND FOOD

Many dogs need double their normal food intake on strenuous or long-distance hikes. You'll learn how much food your dog needs as he or she hikes with you. Yoni eats about 2 pounds of food per day on a long-distance hike. She weighs about 65 pounds.

On a long-distance hike, keep in mind how you binge eat when you get to town. These calories are crucial for you, and the same is true for your dog. When we get to town, I feed Yoni as much as possible, but only dog food! I give her multiple cans of dog food on top of her dry food, which she chows down. I also feed her puppy food, because it has a higher calorie content.

In Yoni's top shape I would only allow her to carry—at most—five days of food, her pack, a section of webbing, and her collapsible bowl. That probably maxed out at 20 pounds. If the stretch was any longer than five days, I carried the rest of her food in my pack and used that food first.

When packing dog food, place it in trash-compactor bags or double-bagged in sturdy zipper bags so it doesn't get wet. Divide the food evenly between two bags, and place one on either side of the pack. Feed your dog out of both sides evenly to keep the weight evenly distributed between the saddlebags.

Whether you send your dog's food along with any mail drops you do is entirely up to you. It can save time, but unless your dog is a picky eater, you can almost always pick up dog food in a town when you stop to resupply. Dog food is heavy, so it can be pricey to ship. I only do it when absolutely necessary and I know the resupply will not have dog food.

WATER

I hardly ever carry any water for Yoni. If I know we're facing a waterless stretch that's over 15 miles and it's really hot out, I will then carry water. From being on the trail so much, Yoni has learned she needs to "camel up" at all water sources and now does so naturally. If you're just starting hiking with your dog, don't anticipate that he will get that approach right away. Start out by carrying a little extra water for him; as he no longer needs it, you can reduce and then eliminate the extra water.

TRAUMA TIP

If you're worried about dehydration and want to carry extra stuff for your dog, they make a powdered electrolyte mix for dogs that you can add to their water bowl. I've used this a couple of times while traveling with Yoni through the desert, and it seemed to work well. You can also add some Pedialyte to their diet if you want to add electrolytes. Check with your vet for the amounts to use, based on your dog's weight.

Yoni needs an extra-large dog bowl because she has trouble getting all the water in her mouth. On the CDT, be prepared to share water sources with livestock.

If you're worried your dog's not getting enough water, carry some extra water until both of you are used to what he will need.

On a lot of trails like the AT or the Long Trail, you probably won't have to carry any water because there are plenty of water crossings. They're generally spaced out at least every 7 miles.

I've heard that dogs can get giardia, but I have never seen or experienced it. I've never treated Yoni's water, and she's had some pretty nasty water. It's up to you if you want to treat your dog's water. It's time-consuming, and when you get to a water crossing it's hard to stop your dog from drinking when he is thirsty.

Still, if Yoni tries to drink from a foul cattle reservoir, and I know there is a better water source not far ahead, I'll try to keep her from drinking that water—though she certainly didn't stop me that one time.

I'm more picky about not letting her drink from puddles on roadways. She could be ingesting oils, rubber, transmission fluid, glycol, and who knows what else. She has drunk from such puddles, especially during long waterless stretches. I'm more concerned about that than a dirty cattle reservoir.

DESERTS AND DOGS

The heat and desert are as tough on your dog as they are on you, especially if your dog has a black coat. I have heard that dogs are not as efficient as people at cooling since they can't really sweat; instead they pant to cool down. Still, I'll never shave Yoni because her coat also serves as her sunscreen. She even seemed to get cow-type spots on her belly after hiking through the snow. I'm guessing it was the sun reflection, and the spots went away after a few months.

If you're in an area where it's hot and waterless, I'd recommend hiking in the predawn darkness until it gets hot. Take a siesta in the shade during the hottest part of the day, and resume hiking when it cools in the afternoon. Yoni prefers this, as do I, and it makes the slog through these conditions a lot easier.

CROSSINGS

One issue you'll face with a dog is crossings. This can be over rivers, fences, and wildlife boundary crossings.

River crossings can be the toughest. Dogs aren't very good at moving through swift water. When crossing a river with Yoni, I'll usually hold her collar in my hand, keeping her downstream. This way she can't take me out if she loses control, and I'll help pull her across as she tries to swim. I do this for any big river crossing. I will let her splash through smaller streams and calm rivers.

The backcountry is littered with fences. These can present a minor challenge at times. The ladders and A-frames over fences and electric fences on the AT are a hassle, but not a big deal. When steps are too small for Yoni to climb, I'll sometimes pick her up and carry her over.

The CDT is full of barbed-wire fences without crossings or gates. In such situations I will raise the bottom of the fence as high as possible and she crawls underneath. Then I climb over the top and inevitably rip my shorts.

ROCK CLIMBING AND TECHNICAL MOVES

If you're going to be doing any technical sections during the trip and your dog is with you, consider bringing a dog harness. You can use the harness to either lift the dog up or to help him make technical moves.

Yoni and I after crossing the headwaters of the Chilliwack River on a cable car. North Cascades, Pacific Northwest Trail, Washington.

SNOW

Yoni likes the snow and cold. Like many dogs, she handles it well. Snowdrifts and snowfields shouldn't be an issue for most dogs, since they can trot through them. Dogs aren't the best on ice. It's like watching them try to run on a wood floor.

Be careful on slopes prone to avalanches. Don't let your dog loose in such areas; it could make the situation dangerous for your dog, you, and anyone else around.

SLEEPING GEAR AND CLOTHES

This depends on your dog and the conditions you're hiking in. Some short-haired dogs can get chilly at night. If you have a short-haired dog, you might need a little quilt or something to put on him. He may want to make a nest to keep warm at night. Some short-haired dogs could benefit from a jacket to keep them warm either during the day or to use

at night instead of a sleeping bag. Most long-haired dogs are okay for three-season camping. Consider a jacket or quilt for your dog for winter camping.

During winter camping, carry a foam pad to insulate your dog from the ground. He will lose a lot of body heat if lying on the ground. During spring, summer, and fall, I don't carry anything extra for Yoni.

Yoni likes to sleep outside. She can also sleep in the vestibule if it's raining and she's wet. If it's going to rain overnight—or if there are mosquitoes—and she's not wet, I'll bring her inside the tent or tarp to sleep.

I would recommend not letting your dog inside your tent, unless he is absolutely miserable outside. The dog will get used to being let in and expect it even if he is dirty, muddy, and wet. A dog's nails

ABOVE: Ascending a ladder in Vermont on the AT. Yoni loves these challenges. BELOW: Yoni taking a little break in North Carolina, showing off her booties during our AT winter hike.

TRAUMA TIP On rainy or snowy days your dog will get wet. It's no fun letting a wet dog in your shelter, where you want everything to be dry. Let your dog sleep in the vestibule area or under your tarp's end, away from you. This will prevent your sleeping bag and dry gear from getting wet—and wet dog on it—all while keeping your buddy out of the weather.

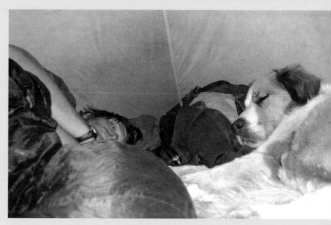

can easily rip the floor of your tent (been there, done that!). Also keep space and weight considerations in mind. If it is a horrible mosquito season and I think I'll have to bring Yoni inside, I'll need a 1.5-person tent at the minimum, which will add at least a few ounces to my pack weight. I can deal with a few ounces here and there, but I can't deal with a sprawling dog taking over the tent or moving around every couple of hours, resulting in a bad night's sleep for me. This is one of the reasons that I prefer to use a tarp. Yoni can come and go, if she wants cover or not, into the foot area of the tarp without waking me up. There's plenty of room and at the right weight savings. These are all things to keep in mind when looking for a shelter if you are going to be hiking with your dog.

DOGGIE DOO

This is an issue of contention with some hikers and nature-lovers. It's a reason dogs aren't allowed in some places, particularly ecologically sensitive places, and why some people don't like dogs on trails. If you're bringing a dog with you, please be responsible and clean up after your pet in the same way you clean up after yourself. Keeping your dog on a leash makes it easier to know when he has done his business. Bury all feces at least 200 feet from water sources and away from campsites and trails.

FIRST AID FOR DOGS

Despite all the miles Yoni and I have traveled together, we haven't had many first-aid issues.

I took her to the vet once during a hike for a sore paw. It was from walking on too much gravel on the CDT. We hitched ahead to the nearest vet. He looked over her paw and kenneled her while I hitched back to the trail and hiked the section. I then hitched back to the vet's. When I got back she was healed, rested, and ready to go.

On the PCT she got foxtail weed in her paw. It manifested as a sore on her leg a couple weeks later. I ended up pulling it out. It never really bothered or slowed her down.

Certain human treatments will also work for dogs. Neosporin is OK to put on your dog's cuts. Make sure he doesn't ingest it.

Dogs can also have aspirin. Before you leave on a trip, ask your vet how mush aspirin can be given. It can help with his pain relief and injuries—same as you—but be careful and limit your dog's ambitions. If your dog thinks he is feeling better, he may be overzealous, which can cause further injury.

Check your dog's body for ticks regularly when hiking in tick country. You may also consider using a Frontline-like chemical to help repel ticks.

PAW CARE

Just like you, your dog's feet are constantly in touch with the ground. You'll usually have shoes or boots on to help protect your feet. Some of the hardest hiking for dogs is on hot pavement. Luckily some companies, like Granite Gear, have designed booties that protect your dog's pads from the searing heat of pavement in summer, gravel, sharp rocks on mountains, and snow in the winter.

Dog booties take some time for your dog to get used to. When first wearing them, your dog will walk funny. After you put them on for the first

time, do something fun with them on. Your dog will soon forget he is wearing them. Booties are great for salted roads in New England or the Midwest, sharp rocky terrain, spring corn snow, walking on pavement on a hot day, and to protect an injured foot pad. Find a pair of booties that fit your dog well, doesn't irritate his dewclaw, and don't come off too often in snow.

Companies also make foot-pad creams to protect your dog's pads from cracking or to prevent snow from accumulating on his feet. If both of you are hiking through the snow, and your dog's not wearing booties, consider a protective cream, such as Musher's Secret.

THRU-HIKING WITH A DOG

I am often asked how to thru-hike long trails with a dog, because each major trail has a section that doesn't allow dogs.

I've been lucky. I've had friends in key places who have watched Yoni when she can't hike with me. They've also been able to meet us, pick her up, and drop her off. (Yoni and I thank you all!) There are other options for your dog on those sections he can't hike with you—on most trails.

APPALACHIAN TRAIL: There are only two places on the AT that don't allow dogs: Great Smoky Mountains National Park in Tennessee and Baxter State Park in Maine. Both are easy to deal with because the AT has enough hikers with dogs that there are services to help.

Kennels in Tennessee will pick up your dog at Fontana Dam or the northern end of the park and kennel your dog for however long you think it will take you to hike through the park. They'll bring your dog to you at the other side of the park. It's a little pricey, but not too bad considering it is a long drive. The names of kennels offering such services are listed in some AT guidebooks.

Baxter is also relatively easy for both northbounders and southbounders. Northbounders hit Abol Bridge on the Golden Road before entering Baxter State Park. The Golden Road gets a fair amount of traffic in summer and goes straight into Millinocket, Maine. You can hitch into town with your dog or walk the distance.

After you summit Mount Katahdin, you'll end up on another road that goes to Millinocket. You can hitch a ride back to town. It's the reverse for southbounders.

You can drop your dog at a kennel in town or find a hotel that allows dogs and book the room for two nights. Only do this second option if you know your dog is really, really well behaved. You then have to cover the mileage from Abol Bridge to Katahdin and get back to Millinocket in one day. Put the "Do Not Disturb" sign on your room door and get a ride back to Abol Bridge in the morning. Summit Katahdin, and return to the hotel room.

> ## TRAUMA PICK
>
> I like a streamlined dog pack that contours well with the dog's body. You don't want the bottom of the saddle bags rubbing on the ground. Make sure it is correctly fitted to the dog so it doesn't chafe the back of his front legs, front of his back legs, or his chest. Make sure you can adjust it properly so it fits well and it isn't so big that you have a tendency to overpack it and weigh the dog down. Dog packs also take a lot of abuse if they are used a lot because dogs don't know to be careful with their gear. It can take a dog a little while to realize that he just got wider and can't fit between those trees, so make sure your dog's gear is made of high-quality materials.
>
> **RECOMMENDED DOG GEAR:** Granite Gear Long Howl or Alpha Dog Pack (discontinued), Granite Gear mush booties, Bison Designs Dur-A-Bowl, 2 trash-compactor bags

Yoni peers into Mexico, scoping "coyotes" at the PCT's southern terminus in Campo, California.

PACIFIC CREST TRAIL: Dogs are not allowed on trails in California state parks and most national parks on the PCT. Most California state parks on the PCT are in Southern California close to Scissors Crossing. You can bypass this by a road that parallels the trail.

The longer, more difficult area is from Kennedy Meadows north to Sonora Pass in California's Sierra Nevada range. This long stretch goes through three national parks (Sequoia, Kings Canyon, and Yosemite). You can kennel your dog either in Mammoth, California, at the north end of the section, or in Reno, Nevada, even farther north, while you hike this section.

If you're northbound, you can hitch a ride from Kennedy Meadows or hike to Olancha Pass and down to Olancha, California. Get to US 395 and hitch to Mammoth on the north end of the section or Reno on the south end of the section. Kennel your dog, then hop on the Inyo-Mono transit back to where you left off on US 395. The Inyo-Mono transit also runs all the way up to Reno, Nevada, and down through the Lancaster-Palmdale area to the south.

Yoni and I at the famous buoy in Key West, Florida, the southernmost point of the United States, after hiking from Cap Gaspé, Quebec.

Yoni and I at the New Mexico–Mexico border, heading for tacos in Mexico after finishing our 10,000-mile trek.
Photo by Shawn Forry

If you're southbound, hitch to Mammoth or Reno with your dog from Bridgeport or South Lake Tahoe, California.

After completing the section, take the Inyo-Mono transit back to where you kenneled your dog and hitch back to where you left off. It's a bit of a hassle, but hitching is usually pretty easy on US 395.

Roads parallel the PCT both through Lassen National Park in California and Crater Lake National Park in Oregon. You can legally walk through the parks with your dog on the roads.

In Washington's North Cascades National Park, dogs are allowed only on the PCT. This is convenient.

CONTINENTAL DIVIDE TRAIL: Dogs aren't allowed on backcountry trails in national parks along the CDT. This includes Glacier, Yellowstone, and Rocky Mountain (sort of). The CDT's dog options are simple.

Glacier is easy to deal with. It's either at the start or end of your journey, and you have one of two options. You can day-hike it. Three roads lead into the park. You can use them to get in and out and leave your dog at a hotel for the day—again, only if you know your dog is well behaved. Make sure you put the "Do Not Disturb" sign on the door

when you leave. You could also kennel your dog for a few days in Montana's East Glacier, West Glacier, St. Mary, or Kalispell. Kenneling your dog in one of these locations can be a little inconvenient.

For Yellowstone you can take the Continental Divide Trail Alliance (CDTA) route and not the Mack's Inn cutoff. You can hike into West Yellowstone. From there you can resupply and road-walk through the park and camp at non-backcountry sites. This is all completely legal. You can meet up with the rest after the south end of the park.

The CDT follows a loop through Rocky Mountain National Park. Most CDT hikers don't do it. They road-walk into Grand Lake, Colorado, to resupply and bypass the loop. This is easy. Then you can road-walk out of Grand Lake and meet up with the trail at the southern border of the park.

JOHN MUIR TRAIL: Don't even bother trying it. There's no way around it. There are no dogs allowed, since this trail is pretty much all in national parks (except for a little bit around Mammoth Lakes, California). Leave your dog with a friend or take him to the doggie hotel for some playtime with friends for a week or two while you hike the trail.

Atop Mount Kenya (4,985m/16,355 ft.) at dawn on a cold, icy morning

Ascending Mount Kenya

A Masai I met while hiking through Kenya. I played in a great pickup soccer game with his village and drank fresh, unhomogenized, unpasteurized cow milk that evening. They even offered to let me stay so I could help teach soccer to the villagers.

Walking behind some Ethiopians headed to market

HIKING ABROAD

Hiking internationally can be as daunting as it is awesome. It means stepping out of your comfort zone and experiencing new languages, cultures, landscapes, rules, and food.

PLANNING

You'll need to do a lot of research to plan an international hike. You'll be farther from your support structure. You simply can't call up a buddy and say, "Can you pick me up in Bangladesh? This just isn't working out."

When devising your plan, use guidebooks, the internet, Google Earth, topographic maps online, atlases—anything you can glean from the library. The Lonely Planet country guidebooks are very helpful, giving a general overview of travel to the specific country. The US State Department's International Travel Information web channel is very useful. Talk to other people who have visited the area.

Look at general maps to get an overview of the regions you plan to hike. Research the towns and cities that will be your potential resupply points.

Sometimes it is hard to find detailed maps of a region or country. Often you can track them down by contacting someone in that region, like a guide service or tourist agency. Omnimap.com (recently acquired by East View Companies) is an online map store in the United States that offers a lot of international maps. They can be pricey.

Stanfords in the U.K. is another good option for international maps (stanfords.co.uk). Sometimes you can find maps on the internet as free downloads, which makes it really easy to draw your planned route right on the map.

As you review these detailed maps, look more closely and start devising a possible route. Look for trails, water sources, nearby towns, and anything else that may be pertinent to the trip.

TRAUMA TIP When traveling abroad and hiking in developing countries, pay attention to what you wear. It's helpful not to draw too much attention to yourself. You don't want to show signs of wealth. Doing so can make you a target for being ripped off by merchants or for theft. For instance, in a lot of countries a camera, smartphone, GPS device, or nice altimeter watch is a sign of wealth. Be careful where you take your camera out. Do not show all your money when making purchases.

Measure distances on the maps between towns, resupplies, trails, and trailheads. Write all of this on your map or in a data-book so you'll have an idea of distances between resupplies, obvious daily landmarks, and water sources.

When you're organizing your trip, make sure you learn about all required permits, visas, and vaccinations. They can take up to six months to acquire. Some vaccinations must be taken over time. If you're at risk of malaria at your destination, see a travel doctor.

All this is worthwhile because it should leave you feeling prepared and confident to set out on the trip.

TO GUIDE OR NOT TO GUIDE

There is a major difference between hiking in a developed nation and a developing nation. In a first-world country most people hike without guides and porters and don't need agents to book the trip. Bureaucracies in developing nations can be a headache to work with. This is another reason more preparation is needed.

Pepper walks toward a gompa in Olangchung Gola in the Nepalese Himalayas.

TRAUMA TIP

Put dryer sheets in your luggage, shoes, and pack to help keep things from smelling when you're traveling to and from the trail. You'll definitely need this for used gear that you are taking home with you!

Loading a huge duffel onto a typical "mini car" in Kathmandu

In third-world countries the majority of people go on guided treks. It can be overwhelming to do all the planning and hike alone in a foreign country. Some places, like Nepal, mandate that trekkers must have guides, or at least a partner. There are pros and cons to either a guided or non-guided trek. It depends on what you like and the situation.

Many guided treks also include the option of cooked meals, camp setup, and portaging your equipment. This can make your trip hassle-free.

I've never had good luck with guides; then again, I am not the normal client. I often feel like they look at me and see dollar signs. I often end up caring for guides and have to make sure they're OK. Hiking with a guide slows me down and takes away my freedom of exploration.

While hiking through Africa, by myself, I went to Mount Kenya National Park. The Kenyan government requires people to have a guide or hike or climb in a group of two or more. I had to hire a guide to even enter the park.

In the nearby village I conducted a survey of the potential guides. It was like I was Regis Philbin and they were contestants on *Who Wants to Be a Millionaire?* Me: "How far can you walk in a day?" Them: "10 Miles." Me: "Is that your final answer?" They nod. Me: "Sorry; go home. Next contestant." It went on.

Finally I picked a young guy who seemed fit and up for a challenge. He said he had all the gear he needed. He retrieved a school bag–size red knapsack. It lacked a hip belt, was barely 1,500 cubic inches, and already had one shoulder strap that was ripping at the seams. I thought, Uh-oh, this could be trouble. There was no turning back now. I was ready to get moving. I calculated that this stretch should last about two days.

We headed up with only a few hours of daylight left and about 9 miles to go. We talked during the first hour, but he soon slowed and told me to go ahead. I reached a hut at about 14,000 feet and waited. I ate dinner. He rolled up about an hour after I finished dinner. The shadow of the mountain was fading into the twilight landscape, and the stars were starting to show.

He was flabbergasted by my speed. He said we probably wouldn't have to start at 2 a.m., like most people do on summit day. I figured he was tired and needed some extra rest.

I knew I wanted to summit, complete the five-pass circuit, and get back down and out of the park the next day. He was skeptical. I said we could leave at 4:30 a.m. and summit during sunrise.

We left at 4:35 a.m. and reached the summit just as the sun peeked over the horizon. He thought we summited from the hut in a record time and was immensely proud of himself. I led down the south side of the peak to continue on the circuit I'd planned to hike. We encountered steep snow and ice, so I kicked steps for him. He was nervous and his legs were shaking in his boots. I helped him down the slope, and we continued on our way.

At about 10 a.m. he hit a wall and said he needed a break. He had no food with him at all. He was counting on the hut's caretaker to feed him. We weren't far from the hut, so I gave him a couple of my Lärabars. We reached the hut by 11 a.m. and took lunch. We had one more pass to go over and then a 15-mile downhill hike that dropped more than 10,000 vertical feet. But he was done.

After he ate, he couldn't stand up. He did the thru-hiker shuffle: walking like he was more than 100 years old. When I asked if he was OK. He responded that he couldn't believe we hiked that much by 11 a.m.

He told me I was the strongest person he'd ever met—strength must be measured differently in countries where they still walk for all their supplies as part of their daily routine. I told him that I can walk really far but am not that strong. I held up my T-Rex thru-hiker arms and flexed my nonexistent biceps, and we both started laughing hysterically.

He told me to go on without him because he couldn't hike anymore. I asked him if my permit would get checked or if I would get in trouble. "No," he said. "We will let the ranger at the other gate know not to bother you. You know what you are doing. You will be safe." I hiked on alone, as I had the rest of the trip. I made it out of the park that night as planned.

People tell me I should start a guiding business and take people into the backcountry. I'm not so sure about that.

TRAUMA TIP Before you leave, call your credit-card companies and banks so they'll know you're abroad and don't freeze your accounts. Also make at least two copies of your credit cards as well as your passport. Leave one copy of your passport with someone you trust, and hide a copy in a locked resupply duffel. With your credit cards, jot down the contact numbers so you can call even if you lose your cards. It can also be helpful to save copies in Dropbox or in the cloud so you can access them overseas if necessary.

Scrambling to organize before setting out on a big international hike

LANGUAGE

It's helpful and respectful to learn at least a few words of the local language where you plan to travel. It shows locals that you're making an effort to try to communicate in their language. They really appreciate it and will likely make you feel more welcome and hospitable. If the situation were reversed, you'd probably be more likely to try to help someone who tried to speak your language than someone who assumed automatically that you knew theirs.

PHOTOGRAPHY

Be careful when taking out your camera. Always ask permission before taking someone's photo. It's often considered rude for strangers to snap pictures without asking. If someone says no, please respect that. It's also customary in some places to leave a small donation or gift in exchange for taking a photograph.

HANDOUTS

This is touchy because I don't like giving handouts. I hate going to places where people are accustomed to getting handouts from foreigners. It really doesn't encourage them to do positive things for themselves. I have no problem buying things from locals. In my opinion, giving things away to them doesn't encourage anything more than begging.

I know there are parts of the world where there are no jobs. Rewarding begging encourages more beggars, especially when local people see foreigners.

Some people give out pens, candy, or other trinkets. People have told me I should do it too. I disagree. If you truly want to help locals, volunteer your time. Help people build a community, a school, a water source, or develop a small business.

Hiking Abroad Tips

- Most countries have some general delivery system. It is called poste restante. This may be a good resupply option in developed countries. It is more dubious in developing countries. Hence, I do the duffel bag "bounce box."

- In town wash your clothes in the sink, tub, or shower; wring out; and hang to dry (or save time and combine while taking a shower). That way you don't have to worry about finding a washer and dryer.

- Aggressive dogs and rabies are concerns in developing countries. People in developing nations often use dogs to help guard their area. Such dogs often get rocks thrown at them by people. You can probably keep them at bay by picking up a rock and pantomiming the action of throwing it at them. That will usually tell them to leave you alone. When you encounter a dog that's undeterred by the action or one that's foaming at the mouth, back away while maintaining eye contact. Never turn and run.

- Bring appropriate medications with you as a precautionary measure. It's helpful to have Diamox, used to prevent symptoms of altitude sickness, in the Himalayas. You also should consider bringing vitamin I (ibuprofen), other painkillers, ciprofloxacin (for urinary tract infections and diarrhea), metronidazole (used to treat giardia and other parasitic and bacterial issues), and petroleum jelly for chafe. You might also consider bringing arnica or turmeric to reduce inflammation, astragalus to boost your immune system, or other common herbs used to treat traveler's diarrhea and cold and flu symptoms or to increase your energy. I would recommend consulting an acupuncturist or herbal specialist before taking them to avoid ingesting herbs that conflict with other medications.

- I separate my money before I get to town. I keep my small bills accessible and my larger bills hidden. This allows the locals to only see the small bills I am carrying when I pay for something. It doesn't draw any unnecessary attention.

- Dress appropriately for the culture and climate. In certain Muslim countries, women are still held to strict dress codes. They wear an outer garment called a burka that covers their entire body while in public. If you are a woman hiking in a strict Muslim country and wear clothing that does not hide your body—even if you are obviously a foreigner—locals may glare at you and make you feel very uncomfortable. Respect their culture. You'll feel a lot more comfortable in it,. and you'll draw less attention to yourself.

- Calibrate your GPS unit to the local datum as listed on the map. The unit will not work correctly if it is not calibrated properly. The datum is usually listed in the map legend. This isn't an issue in the United States but can be internationally.

Cooking dinner in a rural Nepali village with the usual audience. Three times as many people were watching a few minutes later.

SAFETY AND HEALTH

Often, people say they're scared about their health and safety in developing countries, so they avoid traveling abroad. Many health issues are preventable. The list of potential setbacks includes malaria, cholera, dysentery, yellow fever, encephalitis, robbery, mugging, and kidnapping. One of the biggest concerns is traveler's trots (diarrhea).

Generally, you're safer in the wilderness than in a big city, regardless of whether you're in a developed or developing nation. Wherever you are, you should always stay alert.

Always keep an eye and a hand on your pack and your possessions. Don't give people an opportunity to take easy advantage of you. That follows the idea of not drawing unnecessary attention to yourself. Don't wear fancy jewelry or accessories while traveling or hiking.

It's very important with international travel to always leave trip details with someone at home. ALWAYS! When traveling internationally, always make sure someone in your home country also has a copy of your passport.

THE NASTY M&M'S: Although mosquitoes and malaria are not common at high altitudes, you should still follow all recommended precautions.

Mosquitoes in the United States are primarily an annoyance. There are cases of West Nile, encephalitis, and Zika but they are relatively uncommon. In a lot of the world, especially around the equator, there are serious issues. Get anti-malaria pills before you leave, and test them out to make sure the side effects aren't too severe. There are a few options. Make sure you get a prescription that will work for you. Take the same precautions against bugs that you would for hiking on the AT in August. Use DEET, cover up with bug netting, spray your clothes with permethrin before you leave, and wear light-colored clothing.

GEAR CONCERNS

When going overseas to hike, bring equipment you know is durable and will last. It's often very hard to find recreational or outdoors equipment in a developing nation, particularly in the backcountry. Don't pack too much. You want your pack to remain as small as possible. You should be able to bring it on crowded buses and keep it on your lap or between your legs.

It's almost inevitable that you'll take some type of public transportation during your trip. It might be to get to the trailhead, to resupply, or to return from the end of your trip. If your gear's with you, don't let go of it or take your eyes off it. If you have a big pack (larger than 4,200 cubic inches), you'll most likely have to strap it to the roof of the vehicle. This can add unneeded stress to the seams and fabric.

When hiking internationally, I recommend carrying a tent—or at least some sort of tarp that drops close to the ground on all sides. It will give you some privacy. It also hides your gear from the locals, and they won't know how expensive it is. A tent is more versatile, and people are more accustomed to them.

RESUPPLIES

On long international hikes through developing countries, I usually rely on local towns for resupplies. When it comes to swapping out shoes or getting new gear, I usually plan my route and trips to the trail accordingly, setting up resupply stations before actually starting the hike. I stop in my planned hubs in cities and towns. I pay a little extra for a one-night stay at a hotel that I feel safe in. I have them store a duffel and use it as a local hub while in that area. Sometimes I have to hike back through the city itself. Other times, when I get close to it I'll take a bus back and forth to the trail. I'll use the hotel as a resupply. It's nice to know I can get gear and some food I brought from home on at least a few intervals through the trip.

COOKING

Two options are best for international cooking: alcohol stoves and multi-fuel stoves. Alcohol is found throughout most of the world and comes in numerous forms and names. Multi-fuel stoves give you a lot of options for fuel no matter where you are.

Denatured alcohol is often used for window cleaning. Names vary from rod spirit (brand name T-Röd) in Iceland to methylated spirits in New Zealand. It is often colored purple so people don't drink it. It can be found in supermarkets and gas stations in many countries.

For more on cooking options, see the "Stoves" section.

Hiking through Colorado's Gore Range on the Continental Divide Trail in flower season

Resupply caches along the Hayduke Trail

Yoni and I, soggy after a week of rain, at the culmination of our northbound Pacific Crest Trail thru-hike, 2004

THRU-HIKING TRICKS

Here's some information on long-distance hiking and thru-hiking that's immensely helpful. It will help you plan a trip, make an itinerary, and schedule your resupplies.

One of the most important things about thru-hiking on a long trip is to enjoy yourself. If you're not having fun, don't do it! If you want to complete the trip, you've got to be having a good time.

Don't focus on the long haul, the hundreds or even thousands of miles ahead of you. It can get overwhelming. Enjoy each segment as you hike through it. Look at a trip as a bunch of segments (resupplies), with each town stop as its own goal. The larger plan becomes much smaller. This is the key to success.

RESUPPLYING

On an unsupported thru-hike, most people resupply by going to town and either buying food as they go or using mail drops to resupply at preplanned locations. Both methods have their pros and cons.

MAIL DROPS

Mail drop pros:

✓ You can buy your food in bulk before you head out. This saves money. You can pack your favorite foods. You can also pack maps for different sections and other clothing.

✓ You can prepackage everything so you can just dump your box into your food bag and go.

Mail drop cons:

✗ You can't cater resupplies to your cravings once you've packed them. You're tied to the post office's schedule.

✗ Postage can really add up, especially if you're traveling internationally.

✗ The postal system can be a hassle in the United States and even worse abroad. For example, if you reach your mail drop in a rural town on a Friday after the post office has closed—and it doesn't have hours on the weekend—you end up waiting an extra two days for a resupply.

BUY AS YOU GO

Buy as you go pros:

✓ You can usually choose what you want to eat.

✓ You don't have to pay for postage or rely on the postal system.

Buy as you go cons:

✗ Some remote towns only have small convenience stores with limited food and other selections. They might not have food that meets your dietary restrictions or needs.

✗ Rural stores can be more expensive.

I prefer the buy-as-you-go method and try to do this as much as possible. It's sometimes more convenient to do mail drops. Before I leave on a trip, I try to research the size of each resupply town and its amenities. If the town has a supermarket, I'll buy as I go. Sometimes the supermarket is on the outskirts of town. The last thing you want to do when you get to town is walk more! On most trips I combine these two methods.

THE BOUNCE-BOX TRICK

Long-distance hikers use a bounce box in the United States. This trick is really handy. Basically you pack maps for later sections, extra clothing layers you're likely to need, and maybe a few other odds and ends like a camera charger. Then you mail them to yourself addressed as: Your name, C/O General Delivery, Town Name, State, Zip Code. Go to the post office, tell them you have a general delivery package, and show them your ID. If you mailed the package to yourself using priority mail but don't open it, you can forward the package for free! This works really well for spare gear like extra shoes, clothes, and maps—things you might need soon but not quite yet. You can bounce this stuff the entire length of the trail without carrying the extra weight and have access to it every few stops.

THE SUPERMARKET COMBO

When I know I'll hit a town with a good supermarket but the next couple of towns don't have supermarkets, I'll buy food for two or three stretches, divide it up, and mail it ahead for the next few stops. It's a combination of mail drops and buy as you go that works nicely in some situations. If you think you don't need some of the gear you were carrying with you, you can put it in your mail drop. This also helps save on postage, since you're mailing the package from a nearby location rather than from a home base far away.

Postage Tricks

- Tyvek Priority Mail envelopes and post office flat-rate boxes can be turned inside out and used for regular mail—when their insides aren't printed on. You end up with a free envelope, and you don't have to pay Priority Mail prices to ship it.

- If you're shipping a package that needs tape and don't have any with you, consider shipping it Priority Mail. The post office has to let you use their specialty printed Priority Mail tape to secure it. That might be cheaper than buying a whole role of tape. Check out your options based on package size and weight.

- Shipping camping fuel can be a touchy subject with US postal employees, but if you go in knowing your rights, you should be fine. I have never had them deny me domestic shipping. Do not try to mail internationally, though, and make sure to label the package on the address side. All you need to know is: Propane camp stove fuel, up to three small canisters of isobutene fuel canisters, can be shipped if labeled: Surface Mail Only Consumer Commodity ORM-D. Alcohol: Can ship in a metal container, not to exceed 1 quart; a nonmetal container must not exceed 1 pint. The primary receptacle must have a screw cap with a minimum of 1.5 turns, soldering clips, or other means of secure closure (friction tops are not acceptable). Only one primary receptacle per mail piece, and there must be enough cushioning to prevent breakage and absorb any potential leakage. Must be marked with (if it is denatured alcohol, the flashpoint is used below): Surface Mail Only Consumer Commodity ORM-D Flashpoint 13C/55F. Esbit: Esbit can ship less than 1 pound of Esbit tablets surface mail (ground). You must box the tablets in something larger than their original packaging, and the package must be 25 pounds or less. The label shall read: Surface Mail Only Consumer Commodity ORM-D. Matches: Only certain types of matches can be shipped. Those types must be shipped by ground transportation only and be 25 pounds or less. Strike-anywhere matches are not legal to ship via USPS. It must be labeled: Surface Mail Only Consumer Commodity ORM-D Book of Matches (or other type of matches inside).

WEATHER FORECASTING

Many small details can help you predict the weather. A barometer with your watch or GPS unit can tell you when the weather is changing. The weather can change fast. If you watch the Weather Channel, you know it's impossible to predict exactly what will happen. If you're educated about weather indicators and prepared for weather conditions you're likely to encounter, you'll be much better off. You should also consider the wind's direction as well as the shape and movements of the clouds.

CLOUDS: When high-level cirrus clouds—high, wispy clouds or streaks—are building, it means a storm can be heading your way within 48 to 72 hours. Lenticular cirrus clouds echoing a peak as they raise into the sky—like the profile of a lens—also mean a storm is headed in within about 48 to 72 hours. A blanket of cloud cover and spindrift can mean high wind on the peaks.

The march of a storm has a specific pattern. First, the cirrus clouds come in. They're followed by cirrocumulus clouds—small, puffy clouds that can be rows or ripples. Next is the cirrostratus clouds that cover large areas. Those are followed by altostratus—smoky midlevel clouds—and nimbostratus clouds that bring the precipitation.

Keep an eye on cumulus clouds. These might be the nice, puffy cottony clouds you see at the beginning of *The Simpsons TV* show. These cumulus clouds can accumulate and quickly turn into nasty cumulonimbus clouds. They are the breeding

Photo by Shawn Forry

grounds of fierce thunderstorms and other violent bursts of weather.

Thunderstorms can build from friendly cumulus clouds in minutes in the Rockies. On the AT, a warm humid day can quickly turn into a torrential downpour and thunderstorm.

WIND: Wind direction also plays a major role in predicting the weather. If you understand weather patterns, you would know that in the Northern Hemisphere, winds around a low-pressure movement circle counterclockwise. If you're hiking in the Sierra Nevada and winds strengthen and start coming from the south or southwest, a storm might be coming. If you're hiking in New England and the winds start coming from the north or northwest, temperatures are probably going to get colder.

- -

TIP: Clear night skies can mean a cold night, especially after a storm passes.

- -

LIGHTNING: Lightning is the biggest concern on most trails in the United States. While the cause of lightning is somewhat debatable, its cohort, thunder, is caused by lightning. All thunderstorms have lightning. Thunder happens because lightning forces air in a cloud to rapidly expand and contract. That movement creates the sonic wave of thunder.

Lightning's no joke. When you hear thunder or see lightning, it's time to get off high ground. Seek cover in a forested area or low spot. Don't hide under the tallest tree around. Sit on your sleeping pad because it helps insulate you from the ground. The current from lightning can travel through the ground if it strikes close by.

You can use a combination of sensing thunder and lightning to get an idea of how far away the danger is. When you see a flash of lightning in the distance, you should start counting the seconds until you hear thunder. It depends on your altitude. Sound generally travels at 1 mile every 5 seconds. If you hear thunder 20 seconds after seeing lightning, the storm is about 4 miles away.

Keep tabs on this. It'll let you know whether the storm is getting closer to you or farther away. Storms may not be moving away as fast as you think. They can quickly re-form around high peaks. If you're comfortable where you are, then sit and wait it out. You can hike through it to get out of alpine regions quickly.

TIP: Be extra careful if you see lightning in the desert. It can mean heavy rains. Do not camp or be caught in slot canyons, washes, or other potential water paths. It might not be raining where you are, but rain accumulation from far away can rapidly build to a wall of water coming through a canyon. It can happen within minutes.

TRAUMA TIP

If you're in an area like the Rockies, known for afternoon lightning and thunderstorms in summer, and know you have to travel on exposed ridges, get going early in the morning. Get through alpine areas and exposed ridges before storms hit. An early start to the day is called an alpine start, for just these reasons!

WINTER CAMPING

Winter camping is awesome. You're facing colder temperatures, but there are no crowds and no bugs. The chance of seeing other people is minuscule compared to summer months. In winter the backcountry is yours.

Winter also offers exciting backcountry adventures beyond hiking. In winter you can camp and go alpine and cross-country skiing, Telemarking, snowshoeing and snowboarding, splitboarding, or do a combination.

Wherever you're going, you should consider some of the additional backcountry dangers. There are avalanches and whiteouts. If you're headed into avalanche country, beacons, probes, and shovels are mandatory, and you need to know how to use them.

Before you leave on a winter trip, you must check the weather. Check it again at any resupplies so you'll know what to expect and can plan or modify your trip accordingly.

In the winter, always carry some extra food. You may run into bad weather and have to wait out a storm, or fresh snow can slow you down. Your body burns more calories to keep warm during winter trips, so you'll probably also be a lot hungrier than during summer trips.

Days are short and nights are long in the winter. Make sure you have enough batteries for your headlamp and for any nighttime activities. I tend to carry a little heavier and stronger headlamp on winter trips.

Shorter days, extra clothes, and snow are all factors that can slow you down. The amount of distance you can travel in a day will be reduced. On the other hand, if you're using cross-country skis

Ascending Mount Moosilauke in fresh snow during our winter hike of the AT.

Above tree line on Mount Moosilauke (1,464m/4,802 ft.). After days of snow and low-lying clouds, we finally got a stunning view of New Hampshire and its snow-covered mountains.

TRAUMA TIP Taking shorter breaks or eating while on the move will help prevent you from getting cold. When you do take a break, put on another layer before you get cold. Your body uses more energy to heat back up than it does to maintain the same temperature.

Somewhere near Lumbha Sambha La Pass (5,100m/16,732 ft.) during a complete whiteout

or other means of human transportation, you may travel father distances than you could hike some days. When planning, account for the equipment you'll be using and carrying as well as your traveling pace while using that gear.

Ideally, you'll want to bring a winter shelter or make a shelter, have a warmer sleep system, carry extra layers of clothes, and bring a couple pairs of gloves or mittens.

It's important to stay dry in the winter. Don't wear so many layers while traveling that you end up overheating or sweating. Balance it out so you're neither too cold nor too hot. Wearing too many layers and getting hot and sweaty will only make you colder in the long run.

WATER IN THE WINTER

Frozen water in the winter can be a problem. With a few tricks you can keep water from freezing and still treat it.

Keep your water bottle from freezing by placing it upside down in your pack's side pocket. This prevents water from freezing in the bottle's mouth—unless it's really cold out. In extreme cold keep your water bottle in an insulated pouch. You can also warm or boil your water before putting it in the pouch. Or you can keep your water in a thermos.

Melting snow takes a lot of time and fuel. If you know you'll be melting snow, remember to carry more fuel to account for the addition. Adding a little water to the pot when melting snow will make it melt significantly faster and prevent the snow from scalding.

Water filters aren't ideal for winter camping. Their cartridges will freeze and break. You can treat water with chemicals or a SteriPEN. Chemicals take more time in winter to be effective. A SteriPEN works in the winter, if the batteries work. Make sure the batteries are warm before you need the device.

DRYING AND PREVENTING GEAR FROM FREEZING

Your winter gear is likely to get wet. Your boots from hiking through snow all day and your gloves, socks, and layers of gear tend to get wet.

Winter temperatures usually don't get above freezing; the only way to dry gloves and clothes is to wear them, hang them in your shelter at the top, or sleep with them in your sleeping bag.

When I have moist—not soaked—clothes and soft items at the end of the day, I prefer keeping them with me in my sleeping bag. I'll either wear them to bed or put them in dead space within the sleeping bag.

Frozen footwear is painful to put on and wear until it's thawed. To keep your boots, shoes, or boot liners from freezing overnight, sleep with them in your sleeping bag's toe-box or underneath it. If your boots are wet, put them in your pack liner or a stuff sack first—even if they're not going in your sleeping bag. Shake any dirt, mud, or excess snow off them before putting them in your sleeping bag or a stuff sack.

Overboots can be a nice addition in cold weather. They can prevent your shoes from getting wet and help add a lot of warmth to your feet.

TIP: If fresh batteries aren't working in winter, it's most likely because they're too cold. Warm them up in an inside pocket or close to your skin. You may also want to carry them in your pocket for a while before you stop for the evening.

THE WINTER SLEEP SYSTEM

In winter you want to keep warm at night. It doesn't necessarily mean you need to go out and buy a -40°F bag. You can use your 20°F or 30°F sleeping bag and, by adding some additional layers, make it comfortable in subzero conditions.

It's nice to have a quiver of sleeping bags for different conditions. You can create a very versatile winter sleep system without having to spend a lot on an expensive winter sleeping bag.

A warm-weather (40°F or 50°F) bag that fits inside or around your normal sleeping bag will add about 20 degrees of warmth. Most cost $100 or less. This is significantly less than -15°F bag, which can easily cost more than $200; some cost upwards of $500. A bivvy sack or bag over that adds 10 degrees of warmth. A sleeping bag liner can add up to 10 degrees of warmth or more, depending on the

A frosty, high camp in the Nepalese Himalayas
Photo by Shawn Forry

If you don't have enough gear with you to keep you warm; improvise. Zippered plastic bags and bread bags can be used as de facto vapor barrier liners and add significant warmth to your hand and foot systems.

thickness. Sleeping in clothes can keep you even warmer. A tent will add another 5 to 10 degrees of warmth. I like a layered system. It is more versatile and can be directly tailored to the conditions. For example, it can be very wet and stormy on the PCT in winter but also cold at times. We layered a 20°F down bag with a 35°F–40°F synthetic cover bag. This combination helped save on weight while creating a versatile system that prevented condensation within the down bag.

In the winter your sleeping bag will absorb some moisture from your perspiration. The moisture will collect in the bag's insulating lofting materials, compacting them and making them less effective. Over multiple days, the effect is magnified. It's important to take some steps to keep your bag dry.

If you're on a long trip and stopping for resupplies, thoroughly dry your sleeping bag whenever you stop in a town. When I'm shopping during a short stop in town, I'll even drape my bag over the shopping cart to help it dry out, if need be.

If you're just out for a multiple-day trip, try to lay your bag out in the sun during a break. That will help it dry out—at least a little bit.

While I'm not a fan, you might also consider using a vapor-barrier liner. I don't like them because I get clammy in them. I prefer to air my bag out.

You might want to consider using two sleeping pads to further insulate you from the ground in the winter. You can use your pack for the lower half of your sleeping pad. It should work fine, since it's thick, has foam, and the extra gear in it will add more insulation. If you use two pads, a closed-cell foam pad on the ground, covered with an inflatable pad, will give you the most insulation.

WINTER SHELTERS

In the winter you can use an all-season tent, but you have other options as well. You can make snow caves, igloos, trenches, or quinzhees. Each is a great option for winter camping. Each is time-consuming to make, about 2 to 3 hours, if you're doing it by yourself. A trench is the fastest system.

An igloo is the most time-consuming and not the best method for lightweight hiking and backpacking because it can require a snow saw. It takes a lot of packing.

A quinzhee (or quinzee) is basically a snow cave, except you pile snow into a dome to make the cave because there isn't enough snow to dig out a cave. If you're making a quinzhee, make sure snow settles enough to bond together. This can take a few hours. You'll need to check it over time.

Snow caves require a lot of snow and an area that's out of avalanche danger. Look for a snowbank or drift to build a snow cave in.

1. Start by digging a tunnel for the cave. The tunnel should be wider than your shoulders and should slope up toward the cave. Cold air will settle outside the cave.

2. Hollow out a cavity in the snow for the cave. Make it tall enough to sit upright in and big enough for you and your companions to lie down.

3. Pack the roof of the cave and smooth the surface so it doesn't drip on you or your equipment.

4. If you have space in the cave, you can make benches out of the snow. This will keep you off the ground and above some of the cold air.

5. Poke a trekking pole, ski pole, or probe through the ceiling of the cave for ventilation.

TRAUMA TIP

Caffeine restricts blood flow and cools extremities. If you get cold easily, you may want to steer clear of caffeine during winter camping trips.

6. Cover the floor or the benches with waterproof material.

7. Put your backpack or sled in the doorway to keep the cave warmer.

Snow trenches are the easiest and fastest winter shelters to make. They're not as comfortable or as warm as a snow cave. They're not recommended if you're expecting a lot of snow, because they don't provide a strong roof.

1. Dig a trench at least 3 feet deep and 3 to 4 feet wide for each person. Make it about 6 feet long. Make an entrance at one end.

2. Lay your poles, skis, or branches across the width of the trench.

3. Lay your tarp, rainfly, or emergency blanket over the trench. Anchor the sides by covering the edges with snow, tree branches, or rocks.

SLEDS

Instead of carrying a pack in the snow, you might consider dragging a sled—especially if going on longer trips. Sleds can work really well on hut trips in Colorado and other types of winter base-camping trips. It depends on the terrain and conditions.

If you're traversing steep terrain, a sled can be a hassle to haul. Check the geography before you decide to drag one. Make sure your sled has a comfortable harness system. It can become a pain to drag real fast.

GOING TO THE BATHROOM IN THE SNOW

Pack out your waste and toilet paper. Go 200 feet away from trails and water to do so. Cleanwaste makes specific bags that will trap your waste called WAG BAG waste bags. These can be used in areas where toilets are required. If you can dig into the ground, follow the same steps for a cat hole as you would in the summer.

TIP: You can use an alcohol stove in the winter. It just needs a little starter. Light a dry piece of paper or toilet paper and hold the lit end to the alcohol. it will warm the fuel up and catch in a couple of seconds.

Sonora Pass, California, on the PCT, with ground and road at least 10 feet down

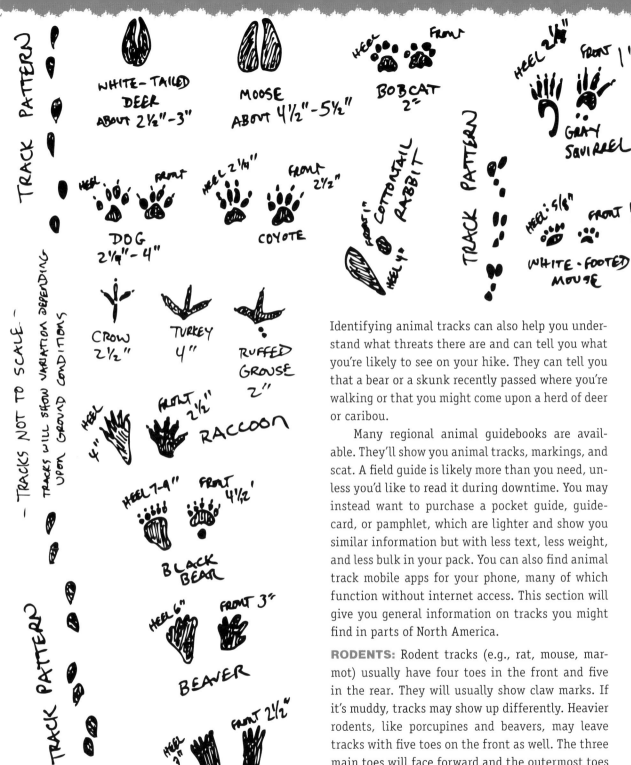

WHITE-TAILED
DEER
ABOUT 2½"-3"

MOOSE
ABOUT 4½"-5½"

HEEL   FRONT
BOBCAT
2"

HEEL 2½"   FRONT 1½"
GRAY
SQUIRREL

HEEL   FRONT
DOG
2⅛"-4"

HEEL 2¼"   FRONT 2½"
COYOTE

FRONT 1"   COTTONTAIL RABBIT
HEEL 4"

TRACK PATTERN

HEEL: ⅝"   FRONT ¼"
WHITE-FOOTED
MOUSE

CROW
2½"

TURKEY
4"

RUFFED
GROUSE
2"

HEEL 4"   FRONT 2½"
RACCOON

HEEL 7-9"   FRONT 4½'
BLACK
BEAR

HEEL 6"   FRONT 3"
BEAVER

HEEL 3"   FRONT 2½"
PORCUPINE

-TRACKS NOT TO SCALE-

TRACKS WILL SHOW VARIATION DEPENDING
UPON GROUND CONDITIONS

TRACK PATTERN

Identifying animal tracks can also help you understand what threats there are and can tell you what you're likely to see on your hike. They can tell you that a bear or a skunk recently passed where you're walking or that you might come upon a herd of deer or caribou.

Many regional animal guidebooks are available. They'll show you animal tracks, markings, and scat. A field guide is likely more than you need, unless you'd like to read it during downtime. You may instead want to purchase a pocket guide, guide-card, or pamphlet, which are lighter and show you similar information but with less text, less weight, and less bulk in your pack. You can also find animal track mobile apps for your phone, many of which function without internet access. This section will give you general information on tracks you might find in parts of North America.

RODENTS: Rodent tracks (e.g., rat, mouse, marmot) usually have four toes in the front and five in the rear. They will usually show claw marks. If it's muddy, tracks may show up differently. Heavier rodents, like porcupines and beavers, may leave tracks with five toes on the front as well. The three main toes will face forward and the outermost toes will splay to the sides.

ANIMAL TRACKS

You're likely to see a lot of animal tracks when in the backcountry. I love trying to piece together what was going on when I see animal tracks. With a little knowledge, it gets easier to figure out the clues that tell what happened before you came upon the scene.

CANINES: The tale of canines (e.g., fox, coyote, wolf, dog) in North America is told by a couple of markers. Both their front and back paws leave tracks with four toes. Most wild canines leave tracks in straight lines, with the rear foot landing in or near the front foot of the same side. Domestic dogs usually leave a more wandering path and have less of a tendency for their back feet to land in their front foot's print. Canine toes have an oval shape and a less-present heel pad than felines. You'll likely see nail marks.

FELINES: Felines (e.g., bobcat, lynx, ocelot, mountain lion) leave tracks with four toes on each foot. They have a more pronounced heel pad than canines. In North America, you won't see claw marks. Mountain lion, bobcat, and lynx have retractable claws they can't extend as they walk or run. Felines' footprints are more rounded than canines'.

WEASELS: Weasels (e.g., mink, badger, wolverine, pine marten, fisher, otter) leave tracks with five toes on each foot. Their footpad leaves an upside-down "V" shape. Claw marks are visible but not as distinct as those of canines. Back feet land close to the front feet because these animals have a leaping gait.

UNGULATES: Ungulates (e.g., deer, moose, elk, caribou) have cloven hooves and leave a two-toe mark. The main difference between the tracks are their shape and size. In addition, ungulates leave pellet-like scat. Deer leave the smallest pellets and moose the largest.

BEAR: Bear tracks are distinct from other North American wildlife. Their feet leave tracks with five toes on the front and back. The back paw prints include a large pad. Their scat is found in large piles. Bears also scratch tree bark and can leave deep scratch marks on trees. Pay attention to all these indicators, and don't camp in an area with a lot of freshly scratched trees or bear prints.

RACCOONS: Raccoons leave tracks with five toes on the front and back. Their tracks look like a small human hand.

SKUNKS: Similar to the weasel family of prints, skunk tracks have five toes on each foot, with large claws in front of the toe imprints.

RABBITS: Rabbits leave tracks with four toes on all feet. The impressions from back feet are larger than the front.

TRACK PATTERN

WEASEL
½"–1"

FISHER
2¼"

KNOTS

SLIP KNOT: This is one of the easiest and most handy. It makes it easy to set up and break down your shelter quickly, even when it's raining or your hands are cold.

CLOVE HITCH: A clove hitch is helpful for tying cord to your shelter's stakes; you can tension the cord by pulling on the knot, making it really tight. When you pull up the stake, you can pop the knot out easily.

Photos by Russ Sackson

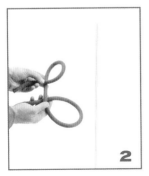

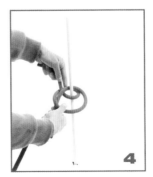

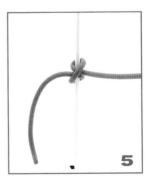

You don't need to know many knots for basic hiking and backpacking, but knowing a few types of knots can really come in handy when setting up your shelter. If you're on a trip where you'll be doing some ice climbing, rock climbing, or other technical moves, you'll need to know more knots than these, but here are a few of the basics.

TRAUMA'S SIMPLE TRUCKER'S HITCH: A trucker's hitch is used to tension a rope to make the rope really tight. I use a slip knot as the leverage spot instead of the typical trucker's hitch. This helps you break down your shelter fast and keeps the rope or cord from developing kinks and knots that are hard to untie.

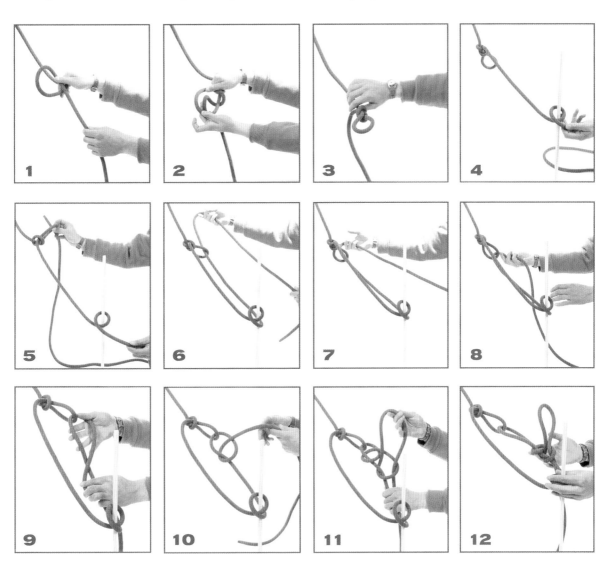

Rally car driving on our way to start our Himalayan traverse in eastern Nepal

Getting ready for the sketchy prop plane flight from rural Nepal to Kathmandu at the end of the Nepal section of our Himalayan traverse

Counting down the miles. A bittersweet moment—1 mile from the Mexico border, the end of the CDT and our yearlong, 10,000-mile hike.
Photo by Shawn Forry

TRAUMA TIP

One of the riskiest things you do on a hike is leave your car at an unattended trailhead. Some trailheads are notorious for break-ins. Ask rangers or park offices if certain trailheads are safe places to park. Never leave valuables in your car—particularly not in open sight—while you're hiking, and park in an open and visible area of the lot. If you are in a bear area, don't leave food or scented items in your car.

GETTING THERE AND BACK

There are a lot of ways to get to a hike. Doing a loop is easy if you have a car. Drive your car as close to the trailhead as possible, then park and go.

If you're doing a point-to-point hike, it gets a little more complicated. If two or more people with cars are hiking, you can park a car at either end of the hike. If you have one car, you can arrange a shuttle with a friend or family member. You can either drop your car at the end of the hike and get a ride back to the trailhead or park it at the start and have someone shuttle you back to where you parked.

On a long-distance hike, things get even more complicated. You can get to the start of a long-distance hike by plane, bus, hitching, and trail angels. If trail angels help you, be appreciative and offer them a donation. Returning home can be done in the same way. You can also store a vehicle near either end of the trail. I don't recommend it, because you have to travel back to pick it up.

AT: There are plenty of trail angels near the AT's terminuses because it receives so much traffic.

At the southern end a lot of people fly or take a bus to Atlanta and then the Greyhound to Gainesville, Georgia. The trip to Georgia's Amicalola State Park, where the trail starts, is still pretty far.

To get to the northern terminus in Maine, you can take a Greyhound on I-95 and hitch or take a shuttle to get to the trailhead.

Check current guidebooks and the internet for information about shuttles and rides to the trail. Handy sites are the AT-L info page (backcountry .net/mailman/listinfo/at-l) and whiteblaze.net.

PCT: To get to the southern terminus of the PCT, you can fly to San Diego. Take public transportation all the way to Campo, California. Some trail angels might be able to help you get from San Diego to the start. Find the latest information about PCT trail angels on the internet. There is also a forum for the PCT called the PCT-L (mailman.backcountry .net/mailman/listinfo/pct-l). It is very useful and can help with rides and other information.

The northern terminus at Manning Provincial Park in British Columbia, Canada, is accessible by Greyhound from Vancouver.

CDT: The northern terminus of the CDT is in Waterton/Glacier International Peace Park at the Canada-US border. Waterton Lakes in Canada or the Chief Mountain Border Station (depending on which route you take) is accessible by bus from East Glacier Montana. East Glacier is accessible by Amtrak.

The southern terminus of the CDT at Antelope Wells or Columbus, New Mexico, is not easily accessible. Your best bet is to hitchhike to Lordsburg or Deming, New Mexico, then take Greyhound to Las Cruces, New Mexico, or El Paso, Texas.

The Continental Divide Trail Society (CDTS) has also been running shuttles to the southern terminus of the trail annually during the start of thru-hiking season There is a forum for the CDT, called the CDT-L (mailman.backcountry.net/mailman/listinfo/cdt-l), where you can get the most recent information on logistics and other information about the trail.

Descending to one of the few alpine lakes in Nepal. This is after passing an amazing spring we named the Fountain of Youth. The holy retreat is just beyond the lake. Gosainkunda trek, Nepal. *Photo by Shawn Forry*

GEAR LISTS
FOR DIFFERENT SEASONS

Always pay attention to the weight of your gear in every season you backpack. Research the conditions you're likely to encounter, and be prepared for them. Don't go crazy and overpack. The ultralighter's pack is filled with necessary and versatile gear. Cut out as much weight as you can. If you're on a long hike and pack more then you need, mail extra gear home or put it in a bounce box.

Here are sample gear lists. They change based on the locations, conditions, places, and seasons. Basically, the sleeping bag, shelter, and layering system changes to minimize weight and adapt to conditions.

These are associated with the main long-distance hiking trails in the United States. Some gear is likely to change throughout the hike—particularly as it approaches shoulder seasons (spring or fall). That's when I'll pick up or drop a layer, a lighter or warmer sleeping bag, or beanie. I can call home for it, or I can have it ready to go in a bounce box.

Most of my pack weight and volume is food. My gear usually fits in the bottom third of my pack. The remaining two-thirds is food, maybe even more on longer stretches with five or more days between resupplying. As the food evaporates, my pack gets lighter and emptier. I love hiking into town that last day when my pack feels like it's empty!

THE DITTY SACK INCLUDES: The book that I am reading, important information, like resupply info and rough itinerary written on a piece of paper (waterproofed and laminated by layering packaging tape over it), a pen, Princeton Tec headlamp,

and a small Gerber multi-tool, which has nail clippers as one of its main features.

TOILETRIES INCLUDE: A small tube of toothpaste, toothbrush, contact lens case, small saline solution, glasses, 2 Placker's dental flossers (strongest and longest-lasting ones I have found), and small sunscreen.

COOK SET INCLUDES: A 0.9-liter Evernew titanium pot, Sidewinder Ti-Tri alcohol stove, Platypus 0.5-liter or 1-liter fuel bottle filled with denatured alcohol or HEET from a yellow bottle (about 1 ounce per day), and a titanium spork.

Getting our packs and duffels with extra gear sorted at a hotel in Nepal before starting the hike

NOTE: Weights of certain items reflect their size. They will vary slightly for smaller and larger people.

RAINFOREST, VALLEYS, AND HIGH ALTITUDES

WEIGHT

SUMMER TO FALL (WASHINGTON STATE IN THE CASCADES)

Carrying	Ounces	Grams
Backpack: Granite Gear Crown, with Mountain Laurel Designs hip-belt pocket	32	907.2
Sleeping bag: Montbell U.L. S.S. Sleeping bag Down Hugger #37	24	481.95
Sleeping pad: Thermarest Prolite X-small	7	198.45
Mountain Laurel Designs Cuben Patrol Shelter and 6 titanium stakes	8.3	235.305
Trash-compactor trash bag	2.2	62.37
Extra pair of socks	1.5	42.525
Montbell Versalite rain jacket	7	198.45
Montbell U.L. wind parka	3	85.05
Montbell Thermawrap	8	226.8
Montbell rain pants	4	113.4
Food bag: Granite Gear Air Zippsack stuff sack (medium)	1.7	48.195
Ditties (All fit in a medium-size Granite Gear Air Pocket.)	8	226.8
Toiletries (All fit in a Granite Gear #1 Air Bag.)	6.6	187.11
Granite Gear trail wallet with credit card, ID, and cash	3	85.05
Camera and Aloksak for waterproofing	6	170.1
Cook set	10	283.5
SteriPEN Ultra Journey	5	127.575
Water bottle: Vargo Titanium water bottle with lid (or 20 oz. Gatorade bottle with squirt top)	3.9	56.7
1.5-liter Platypus Evernew water carry	1.3	36.855
Mountain Laurel Designs U.L. ground cloth	1	28.35
Extra insoles (a pair of Crocs or Waldies [foam clogs] that I have cut and ground down into insoles to fit my shoes; done before I begin a hike)	3	85.05
Sunglasses with case	3	85.05
Total in ounces/grams	**140.1**	**3971.835**
Total in pounds/kilograms	**8.75625**	**3.971835**
Wearing		
Highgear/Suunto watch	3	85.05
Icebreaker wool boxers	3.4	96.39
Wool Socks	1.4	39.69
Icebreaker merino wool half-zip long-sleeve shirt	9	255.15
Montbell shorts	8.9	141.75
Hat or visor	3	85.05
Leki carbon ultralite poles	12.6	357.21
Trail running shoes with Superfeet insoles	26	737.1
Total in ounces/grams	**63.4**	**1797.39**
Total in pounds/kilograms	**3.9625**	**1.79739**

gear lists for different seasons

NOTE: Weights of certain items reflect their size. They will vary slightly for smaller and larger people.

ALPINE | WEIGHT

SUMMER TO FALL (ROCKIES OR SIERRAS)

Carrying	Ounces	Grams
Backpack: Granite Gear Crown, with Mountain Laurel Designs hip-belt pocket	32	907.2
Sleeping bag: Montbell U.L. sleeping bag S.S. Down Hugger #3	23	652.05
Sleeping pad: Thermarest Prolite X-small	7	198.45
Mountain Laurel Designs Cuben Patrol Shelter and 6 titanium stakes	8.3	235.305
Trash-compactor trash bag	2.2	62.37
Extra pair of socks	1.5	42.525
Montbell Versalite rain jacket	7	198.45
Montbell U.L. wind parka	3	85.05
Montbell Ex Light down jacket	5.5	155.925
Montbell rain pants	4	113.4
Montbell U.L. wind pants	2	56.7
Icebreaker wool beanie	2	56.7
Icebreaker wool gloves	2.5	70.875
Food bag: Granite Gear Air Zippsack stuff sack (medium)	1.7	48.195
Ditties (All fit in a medium-size Granite Gear Air Pocket.)	8	226.8
Toiletries (All fit in a Granite Gear #1 Air Bag.)	6.6	187.11
Granite Gear trail wallet with credit card, ID, and cash	3	85.05
Camera and Aloksak for waterproofing	6	170.1
Cook set	10	283.5
SteriPEN Ultra Journey	5	127.575
Water bottle: Vargo Titanium water bottle with lid (or 20 oz. Gatorade bottle with squirt top)	3.9	56.7
2 1-liter Platypus Evernew water carry	1.3	36.855
Mountain Laurel Designs U.L. ground cloth	1	28.35
Extra insoles (a pair of Crocs or Waldies [foam clogs] that I have cut and ground down into insoles to fit my shoes; done before I begin a hike)	3	85.05
Sunglasses with case	3	85.05
Total in ounces/grams	**150.1**	**4255.335**
Total in pounds/kilograms	**9.38125**	**4.255335**
Wearing		
Highgear/Suunto watch	3	85.05
Icebreaker wool boxers	3.4	96.39
Socks	1.4	39.69
Icebreaker merino wool half-zip long-sleeve shirt	9	255.15
Montbell shorts	5	141.75
Hat or visor	3	85.05
Leki carbon ultralite poles	12.6	357.21
Trail running shoes with Superfeet	26	737.1
Total in ounces/grams	**63.4**	**1797.39**
Total in pounds/kgs	**3.9625**	**1.79739**

NOTE: Weights of certain items reflect their size. They will vary slightly for smaller and larger people.

DESERT

SPRING AND FALL (UTAH)

Carrying	Ounces	Grams
Backpack: Granite Gear Crown, with hip-belt pocket	32	907.2
Sleeping bag: Montbell U.L. Sleeping bag S.S. Down Hugger #3	23	652.05
Sleeping pad: Thermarest Prolite X-small	7	198.45
Mountain Laurel Cuben Designs Patrol Shelter and 6 titanium stakes	8.3	235.305
Trash-compactor trash bag	2.2	62.37
Extra pair of socks	1.5	42.525
Montbell Versalite rain jacket	7	198.45
Montbell U.L. wind parka	3	85.05
Montbell Ex Light down jacket	5.5	155.925
Montbell rain pants	4	113.4
Montbell U.L. wind pants	2	56.7
Food bag: Granite Gear Air Zippsack stuff sack (medium)	1.7	48.195
Ditties (All fit in a medium-size Granite Gear Air Pocket.)	8	226.8
Toiletries (All fit in a Granite Gear #1 Air Bag.)	6.6	187.11
Granite Gear trail wallet with credit card, ID, and cash	3	85.05
Camera and Aloksak for waterproofing	6	170.1
Cook set	10	283.5
SteriPEN Ultra Journey	5	127.575
Water bottle: Vargo Titanium water bottle with lid ;or 20 oz. Gatorade bottle with squirt top)	3.9	56.7
1 2 liter Platypus1.5-liter Evernew water carry	1.3	36.855
Mountain Laurel Designs U.L. ground cloth	1	28.35
Extra Insoles (a pair of Crocs or Waldies [foam clogs] that I have cut and ground down into insoles to fit my shoes; done before I begin a hike)	3	85.05
Icebreaker wool beanie	2	56.7
Icebreaker wool gloves	2.5	70.875
Sunglasses with case	3	85.05
Total in ounces/grams	**150.1**	**4255.335**
Total in pounds/kgs	**9.38125**	**4.255335**
Wearing		
Highgear/Suunto watch	3	85.05
Icebreaker wool boxers	3.4	96.39
Socks	1.4	39.69
Icebreaker merino wool half-zip long-sleeve shirt	9	255.15
Montbell shorts	5	141.75
Hat or visor	3	85.05
Leki carbon ultralite poles	12.6	357.21
Trail running shoes with Superfeet	26	737.1
Total in ounces/grams	**63.4**	**1797.39**
Total in pounds/kilograms	**3.9625**	**1.79739**

NOTE: Weights of certain items reflect their size. They will vary slightly for smaller and larger people.

HOT AND HUMID SUMMER ENVIRONMENTS

(EAST COAST)

Carrying	Ounces	Grams
Backpack: Granite Gear Virga 2 or Virga 26L Meridian Vapor without lid or crown, with hip-belt pocket	19	1020.6
Sleeping bag: Montbell Down Sleeping Wrap #5 or U.L. down inner sheet	12.2	311.85
Sleeping pad: Thermarest Prolite X-small	7	198.45
Mountain Laurel Designs Cuben Patrol Shelter and 6 titanium stakes	8.3	235.305
Trash-compactor trash bag	2.2	62.37
Extra pair of socks	1.5	42.525
Montbell Versalite rain jacket	7	198.45
Montbell U.L. wind pants	3	85.05
Food bag: Granite Gear Air Zippsack stuff sack (medium)	1.7	48.195
Ditties (All fit in a medium-size Granite Gear Air Pocket.)	8	226.8
Toiletries (All fit in a Granite Gear #1 Air Bag)	6.6	187.11
Granite Gear trail wallet with credit card, ID, and cash	3	85.05
Camera and Aloksak for waterproofing	6	170.1
Cook set	10	283.5
SteriPEN Ultralight Journey	3	127.575
Water bottle: Vargo Titanium water bottle with lid (or 20 oz. Gatorade bottle with squirt top)	3.9	56.7
Mountain Laurel Designs U.L. ground cloth	1	28.35
DEET	2	56.7
Extra insoles (a pair of Crocs or Waldies [foam clogs] that I have cut and ground down into insoles to fit my shoes; done before I begin a hike)	3	85.05
Sunglasses with case	3	85.05
Total in ounces/grams	**126.8**	**3594.78**
Total in pounds/kgs	**7.925**	**3.59478**
Wearing		
Highgear/Suunto watch	3	85.05
Icebreaker wool boxers	3.4	96.39
Socks	1.4	39.69
Icebreaker merino wool half-zip long-sleeve shirt	9	255.15
Montbell shorts	5	141.75
Hat or visor	3	85.05
Leki carbon ultralite poles	12.6	357.21
Trail running shoes with Superfeet	26	737.1
Total in ounces/grams	**63.4**	**1797.39**
Total in pounds/kilograms	**3.9625**	**1.79739**

NOTE: Weights of certain items reflect their size. They will vary slightly for smaller and larger people.

WINTER OR COLD WEATHER   WEIGHT

(WINTER AT HIKE)

Carrying	Ounces	Grams
Backpack: Granite Gear Crown with frame sheet taken out and some extensions on the cordage for snowshoes (34 ounces); Meridian Vapor without lid, crown; or Nimbus Meridian if extra capacity is needed, with hip-belt pocket	56	1,587.6 at most
Sleeping bag: Montbell U.L. sleeping bag S.S. Down Hugger #0 or #2 (depending on location and time of year)	45	1,275.75 at most
Sleeping Pad: Thermarest Prolite X-small	7	198.45
Mountain Laurel Designs Solomid XL in DCF (19 oz.); Big Agnes Fly Creek tent and 6 titanium stakes	23	652.05
Trash-compactor trash bag	36	1020.6
Extra pair of heavier socks for sleeping	4.5	127.575
Montbell U.L. wind parka	3	85.05
Montbell U.L. down inner parka	9	255.15
Montbell U.L. wind pants	2	56.7
Food bag: Granite Gear Air Zippsack stuff sack (medium)	1.7	48.195
Ditties (All fit in a medium-size Granite Gear Air Pocket.)	8	226.8
Toiletries (All fit in a Granite Gear #1 Air Bag.)	6.6	187.11
Granite Gear trail wallet with credit card, ID, and cash	3	85.05
Camera and Aloksak for waterproofing	6	170.1
Cook set	10	283.5
SteriPEN Journey	4.5	127.575
Aqua Mira in Small dropper bottles 2 ounces		
Water bottle: Vargo titanium water bottle with lid or 20 oz. Gatorade bottle with squirt top)	3.9	56.7
1.5 Liter Platypus Evernew water carry	1.3	36.855
Mountain Laurel Designs U.L. ground cloth	1	28.35
Granite Gear Uberlight Dry Sack to compress sleeping bag	0.6	17.01
Extra insoles (a pair of Crocs or Waldies [foam clogs] that I have cut and ground down into insoles to fit my shoes; done before I begin a hike.)	3	85.05
MLD eVent mittens	2	56.7
Fleece glove liners	3	85.05
Sunglasses with case	3	85.05
Total in ounces/grams	**241.2**	**6838.02 at most**
Total in pounds/kgs	**15.075**	**6.83802 at most**

NOTE: Weights of certain items reflect their size. They will vary slightly for smaller and larger people.

WINTER OR COLD WEATHER (CONTINUED) — WEIGHT

(WINTER AT HIKE)

Wearing	Ounces	Grams
Highgear/Suunto watch	3	85.05
Icebreaker wool boxers	3.4	96.39
Icebreaker leggings	5.5	155.925
Socks	1.4	39.69
Icebreaker merino wool half-zip long sleeve shirt	9	255.15
Montbell Versalite rain jacket	7	198.45
Montbell rain pants	6	170.1
Hat or visor	3	85.05
Leki carbon ultralite poles	12.6	357.21
Trail running shoes with Superfeet or leather boots (47.6 oz.), depending on conditions. Trail runners preferred	26	737.1
Icebreaker wool beanie	3	85.05
Icebreaker wool gloves	2.5	70.875
Thermawrap parka	12.8	362.88
Total in ounces/grams	**95.2**	**2698.92**
Total in pounds/kgs	**5.95**	**2.69892**
Additional Equipment	Ounces	Grams
Iridium satellite phone, 9550 (Extreme model is lighter.)	9.4	266
Smartphone with navigation app or trail specific app (iPhone)	6.2 oz.	
Total in ounces/kgs	**12.7**	**3.6**

"Pack explosion": What thru-hikers do to try to dry their gear. This occurs when they get to a hotel room or town after a few soggy days in the rain.

I only had 450 miles left

on my first PCT thru-hike. It was September. I had just entered Washington and was near Mount Adams. I'd set up camp and was relaxing when another thru-hiker walked up. The site was big enough for two, so he camped there as well. We talked and found that we had seen each other's names on trail registers throughout the trip but had never met.

He was an extreme ultralighter with a base pack weight under 5 pounds. He was using mail drops to resupply. We had used different resupply stops for supplies and inevitably were flip-flopping past each other at many of these points without ever meeting. We hit it off.

It started raining in the middle of the night. The temperature plummeted and the rain became mixed with snow. It rained through the morning. We tried to wait it out, but the rain was relentless.

My new friend broke down his poncho, which he was using as a shelter, and threw it on. By the time he broke it down, he was sopping wet. I put on my rain gear then packed up my tarp for the day. We left at the same time and hiked together throughout the rainy day.

We passed a group of unprepared Boy Scouts. Their sleeping bags were sponging water on the outside of their packs, which weren't waterproofed. They were wearing cotton and were showing some signs of hypothermia. We talked to their troop leaders and helped them start a fire out of soaking-wet wood. It could have been a disaster.

We left them safer than before and continued on to keep warm. By the evening my friend was getting cold even while hiking. He was exhibiting signs of hypothermia like the Boy Scouts. He just had higher-tech gear than they did. We stopped to camp and get warm. I set up my tarp in a couple of minutes, took my wet clothes off, put on dry layers, got in my sleeping bag, and started to cook my dinner.

He'd taken off his poncho tarp and was struggling to tie the super-thin Spectra cord he was using as the shelter's guylines. When you're cold you lose dexterity in your fingers, and simple tasks like tying or untying your shoes can become difficult if not impossible.

I asked him to join me under my tarp and get warm. He could deal with setting up his shelter after warming up. He refused. Thirty minutes later I was warm, fed, and ready for sleep. He was going downhill. His skin was pale. He was still trying to set up his tarp and refusing my offer.

Upon further insistence, he finally came under my tarp. He crawled in and sat in his wet clothes. He wasn't thinking rationally anymore and was scared to get his sleeping bag wet. I told him he needed to strip down, get dry, and get into his bag. I told him multiple times. He said he didn't have any other layers of clothes to wear. He only had his sleeping bag and a down jacket and didn't want to get them wet.

Some time had passed and he'd stopped shivering, but he still wasn't making rational

TRAUMA TRAIL STORY

decisions. I also cooked up one of my extra ramen noodle packets for him, since he wasn't carrying a stove and had no opportunities for hot food. He finally stripped down and got in his sleeping bag, ate the hot noodles, and started to improve. He ended up staying the night under my shelter.

It was still raining when we got up in the morning. We started to hike again in the rain. He told me he had decided to wait to switch to his "bad-weather" shelter because the weather had been good. He was unprepared for Mother Nature's changing mood. We decided to stay together until he could get a better shelter. He called home from White Pass and had his other shelter, a little bigger tarp that wasn't also his rain gear, mailed to Snoqualmie Pass. He also added an ultralight rain jacket to his kit. He only added about half a pound to his base-pack weight.

But now he was better prepared, and ready to finish his hike safely!

Yoni and I on the PCT near Trap Pass,
Alpine Lakes Wilderness, Washington
Photo by Raina Ferran

Heart-shaped cottonwood leaf on the Hayduke Trail in Utah *Photo by Shawn Forry*

KEEPING IN TOUCH

Keeping in touch with family and friends during a long hike is very important—for both your safety and their peace of mind.

Checking in, reporting your progress on the internet, and having a reliable emergency system in place—all are important. After all, you don't want to be the person who forgets to make a weekly call home and whose family sends out Search and Rescue for absolutely no reason. Nowadays, there are plenty of options to stay in touch.

In the "old days" a thru-hiker would have to be in town, get a chunk of change, and search for a pay phone. Pay-phone calls are antiquated and probably not the best way to do things. After all, pay phones are endangered species these days; when they break down, they're ripped out instead of repaired. Then came calling cards. Calling cards can be used with pay phones or other restricted landline telephones. They're great for hotels because you can make a call without paying exorbitant hotel call rates.

It's nice to call everyone while lying in bed with the TV on, surrounded by food. This is definitely better than standing in the cold rain on a pay phone. There's an even easier option: cell phones. As long as you have reception, cell phones are probably the most convenient way to make calls when you get to town. Cell phones can also serve as an emergency system when you are hiking in an area with good coverage (I think much of both the AT and PCT get cell coverage now). If you're in a remote area with poor coverage, like on some of the CDT or other lesser-used or international trails, a cell phone is dead weight.

If you do carry a cell phone, be mindful of using it on the trail. It's a pet peeve for many. Why bother hiking in nature if you're acting like you're walking in the city?

Smartphones also are handy because you can text, e-mail, post pictures online, and update Facebook pages and blogs while hiking.

I usually consider carrying my cell phone in my pack, or at least putting it in my bounce box so I can make calls when I get into town. If you're bringing a phone with you, you have to be able to charge it. You can carry a charger or keep it in your drop box. Solar might seem ideal, but I'm not thrilled with today's portable solar chargers. I wouldn't count on them as a great option until the technology improves and weight decreases. With today's technology, I think solar isn't worth the weight. It won't charge well when on a backpack or moving so, in my opinion, isn't worth the weight to carry. A backup battery may be a better option, but it can get zapped if the temperatures are cold.

Computers offer you a range of ways to communicate, whether or not you carry a cell phone or calling cards. In addition to using tools like e-mail or Skype, you can also update blogs (like on Trail Journals or Post Holer), route maps, upload pictures or videos, do online banking, or trade stocks. Sometimes finding a computer to use isn't easy. You can usually find computers at public libraries (usually free of charge); hotels or motels, especially those with business centers; hostels; and coffee shops.

Independent coffee shops are more likely to have public computers than Starbucks or other chains. Some towns also have internet cafes or storefronts with blocks of computers for the internet. I find this to be the case internationally.

Using Skype to call or IM is inexpensive and easy. You can talk on a computer with a headset, microphone, and speaker or listen with your own headphones.

E-mail is another means of staying in touch. Many thru-hikers set up an e-mailing list and send out trip updates to interested friends and family. It's easy and efficient, and complements phone calls to immediate family. Today, social media is probably a lot easier way to keep hordes of people posted about your trip and post pretty pictures to make them all jealous.

For adventures in remote regions with less access to cell phone coverage or computers, the SPOT or Garmin satellite messenger or a satellite phone is an option. It gives you some of the same abilities as a cell phone. They're more expensive but can transmit from the trail—or almost anywhere—and are the best choice for an emergency situation.

The bonus of having a satellite phone is that you can make a call or send a text message from almost anywhere. It's a great safety option. Iridium's satellite phones are my favorite. Connection time is usually shorter than Globalstar's phones, and the network drops fewer calls. Iridium also covers the entire globe, while Globalstar and SPOT have some dead spots.

SPOT is not a phone. It can send distress signals and previously planned "OK" messages. SPOT can also upload your location information to Google Maps, and you can invite people to track your trek by e-mailing them a link or by putting a link on your blog or website. It also can save you a lot of time plotting your actual route out after the trip is over.

If you're bringing any of these gadgets, remember that you need extra batteries and/or a means of charging them. It doesn't mean you have to carry chargers with you. The battery on an infrequently used satellite phone will last a fairly long time. You could keep the phone's charger in a bounce box rather than carrying it.

. . . . all the crazy things that happen on the trail

BLOGGING OR JOURNALING FROM THE TRAIL

Hikers can post stories, blogs, and diary updates to the web during a trip. Trail Journals and Post Holer are two popular sites that cater to hikers and are easy to use in the field. These sites let you write your story or journal entry. It's formatted in their template. You can upload photos to both Trail Journals and Post Holer, but you can't embed information from other sources like Google Photo galleries or Google Maps. Facebook, Instagram, and other social media sites are also popular ways to keep people posted and can be quicker and easier for posting photos and text from your smartphone. Just be sure your data plan is ready for that or else you may get a surprisingly expensive cell phone bill, if you're not on wifi when you connect.

If you're interested in stepping it up even more, you'll need to have your own website or blog. You can also set up a blog on sites like Wordpress or Blogger. They have a lot more options and flexibility. This is nice, but it takes more effort to design and set such sites up.

There are different ways to post to your blog when on the trail. When I hiked through Africa and the Himalayas, I posted via a friend, who would take the text messages I sent on my satellite phone and post them to my blog. I also texted my coordinates. My friend uploaded them to Google Maps. You can also send coordinates to sites like itouchmap.com/latlong.html and it logs them into Google Maps. It automatically updates the embedded map on your blog or website.

Some sites, like Wordpress, offer an e-mail posting tool. The site issues you an e-mail address; whenever you send an e-mail or text to it, the site posts the e-mail on your blog. It's pretty handy when you're using a cell phone or a satellite phone in the backcountry, because you can text message to an e-mail address. The Garmin InReach, ZOLEO, and SPOT also provides opportunities to upload messages directly to social media and mapping.

This may seem a little complicated, but it doesn't have to be. Some people want to tell all about the trip, while others want to leave it all behind when they step on the trail. The lesson is that there are lots of ways to keep in touch.

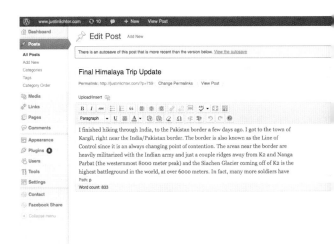

Leaf skeletons and getting creative with photos while waiting for our boat taxi to come pick us up from Ship Cove at the end of the New Zealand hike

Pepper going bull-istic on the Hayduke Trail in Utah

Checking out a waterfall near the base of Mount Meru in Tanzania

PHOTOGRAPHY

On my first few hikes, I only brought a disposable camera. I'm still kicking myself for missing so many great photo opportunities and for poorly documenting those trips. Now a camera is an essential part of my hiking gear.

Photo by Russ Sackson

Hiking offers a great opportunity to take pictures. I've taken some amazing photos on my trips, and I love looking at them. When you're hiking in the backcountry, you are seeing places and things that most people never have the chance to see. No one will see things exactly as you're seeing them—including the weather, cloud cover, lighting changes, and sometimes the geology changes due to natural events. Here are some tips for choosing a camera and taking good pictures:

While there are tons of photography resources out there, these are geared to hikers and long-distance adventurers. I don't cover film-based cameras because they're antiquated, require special care, and aren't the right tool for long-distance hiking, especially ultralight hiking.

Digital cameras, which save pictures on re-placeable memory cards instead of film, are much better for hiking. The cards offer a more secure medium for saving pictures. You can delete some lesser photos if you want to save additional photos to the card.

There are two main options for digital cameras: point-and-shoot and SLR (single-lens reflex). The first is less advanced. It's a camera that usually doesn't have many manual settings. They simplify picture-taking. They're smaller, lighter, and less expensive than SLR cameras, but they allow far fewer options.

Digital SLR (DSLR) cameras are more expensive. The least expensive start around $300, and higher-end versions can cost thousands. That's just the camera body! Interchangeable SLR lenses can cost into the thousands as well. More-expensive cameras have sensors that can record more details in pixels, with some recording more than 16 megapixels in a picture.

The number of megapixels a camera can record in a shot determines how much detail or resolution the camera can capture. More pixels are better and mean the resulting photograph can be printed larger or in higher resolution. Most modern digital camera sensors record so many megapixels that the number is close to being irrelevant, unless you're planning on printing billboard-size photos.

Digital cameras use a number of different formats (RAW, JPEG, TIFF, etc.) to record images. RAW format records the most data and has the least amount of data compression. Most cameras save pictures in JPEG—in file names, usually represented by the .jpg extension—format because of its balance between smaller file size and level of image quality. JPEGs can be viewed quickly and easily on any computer with any operating system.

RAW allows you to do more tinkering with photos in photo editors like Photoshop or GIMP, but RAW files need to be processed into a JPEG or TIFF before you can share them.

Note that I'm partial to using a camera and not my cell phone for photos on hikes. Cell phone cameras are making enormous strides, but I don't think the photos are equivalent to a good point-and-shoot yet. The variety and options aren't there yet, and I'm strongly against using the filters cell phones provide to tune up photos. In my opinion, they just make things look unnatural.

PHOTOGRAPHY FAQS

What kind of camera and supplies do you take on a long-distance hike? I really like the Canon S series now. They have more manual functions than other point-and-shoot cameras. They have a 10+ megapixel sensor and can shoot in RAW and take HDR (high dynamic range) photos. The zoom and battery life are reasonable. DSLRs are heavier and can require extra equipment like lenses and lens filters.

There is no set system for accessories for your camera. The accessories I carry depend on the hike, how long between resupplies, services in towns, and the ease of mailing myself things. I always carry my camera in my hip-belt pocket and in an OtterBox to help keep it dry and safe. I've broken too many cameras over the years, and they're too expensive. This is an area where I will carry a little extra weight to keep my camera protected.

If I were hiking the AT, PCT, or CDT, I'd have my camera loaded with an 8 gigabyte (GB) or larger SD card. I'd mail the battery charger and an extra SD card ahead to myself. That way I wouldn't need to carry an extra battery pack. I would, however, carry an extra battery through the Sierras on the PCT so I won't feel limited as to how many pictures I can take on that stretch of the trail.

When I get to town and my SD card or cards are full, I'll burn all the photos to a DVD or USB drive and mail it home, or upload to the cloud.

HOW MANY MEMORY CARDS SHOULD I BRING?
This depends on your camera's settings, how big your picture files are, whether you're shooting in RAW, and where you're heading. Shooting in RAW takes up a lot of memory. However, prices on memory cards have fallen steeply, so I'd recommend getting the largest one that's in your budget. You may want to carry two in case you fill one up, or in case

View from Thorung La Pass (5,416m/17,769 ft.) framed by prayer flags on the Annapurna Trek in Nepal

one breaks or fails—though that's rare since they are so light.

Hopefully, you'll be able to take as many pictures as you want without stressing about running out of space. If you do run out of memory, you can go back and delete lower-quality photos. Try not to erase pictures you think are just OK. They'll look different when you view them on a larger screen, and some may be better than you think.

SHOULD I GET A CAMERA WITH A CERTAIN TYPE OF BATTERY? HOW DO YOU CHARGE BATTERIES? WHAT'S BEST? Cameras that use AA batteries are convenient because AA batteries are easy to get throughout the world. You can share batteries among multiple devices like cameras, headlamps, and SteriPENs. I previously tried to use cameras that used AA batteries, which helped keep the number of different types of batteries I carried down. The variety of cameras with this has decreased substantially over the last decade. Canon cameras I'm fond of use a rechargeable lithium-ion battery. I've found that it isn't a big deal after all. These last a fairly long time in the right conditions and are lightweight. However, you have to recharge the battery with the factory charger, which means you have to carry the charger or keep it in a bounce box. It also means taking time in town to recharge the battery. Sometimes I'll carry an extra camera battery.

I've never had luck with solar chargers. They never seem to draw enough power to fully charge a battery fast enough to warrant carrying one. I'm also moving most of the time and through various climates and directions, which affects the performance of solar chargers.

For backcountry electronics, rechargeable AA batteries don't seem to hold a charge or handle the cold very well. If you choose to use rechargeable

One of the many flowers that sprang up during the India section of the Himalaya traverse

AAs don't get any under 2300mAh (milliamp hours). You can also buy 2500mAh rechargeable AAs. Each level represents a roughly 12 percent increase in battery life. Get NiMH (nickel-metal hydride) instead of NiCad (nickel cadmium) rechargeable batteries. NiMH batteries are more flexible because they don't have to be fully drained before being charged. If your battery charger is in your bounce box and you run out of battery power, you can pick up AAs anywhere.

A better option is using lithium AA batteries. Lithium batteries last longest and handle cold the best. They are more expensive but worthwhile. You don't have to carry hordes of heavy spare batteries just in case your batteries die.

WHAT IS THE MINIMUM AMOUNT OF ZOOM I SHOULD GET? If you're using a point-and-shoot digital camera, it will have an optical zoom rating and a digital zoom rating. Completely disregard the digital zoom. It creates pixilated, grainy pictures. If you're using a DSLR, it's all about the lens. I like to take good pictures but am not willing to carry a DSLR on a long hike because of its weight and bulk.

Optical zoom is the important feature on point-and-shoots. It makes it easier to take pictures of wildlife, far-off objects, or candid shots of people. The higher the optical zoom, the more you're able to take close-up pictures of things that are far away—like the marmot on a rock 200 yards away.

I use a camera with a 3.8x optical zoom. I have never used anything more powerful than that, and it works for me. Point-and-shoot cameras can have optical zooms up to 10x or more. They are more expensive, bigger, heavier, and the lens usually protrudes from the camera body itself, making it potentially easier to break. It's a trade-off.

WHAT SHOULD I DO WITH MY PICTURES AS I FILL UP A MEMORY CARD? It's inevitable on a long hike that you'll fill up memory cards. Consider carrying an extra memory card. You can also carry a card reader in your bounce box. Then you can burn pictures onto CDs, DVDs, or USB drives and ship them home. Some people burn two CDs or DVDs and mail them to two separate places just in case the post office has a snafu. Walgreens, CVS, and Walmart also have systems that can transfer photo files to discs.

You could also keep an SD card–reading mass-storage device, like a hard drive, in your bounce box and download pictures to it when you get to town. If you're using public computers, you can keep a card reader and/or a few USB drives in your bounce box.

You can also upload photos to an online storage service like Dropbox or Google Drive. Or you can upload photos directly to your Facebook or blog, which makes them easy to share. Uploading to such a site usually takes more time, and often they automatically resize your photos, so you may lose data due to file compression. The result is a small picture that you can't do much work on. Some

TRAUMA TIP Early-morning and evening light is softer. This can lead to great photos with shadows and depth. A lot of my best shots are taken during these times.

Gelada monkeys in Ethiopia

Pasqueflower seed head, also called mouse-on-a-stick, on the PCT in Washington

cameras connect directly to wifi to make uploading easier and prevent you from needing to connect to ao computer for that step.

SHOULD I BRING A TRIPOD? It's a personal preference. If you're taking long-exposure or HDR shots, maxing out the optical zoom, or shooting in low light and need to have the camera steady, a tripod can help. Most cameras have a threaded hole in the bottom for attaching it to a tripod.

If you're hiking with somebody else, you probably won't need to carry a tripod since you can take pictures of each other. When the opportunity presents itself, you can take pictures together.

On some solo hikes, I'll bring a tripod. On others I won't and wish I had. However, I can usually find a rock or signpost to place my camera on and use that to take pictures with the self-timer. Watch out for the wind, though.

There are a lot of lightweight, small tripods available, like the GorillaPod. It weighs just a few ounces and is very versatile—you can wrap it around things, like a tree branch. Another option is a product like the StickPic. It goes on the pointy end of a trekking pole and attaches to your camera like a tripod. You can hold your pole out and get pictures of yourself from a little farther off while also capturing some background. When you hold the camera out and snap a picture of your face, it usually takes up most of the screen. Some trekking poles are designed to double as monopods. All in

A quick Taj Mahal stop after finishing the Himalaya hike

Pepper scopes out tomorrow's route in Nepal. *Photo by Shawn Forry*

TRAUMA TIP

Always keep your camera easily accessible. You never know what you'll see on the trail. That is why I love using a hip-belt pocket to hold my camera. When your camera is handy, it's not a chore to take pictures. A landscape photo or a deer bounding across the trail a foot in front of you can be easily photographed.

Bighorn sheep checking me out in Montana

all, I can usually find a rock or something to use, so I've stopped carrying a tripod.

IS MY CAMERA GOING TO BREAK? Maybe. Hiking, particularly long-distance hiking, definitely isn't easy on cameras. I have broken my fair share. Common things that break cameras while hiking include dirt, grit, water, and drops. I have broken a few while using the self-timer. I placed a camera on a rock, walked into position, and watched an unexpected breeze blow it over. Whoops!

Grit has also broken one of my cameras. Grit and dirt can be largely prevented by putting your camera in a zippered plastic bag before putting it in your pocket or hip-belt pocket, or by using an OtterBox that fits your camera well. It also helps protect the camera from moisture and rain. If I'm expecting a long-lasting deluge, I'll put my camera, still inside the bag, inside my pack and pack liner for extra protection. I hardly have any pictures of my being soaked and miserable, but I'd rather save my camera.

Condensation is another moisture issue that can break cameras or mess up pictures. It's more likely if you leave your camera exposed at night. Dew and temperature differences can allow moisture to build up inside your camera. You can prevent this by leaving your camera inside your hip-belt pocket or keeping it covered up at night. This is more important when you're camped near a creek or meadow and dew is commonplace.

ON TAKING PHOTOS

Get creative. Take a variety of shots of different things to help document your journeys. A million shots of a hazy green Virginia valley on the AT get old. Taking pictures of crazy shelters and people, trail life, and miserable, drenched hikers tells a more complete story that complements those pictures of that verdant Virginia valley. Those are the shots I wish I had more of.

TAKE A LOT OF PICTURES. With digital cameras you can erase bad pictures and don't have to worry about running out of film.

USE THE RULE OF THIRDS. Whenever possible place the subject of the photo about a third of the way in from the edge of the picture. It helps make the resulting picture more interesting to the viewer.

Framing the foreground before you take a picture can give you the full depth of the situation.

GEOTAGGING: Some new cameras have GPS tracking (or geotagging) for photos. I haven't use it yet, but it could be a pretty cool feature if you don't remember or didn't record where you took the picture. This is also helpful when sharing your photos on a site like Flickr, which will show your location on a map. Some cameras have a wireless connection option, which can be very helpful for sharing photos without needing another cable or computer.

TIP: Always shoot with the highest resolution possible. You can always reduce photo size later. You can't increase resolution after you shrink the photo. Higher resolution photos allow you to do more post-picture work and allow for larger pictures.

STEPPING IT UP ○-----→

Putting sewing skills to the test
by sewing slippery silnylon
Photo by Russ Sackson

MAKING YOUR OWN GEAR

Making your own gear can be fun and rewarding. It can also be time-consuming and frustrating.

If you've got a little creativity and don't mind working with different materials, you can make great custom products—like backpacks or even stoves—that are tailored to your needs and lighter than what you can purchase. However, it requires a lot of patience and tinkering.

Considering the time, effort, and the cost of materials you put into making your own gear, you're not going to save much money. Making your own gear is more about the satisfaction of doing it for yourself and seeing your gear perform in the backcountry. That's how Ray Jardine came up with the original Ray-Way Pack design.

SEWING

If you know how to sew and know what you like, you can make some great lightweight products. You can order materials, patterns, and even pre-cut materials online. All you have to do is sew them together.

If you're interested but don't know how to sew, visit online forums for tips. Consider taking a sewing class. Some websites with sewing tips for hikers include thru-hiker.com, questoutfitters .com, seattlefabrics.com, and owfinc.com.

I'm not going to go into sewing your own gear; it would be an entirely separate book. This should help get you on your way to making your own gear.

- Start small. Try making stuff sacks, bivvy sacks, and other simple pieces of gear. When first starting to learn how to sew ultralight fabrics, make sure you catch enough of the fabric in the seam or else it will pull out over time. When you're familiar with sewing techniques and the fabrics you want to use, try sewing the new ultralight materials like silnylon or DCF and work up to bigger projects like backpacks and sleeping bags.

- A seam-ripper will be your best friend when you start sewing. You can always take a seam out and restitch something. Nothing is permanent.

- Make prototypes with cheaper fabrics before using expensive fabrics on the final product.

- Fabric from Walmart or your local fabric shop isn't likely the same quality of genuine fabrics like Polartec or Cordura. They could allow you to make a cheap alternative.

- If you want to design a piece of clothing, try to find a similar but inexpensive item in a thrift store that fits well, like a windbreaker or a pair of pants. De-seam the thrift store item, and use it as a pattern. This makes it much easier for you to get the pattern correct for the right fit.

- You can salvage zippers and other hardware from other jackets and thrift store items.

- Straight-stitch sewing machines will cover 90 percent of the sewing you need to do.

- Learn how to oil, time, and do basic repairs to your sewing machine. Repairs will set you back $80 or more per visit.

HOW TO MAKE AN EASY ALCOHOL STOVE

All you need to make an alcohol stove is a can of tuna or beer and a good paper hole punch. There are plenty of other designs with instructions and descriptions on the internet. The tuna-can stove is nice because you don't need a separate pot stand (although you can always use your Ti tent stakes for the pot stand).

1. Open up your tuna can and eat the tuna—or give it to the cat. Clean it until there's no smell left in the can.

2. Using the punch, make a ring of evenly spaced holes a little bit below the can's rim. Be sure not to punch through the rim.

3. Below those holes, create another ring of holes, offset slightly, so it's like looking at a brick wall.

4. Pour a little denatured or methyl alcohol into the bottom of the can, light it, and set your pot on top. You're set with a new stove—for less than $10.

HOW TO MAKE AN EASY ULTRALIGHT POT

1. Buy a can of Heineken. Their cans are more like a half liter than a normal beer can. The additional volume helps.

2. You can either open it normally and drink the beer or pour out the beer, then start by cutting the top off, right below the lip. Cut it as smoothly as possible.

3. Voilà, you have a new pot! It's the cheapest and lightest weight available. You can either use some aluminum foil or the original top of the beer can as the lid.

4. If you really want to get fancy, you can solder a little baling wire onto the can for a handle that arches over the top. If you don't want to solder, you can punch small holes near the top of the can and wire it through.

MAKE YOUR OWN ALCOHOL STOVE

Photos by Russ Sackson

FORDING RIVERS

Fording a river is one of the most dangerous things you can encounter on a hike. You can't always tell the depth or undertow of the river by looking at its surface. Approach rivers with respect and caution. Depending on the size of the crossing, you can sometimes find downed trees to cross a river without getting wet.

Crossing a seasonal creek in the High Sierras on the PCT

General river dynamics can be good to know. Here are a few helpful concepts. Rivers are deeper under a steep bank and outside of a turn. They are shallower on the inside of a turn. There can be eddies behind rocks, which can help break the constant push of the river.

Scout for a good place to cross the river before starting to cross. Make sure your exit and entry points are safe and that you will be able to get out of the water without a problem. Try to pick a spot where there are no visible rapids downstream, particularly with trees strewn across—known as strainers. If you get swept into them by the current, they could catch and keep you underwater.

Rivers usually get gentler in meadows and when they spread out, although the water may be a bit deeper in such areas. The current is usually gentler, and such meadows are often good places to cross.

Fast-moving water above the knee can knock someone over. It's helpful to use trekking poles or a stick for balance. Test the depth of the water. Glacial rivers are sometimes tough because they are silty. You often can't see the bottom.

If the ford is tough, do not go barefoot! If the river is really gentle, wear shoes when fording a river. They help with traction and protect your feet in case there are jagged rocks in the water.

If the river looks tough and is wide, look for a spot upstream to cross. That could mean miles upstream. There's usually less volume if you go upstream, making it easier to cross. As the river flows down, it picks up more water from its tributaries.

Always watch out for rocks with a green or brown tinge or coating. These rocks are covered with algae and are usually super-slippery. The same is true if you're hiking on the coast, such as near the western terminus of the Pacific Northwest Trail. These rocks have moss on them that makes them dangerously slippery.

HOW TO FORD A DIFFICULT RIVER CROSSING

There are multiple ways to cross rivers. While there are other options, these have worked well for me in some tough situations.

1. Take off anything baggy, like rain pants, that can catch current. Tie your shoelaces and other things that you could trip over well so they can't catch or hinder you.

2. Sidestep across, without crossing your feet. Use your trekking poles for extra balance if you need them. You can also test the depth of the water with them. Walk at a downstream angle, which will make it easier to cross.

3. I leave my sternum and hip-belt straps buckled. Some people say you should unbuckle them so you can get out of your pack quickly if you do fall. I have done both. I find that I really don't like unexpected load shifts when I am in a precarious situation. This can happen when you're not strapped in. So I leave the straps buckled. If I do go under, I'm ready to unbuckle.

4. If you have an extra person in your group, he or she can wait downstream. This person can be a catcher in case someone falls. The catcher should be prepared with a branch, pole, or rope.

Pepper braves the icy-cold water of one of the fords in the remote Dolpa region of Nepal.

TRAUMA TIP

Creeks, streams, and rivers rise and fall throughout the day. If the body of water stems from snowmelt or a glacier, the morning is the time of lowest flow and easiest time to ford. Sometimes the difference is substantial. I have seen creeks rise more than 6 feet between the morning and the afternoon—basically from fordable to completely deadly.

Postholing just enough to wish
we had snowshoes

HIKING IN SNOW

Snow creates unique conditions for hikers. Snow can be different depending on recent weather and the time of the year. You can bomb through a dusting of fresh, powdery snow or slog through miles of deep powder. Spring conditions are much different and change throughout the day.

Snowshoes generally aren't worth carrying for spring snow conditions. In spring the snow often has an icy crust in the mornings. The crust is sometimes treacherous on steep slopes, particularly when you can't kick steps in it. It also makes travel fast and efficient.

When you're on snow you can kick steps in on steeper terrain and when going over passes. Create a little platform by stamping your foot up and down and moving it from side to side on tricky slopes. This helps you get a good position and creates something to push off of as you take the next step, as well as a flat platform to land on. If the snow is getting softer, you can walk normally or dig in with your heels. If you're going downhill, you can slide.

On winter hikes and in spring snow conditions, plan where you camp and wake up early in the morning to take advantage of the best snow-hiking conditions. This will help you make good time on the long gentle ascents before the headwall of the pass. Then you will get to the pass when the snow is hard, but it will just be softening up in the early morning. These are perfect conditions that won't zap your energy or kill too much time. When the snow is soft, these can be long slogs.

Traveling in the morning will be faster since you'll be on top of the snow rather than postholing and expending a lot of energy sinking in rotten snow in the afternoon. Try to stay in shady areas in the afternoon to avoid rotten snow.

It is tempting to want to walk on rocks and get off the snow, but keep this in mind. Snow often melts from underneath. This means you can sink farther or even poke through a pocket under the snow that's deeper than expected. Either take a big step on and off the rocks or walk around them. Watch out for thin snowbridges with water running underneath.

Take big steps when walking on and off snowfields. Snow is often slushy or punchy near the edges. Areas that are firm and solid in the morning may soften up and require postholing in the afternoon.

It's tempting to follow somebody's tracks through the snow. Make sure they go where you want to go. For instance, Pinchot Pass on the PCT is a little confusing, and tracks there can lead to the wrong pass. Check your maps often, and don't follow blindly.

Spring snow is what most PCT thru-hikers hit. The optimal plan for hiking through the Sierra Nevada in the spring is to camp in a basin below the next pass. Wake up early, and take about an hour or two to get up to the headwall of the pass. If you're hiking northbound, the south side of the pass should be in morning sun and will get soft enough to get really good footing. By the time you get to the top of the pass, the north side will be softening up too. In the best snow conditions, you can glissade or boot-ski down the pass, ignoring the switchbacks of the trail, which are buried under feet of snow. This can save tons of time!

Even as you hike down the pass and into basins, snow conditions shouldn't be too soft or rotten. As you get lower into a basin in the Sierras, snow peters out. This is a good place to take a break or have lunch.

If you're hitting another pass the next day, hike through the afternoon until you hit snow again. If you have the energy, posthole to get up into the snow again. If not, camp near the snow line. Get up early the next morning and cruise up to the next pass and onto the face of the pass as the snow is softening with the morning sun and you can start to kick steps easily.

RAUMA TIP

Always consider avalanche danger when hiking in snow. Travel in low-angle areas, and try not to walk under steep slopes. Slopes at a 30-degree angle or greater are more prone to sliding. If hiking in a group through a dangerous spot, move one at a time from safe area to safe area; keep your eyes on the person going through the treacherous spots.

Travel gently. Don't stand on the edge of cornices or try to break them off—unless you're intentionally trying to see if a slope will slide under the weight.

Take all necessary precautions if you are traveling where avalanche danger is high. Travel with a partner and carry a beacon, probe, and shovel. Make sure you know how to use them all efficiently.

In the spring avalanche danger dramatically increases when there's fresh snow. These are usually wet slides that occur when the sun comes back out; they are slower and start as a point release and spread from there. There can also be dry slides if the freshly fallen snow is not binding well to the old snow interface. Rainfall can add weight to the snowpack. Snow is further destabilized from wider changes in temperature during the day and strong solar radiation. In spring, if you're sinking in deeper than your boot top, there's a chance for wet slides, so keep that in mind.

Snow Hiking Tips

- When glissading, descending, or boot-skiing a pass, make sure you first traverse to a spot where there are no rocks or steep drop-offs below. You don't want any rocks in the way, just in case you slip and go for an unexpected ride or can't self-arrest quickly.

- The last place snow refreezes overnight is under trees. If the temps are not dropping below freezing or are near freezing, open areas like meadows and bowls can still refreeze due to radiational cooling. Tree cover prevents long-wave radiation from escaping, keeping such areas warmer. Snowpack is more solid and frozen in open areas and can still be punchy beneath trees. Alternatively, in spring the snow may stay a bit firmer under trees where there is a bunch of tree litter and pine needles. Use these tricks to help plot your route and keep you from postholing.

- When hiking in snow, apply sunscreen early and often. People get roasted on the PCT in the spring. They get burnt from the reflection of sun off the snow. Be sure to put sunscreen on the bottom of your chin, your ears, under your nose, the back of your legs if you're wearing shorts, under your forearms, and any other place where sunlight can bounce off the snow and onto your skin. I have even heard of people burning the roof of their mouth from hiking with their mouth open! Don't forget sunglasses! People go snow-blind in the Sierras in the spring!

- Make a cheap and ultralight case for your sunglasses or goggles out of plastic soda bottles. Cut the top off two plastic soda bottles (2-liter bottles for goggles; smaller bottles for sunglasses). Put your sunglasses or goggles inside one end, slide one end over the other, and you have an ultralight case. Your sunglasses case can double as food bowls. Wash the case/food bowl out after using; otherwise your sunglasses or goggles will get really nasty.

Digging a snow pit to study the snow and determine snow safety while backcountry skiing in the Sierras, California

Going cross-country through a sea of talus. Sometimes getting on a snow patch is the easiest way to travel.

CROSS-COUNTRY

Hiking cross-country is hiking without a trail. This can be fun and rewarding and can take you to seldom-seen places.

When hiking cross-country you need to be experienced and confident in your map reading and navigation skills. Reading a map and being able to visualize terrain and landscape from the map are key to picking the path of least resistance.

If your route selection is bad, hiking can be tedious and slow. If it's good, it can be easy and fast and even provide a more direct route than a trail.

When planning your cross-country route, find a landmark or bearing point on the map and plan your route from there. A straight line isn't always the best route. Look for open terrain, like a forest without brush and low-lying vegetation or an alpine zone. This is often symbolized by a particular color or shading on a map. Following a river, creek, or other water source offers a clear direction and path. Depending on the vegetation, it can sometimes be annoying and choked up. Other times it's the path of least resistance.

When cross-country hiking, check your map regularly. Match your location with the time so you can pinpoint your location and be aware of your progress. This will help in case you aren't sure where you are later on.

Try to stay away from shrubs, tamarisk, chaparral, and other plants low to the ground and rigid, unless absolutely necessary. They make hiking hard and can tear your skin and gear. Sometimes you can find a faint animal trail through these obstacles that will help get you through without as much bodily harm.

Hiking Cross Country Tips

- Most people hike at about 3 miles per hour on a trail but move between 2 and 2.5 miles per hour while hiking cross-country over good terrain. They cover even less ground in an hour on more difficult terrain and while bushwhacking. You'll have to account for the slower pace when figuring out your location.

- Be open-minded when hiking cross-country, and try to consider all the options. The route you scouted and think will work might not. You never know until you see it in person. Sometimes even the best topo map doesn't do the terrain justice. Common questions might be: Is that High Sierra granite ledge impassable? Or is it slippery because it has little ball bearing–size pebbles on it? Did recent rain make what looked possible now seem impossible? Is there still a snowfield that fills in a steep part and makes it easily passable? Sometimes a map can't tell you that information. We ran into some problems like this in New Zealand. The maps we had didn't depict ledges. All it takes is a 15-foot drop or cliff to make passing undoable without technical equipment. Still other slopes looked ridiculously steep on the map but were completely safe because they were scree. We safely ran down scree slopes at about 50 degrees.

- When walking across talus and boulder fields, scope out your route. Look for flat areas on rocks to step on. Try not to step in between rocks with narrow gaps. Stash or carry your poles so you can use your hands and arms as additional points of balance. Using your poles in boulder and talus fields greatly increases the chance of snapping your poles.

OTHER RATING SYSTEMS

The National Climbing Classification System (NCCS) in the United States; British System; Austrian System; French System, including the French Adjectival System (IFAS); and Soviet, West German, and European System are just a few rating systems. Wherever you plan to go, make sure you understand the rating system beforehand.

SCRAMBLING

Scrambling can turn a hike into a new adventure. It opens up opportunities to reach new places, new passes, and new terrain—and it can be a lot of fun.

Guidebooks use a rating system to tell you how difficult the terrain is and whether it requires scrambling or climbing. Ratings are a little subjective to the guidebook and author and depend on your strengths, weaknesses, and comfort levels. They serve as good guidelines.

The main system used in the United States and Canada is the Yosemite Decimal System. It has five classes of difficulty. The fifth class is the most difficult. It has a decimal system and is primarily for rock climbing. The rating system is used as a guide but is sometimes slightly off.

Ratings are made based on the crux—hardest move—on the route. If much of a hike is an easy Class 2 hike but has one Class 4 section the whole route is rated Class 4.

HERE'S HOW THE YOSEMITE SYSTEM GRADING WORKS

CLASS 1: The easiest class, includes hiking, light scrambling, and some rocky gradients. Generally hands are not needed.

CLASS 2: Involves some scrambling and likely use of hands. The most inexperienced may want a rope.

CLASS 3: Moderate exposure may be present. Simple climbing and/or scrambling with frequent use of hands. Consider bringing a rope in case you need it.

CLASS 4: Includes intermediate climbing. Most people want a rope because of exposure. A fall could be serious or fatal. Beginners and most average climbers will want and should have a belay. Usually includes some natural protection.

CLASS 5: Rock climbing that requires rope and natural or artificial protection by the leader to protect against a serious fall. All rock climbing is considered Class 5 or 6.

5.0–5.4: A physically fit person can actually climb at this level with little or no rock climbing skills, using only natural ability.

5.4–5.7: Requires climbing techniques.

5.7–5.9: Rock-climbing shoes, good climbing skills, and some strength are usually necessary at this level.

5.10–5.14+: Excellent rock-climbing skills and strength are needed. This level requires climbing training and commitment. Each category also has a letter grade, like 5.14a or 5.13d, to subdivide each grading. Under this system "a" is easier than "b," and so on.

CLASS 6: Climbing that involves placing the climber's weight on the equipment itself, as opposed to using it only for protection. This is also known as aid climbing.

Ascending Nengla La Pass (5,400m/17,717 ft.) in Dolpa, Nepal, through sun cups and rotten snow on a crisp morning

TRAUMA TIP

Use dotted or dashed lines (see map on the left) to draw your route with mapping software. That way you won't cover up the map's topographic lines or confuse your path with the lines.

MAKING HIKING ROUTES

Making your own hiking routes or adding variations to popular routes is a great way to explore a region. It's exciting and challenging. You have to be ready to make changes on the fly. Sometimes the landscape and route you planned doesn't look the same when you're actually there. The topo lines might not do a great job of portraying a landscape and showing steep terrain.

When I'm planning routes in the United States I use the CalTopo.com website. It allows you to zoom in and out, pan through the map, locate nearby towns and trails, draw on and annotate maps, and plan your route and alternate routes before you print out topo maps. You can print maps of varying scales for overview and more detailed maps for areas you think will be more technical. These maps are also smartphone compatible, so if you would rather go digital, you can.

If I can't use mapping software to research a trip, I'll find road or recreation maps to help plan my routes through a region. I look for maps that show protected and roadless areas, trails, high mountains, towns, and possible resupply locations and any other helpful information. I use multiple maps to figure out how best to link everything with the least amount of road-walking and the greatest amount of trail systems I can hike on.

Once I figure out the general corridor I want to hike, I research local trails and other nearby attractions. Whether or not I'm using mapping software or maps I found, I'll get the most

detailed maps I can find to cover the entirety of the route. These are the maps I will use during the trip—maps that are good enough for cross-country travel and navigation.

I research towns along the route, looking for post offices (in the United States primarily), grocery stores, or other shops to see where I can resupply and where supplies are slim pickings.

After that I draw my intended route, either on the mapping software or on the maps. I mark key points, water sources, and towns on the map and measure the distances between them. If I'm concerned that I may face a cliff or terrain issue, I may draw a couple alternate routes, in different colors, I think might work for the section.

Finally, I add all the distances together and develop an itinerary so I know how many days of food to carry between resupplies. This is also when I figure out the logistics of how to get to the start of the hike and home from the end. I also try to determine when I'm likely to need replacement gear or to swap out gear along the way.

Scampering across talus in the Canadian Rockies

Ascending the steep snow chute to the Banner Ritter Saddle, a Class 3 route in the Minaret Range of the Sierra Nevada, California *Photo by Shawn Forry*

Using the fixed chain on a steep, wet, slippery descent in New Zealand *Photo by Shawn Forry*

ADDING TECHNICAL ADVENTURES ON LONG-DISTANCE HIKES

I define a technical route as anything where there is added risk, danger, or exposure requiring extra hardware or equipment to help minimize the risk. Technical adventures can range from going solo with an ice ax to fully roping up on a three-person glacier team.

When you get comfortable hiking trails, over snowy passes, fording tough rivers, navigating, scrambling, and the other technical aspects of hiking, consider incorporating other skills into your trips. You need to have the skills for the challenge, and the more experienced you are, the more flexible you can be with the gear you carry. After learning how to rock climb, cross glaciers, mountaineer, and rappel, I started integrating those skills into my long-distance routes for more challenges.

If you're ready to incorporate such expeditions into your long-distance escapades, research and planning become even more crucial to having a fun but safe adventure. The more you know ahead of time means fewer unexpected variables.

Throwing a technical section into a long-distance hike takes a lot of homework, but that is half the fun. Research what equipment you'll need for each type of activity, and tailor your gear to the situations. You'll also know how long each section should be and then be prepared with the correct amount of food. Search guidebooks, read posts on internet forums about the trip (like SummitPost), browse the web, talk with local outfitters, call the national park backcountry office, and/or recon the route ahead of time. These are all really helpful.

While planning our Hayduke Trail hike, Pepper and I decided to add some slot canyons into some of the sections. It required climbing and rappelling gear. We researched the slot canyons and figured out how we could line them up so we were headed in the right direction for each. We found out what equipment was recommended for each canyon depending on rappel lengths and protection needed. By the time we got there, we were prepared for everything.

When I first hiked the Great Divide Trail, I marveled at the Columbia Icefield and large glaciers in the Canadian Rockies. I returned a few years later and devised a way to incorporate the ice fields and glaciers into a long-distance hike on the GDT.

Taking in the view and catching my breath on the ascent to Lumbha Sambha La Pass (5,100m/16,732 ft.) in Nepal. It was an amazing bluebird morning after getting about 8 inches of fresh snow overnight, until the clouds rolled back an hour later and the whiteout began again. *Photo by Shawn Forry*

BELOW: A local Nepali kid testing out my helmet, still not sure what it does or if he likes it. Five minutes later he realized he really liked it and started running around showing everybody.

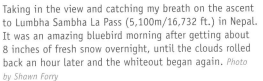

TRAUMA TIP

You don't want to carry your technical kit any longer than you have to—it's heavy and cumbersome. When researching and planning the trip and any technical routes, consider the following: Do I need to carry the technical gear the entire trip or just for the technical section? How can I get it to and from the area so I don't have to carry it the whole trip? Can I ship it to a town before the technical section and ship it back afterward?

TECHNICAL GEAR

Technical gear can quickly turn your pack into a heavy burden. You can incorporate ultralight methods to lighten the load. Figure out creative and safe ways you can use your gear for multiple purposes. If you have a partner or rope team, you will be able to split the weight of some of the communal gear.

GEAR CONSIDERATIONS

Consider comfort, convenience, and consequences as you select the minimum and lightest-weight equipment for the task at hand. Use anchors, tag lines, and everything necessary, but still do what you can to save weight. Carabiners can weigh as little as 23 grams. You can find full-strength ultralight harnesses that weigh 3 ounces.

Know all of your equipment well, and consider potential multiple uses. If you're carrying an ice ax and pickets, also use them for tent stakes. Why not use your climbing rope as a pillow and sleep in all your clothes so you can carry a lighter sleeping bag?

Make sure your gear will work for all the conditions you will face. Are your 'biners too small if you're using mittens or gloves in cold weather? Will your adze and ice ax have enough swing weight to chop a step in ice? Do your crampons have too much flex to front-point efficiently? Weight is important, but your equipment better work.

When I decided I was ready to incorporate the Columbia Icefield into an adventure, I talked with some friends. Pepper and I looked at normal glacier traversing gear and figured out how to incorporate ultralight methods without sacrificing performance. In the end our technical glacier equipment weighed just 4 pounds per person!

The list of ultralight methods to take on technical adventures is long. It's highly customized to the trip you're planning and your skills. This isn't a how-to. It's meant to spur the thought process and advise you where to start—again, research!

TECHNICAL GEAR

There's a wide range of options for your technical adventures. Depending on your skills and what you plan to encounter, you can tailor your gear to the trip.

HELMETS: Climbing helmets also range in size, weight, and function. You can get the classic bowling ball–shaped rock climbing helmets or superlight helmets like CAMP's Speed.

Helmet considerations:

- What are the hazards on the trip: falling, debris from above, crashing into the wall, etc.?
- How likely are such hazards?
- Should I carry a helmet?
- Is it worth the space and weight?

HARNESSES: You can go ultralight with a harness like CAMP's Alp 95 (I call it the G-string harness) or CAMP's Alp Racing. You may also choose a more comfortable or secure harness, up to a full-body harness.

Harness considerations:

- What's the likelihood of taking a fall?
- How long will I be hanging in the harness?
- Do I want or need the padding that's only available from a heavier harness?
- How necessary and convenient are gear loops going to be?
- How many gear loops do I need?

Each feature adds weight to a harness. I have used the Alp 95 on all of my technical hikes. It's a fantastic, lightweight, packable harness.

ICE AXES: Ice axes vary in size and weight. You can get a 7-ounce, 50-centimeter aluminum ice ax like the CAMP Corsa 50 centimeter to a much heavier, all-steel ax. The lighter the ax the lighter the swing weight. A heavier ax will bite into ice much easier than a lightweight one.

Ice ax considerations:

- What is the likelihood of a fall?
- Am I only using it as a self-arrest tool?
- What snow and/or ice conditions will I face?
- Do I need to chop steps or climb a pitch of ice?
- Do I need swing weight?

Technical Gear Tips

- Most of the time you won't remember what you read by the time you get there. It helps to have the info with you. For technical or tricky sections, I often make a small guide to carry with me. I'll copy text and pictures from internet research into a Word document. I shrink pictures and fonts—to a still-usable size—and get rid of extra space on the document. I print it all out double-sided to keep with me. When I'm doing recon in the field or thinking about a place I'd like to come back to, I'll take pictures of the pass or tricky spots with my camera while pointing out the route you're supposed to go, or what looks like the best route. I'll take pictures of guidebook photos of the route. Then I put those in my guide sheet to refer back to when I get to the area—without carrying anything extra. Another option is taking a picture of a guidebook page and keeping it on the memory card in your camera. Make sure you can read it or see the route when you play back the photos, and navigate from that.
- Slings can be very useful on a technical trip. They can double as prusiks, alpine draws, and ice-ax leashes.
- Depending on the technical aspects, you might be able to use a Munter hitch instead of carrying a belay device.
- Use a thinner-diameter tag line to pull your climbing rope to reduce the amount of heavier rope. This can save a lot of weight and makes your technical equipment more packable. It also helps to split the weight of the gear between you and your partner(s).
- You can also add a gear loop on the Alp 95 or Alp Racing by putting a 'biner through the small webbing loop on the side

- Do I need an adze or a hammer to put in gear like snow pickets (also known as snow bars in some countries)?

CRAMPONS: Crampons range from the simple, like Yaktrax or Kahtoola-style spikes, to 6-point in-step, 10-point aluminum, 12-point steel, or a rigid ice-climbing crampon.

Crampon considerations:

- What are the consequences of a fall?
- What shoe will the crampons need to be compatible with?
- What snow and/or ice conditions will I face?
- Will it be mixed with ice and rock?
- How steep are the ascents and descents?
- Will I need to front-point at all?

ROPES: Climbing ropes range from static to dynamic (basically dynamic ropes have stretch; static ropes don't) and from 8mm to 11mm or more. There are also twin, single, and double ropes. Some ropes are coated to repel water, like Sterling's DryCore ropes. This is nice because they don't absorb water and get heavy.

Rope considerations:

- How long a rope will I need?
- What will I use it for?
- Do I need static or dynamic rope?
- Do I need to rappel?
- Am I likely to fall on it? Can I use a tag line?
- How thin a rope do I feel safe with?

PROTECTION: Protection ranges from the passive, like nuts and chocks, to active, like spring-loaded camming devices.

Protection considerations:

- What type of natural protection will I have?
- How far do I feel safe "running it out" between protection?
- What are the consequences of a fall?
- What is my comfort level?
- What type of ice or rock will I climb?
- How wide a range of conditions can each piece of protection cover?
- How likely am I to need each piece?
- Can I get away without it?

HERE'S A SAMPLE GEAR LIST FOR TECHNICAL EQUIPMENT. THIS INCLUDES SOME GLACIER TRAVEL AND MANDATORY RAPPELS.

Technical Gear	Weight	Details
Sterling Ice Thong 7.7mm	49.3 oz.	Half rope, cut to 35m
Sterling Power Cord	TBD	6mm, tag line, 45m, extra for anchors
CAMP XLC 490 Crampons	13.8 oz.	Works well with trail runners
CAMP Corsa Ice Ax	8.8 oz.	60cm; use 2nds for pitched routes
CAMP Nano 23 Biners (6)	4.8 oz.	
CAMP HMS Nitro Lockers (2)	3.8 oz.	
8mm x 60cm Dyneema Runner (3)	2.1 oz.	
8mm x 100cm Dyneema Runner	1.1 oz.	
12mm x 240cm Dyneema Runner	4.8 oz.	
CAMP Stream Ice Screw 22cm (2)	6.2 oz.	V-Threads
CAMP Stream Ice Screw 12cm (2)	8.8 oz.	
CAMP Speed Helmet	7.4 oz.	
CAMP Alp 95 Harness or newer Alp Racing	3.4 oz.	Size medium

Getting ready to defrost, take a break, and warm up while swimming around Lake Tahoe unsupported

MULTISPORT ADVENTURES

Another way to mix things up is to plan a multisport trip. This can be as simple as scrambling or any of the other technical adventures you mix in.

You can build upon hiking and backpacking and add in adventures like packrafting, skiing, snowshoeing, kiting, standup paddleboarding, BASE jumping, paragliding—anything you can think of. These are all nice ways to spice things up if you're starting to feel that the hiking is getting monotonous but you still want to enjoy the backcountry and see new things. The bulk of the gear is fairly similar; you may need just a few new pieces of equipment before you're ready to see things from a different perspective.

Packrafting is one of the most popular forms of multisport adventure. A packraft is a great tool to cross big rivers or float them instead of walking. It can be a lot easier to paddle down a river for 30 miles or so than to walk along the river for the same distance. They are easy to portage if you see some rapids that are too big to float. Packrafts start at about 4 pounds and get heavier depending on size and features. The main downfall with smaller, lighter-weight rafts is that they travel slowly on flat water.

If you're packrafting, you'll also need a paddle, PFD (personal floatation device), and possibly a spray skirt. You can fashion an ultralight PFD out of blown-up water bladders that you put in a custom-made jacket or vest. You can use 1-liter bladders, which you can also use as water reservoirs for camp if needed. It will likely be much lighter and more packable than a traditional PFD.

If you're going to encounter snow, skis make for a multisport adventure with an obvious benefit. They prevent you from postholing in snow and provide mechanical advantage on downhills. Boots and skis can be heavy to carry. They can also be tough in tight, twisting terrain with lots of trees. Snowshoes are better in tight terrain, though you lose the mechanical advantage of skis and the fun of the downhills.

Kites are sometimes used with skis in open areas like Antarctica or on water or frozen lakes. They can greatly increase the distance you're

Raina overlooks Donner Lake on a winter overnighter on the PCT

able to cover. They are a great tool in vast spaces with consistent wind and when you have minimal chances for resupply.

I think multisport adventures are where things are heading. It could be because of people's decreasing attention span or time constraints, like picking up a bike when there's a long section of dirt roads or doubletracks on a trail. I think that may be a small factor. The bigger factor is that it's just plain fun to mix in a bunch of different skills, learn new things, challenge yourself, and mix it up a bit when you're out on a long adventure. More and more people are hiking and finishing the Triple Crown of long trails. There's other trails for bikepacking, rivers for packrafting, mountains to ski, glaciers to kite across. Think about the unlimited options you could have by tying any of those together and the amazing terrain you can see and cover, even if you only have a couple of weeks.

PLANNING

Planning a multisport adventure is just like planning any other trip, but you have to layer in another component. Depending on what the other "leg" will be, you need to look specifically at that area and determine when and where that mode of travel will be best. Is it a section of skiing because you'll be crossing a snow-covered mountain range? What miles will you need the ski equipment for, and what other equipment might you want to change out for this section because of the different conditions you'll encounter? For example, if you'll be on snow for the entire segment, you can probably use your skis for tent stakes. You might want to switch shelters, use a sleeping pad with a higher R value, and add other layers to your clothing system. Then it's important to determine where you can mail this gear swap and where you can bounce the other stuff to when the section is complete so you can switch back. If you're adding weight to your system, you'll want to keep the gear drops as tight as possible to the section you'll need the gear for. It happens sometimes, but it's definitely not ideal to be carrying skis and ski boots through the desert after you've descended from the snow-covered mountains.

Keep in mind as we move through this section with the multisport items, that the base case is typically hiking and backpacking. The core of the gear needed does not change from the typical Big 3. It might pack up a little differently or swap out an item or two from the core components, but generally, once you have the bulk of the gear, you'll just be adding more specialized equipment for the other sport or sports you're looping in.

MOUNTAINEERING/ CANYONEERING/ GLACIER TRAVEL/ RAPPELLING

Mountaineering, canyoneering, glacier travel, and rappelling are all exciting and fun to add into a long-distance route. Some of my favorite trips have added these components into the mix for a stretch or multiple stretches. First and foremost, you have to be practiced and prepared in the techniques to be safe. Knowing how to self-rescue is imperative for all these activities. Practice with your gear and equipment beforehand, and, most important, run through scenarios with your rope partner so you'll be on the same page once you get out on the adventure in the middle of nowhere. There are plenty of books out there on how to do these skills, so I'm not going to dive into those items specifically. I think it is more important to go through some areas where these skills can be used in the mix of a long-distance route and what gear you may need to bring along to add this to your repertoire.

With ten days of food and technical gear, ultralight packs can easily get maxed out and pushed to their carrying capacities. Here with rope, pickets, helmet, crampons, etc.

PLANNING

It is always fun to look at the map and explore what's around. Often I've found that when hiking a long-distance route, I see places the route bypasses for one reason or another. Most of the time it's because it's too rugged or technical, too hard to build a trail, or the snow sticks around too long—all reasons that make me want to explore there. That's what entices me to check out the area and figure out how to incorporate it into the route. My second time on the Great Divide Trail, we devised a route that paralleled and crossed over the Columbia Icefield to mix it up a bit and stay higher toward

the crest from the standard route. In the Himalayas there are a few high passes that can be added into the Great Himalaya Trail that use rappelling for a descent and some low-grade ice climbing/scrambling on the ascent. In southern Utah along the Hayduke Trail, you can add a canyoneering alternative that connects a bunch of canyoneering classics. Technical components can be added in to the Sierras, Wind River Range, Cascades, and Glacier National Park, along with countless other locales if you get creative.

When you're ready to up your game, do research online about the routes and how to connect things. It's very important to look at the direction of travel. Some routes need certain pieces of gear in one direction and not the other. You may need more rope or less rope. In a technical canyoneering situation, you will generally only want to go down the slot canyon, so it's important to note the details and direction of travel. This will also tie into what gear you will need to accomplish that traverse.

Your pack will gain significant weight with the technical equipment, so it's important to know what you need, get creative with how you can use things in multiple ways, and make sure you have a plan so you know when you'll have to carry the technical gear. You don't want to be carrying everything for the entire length of the trip if you won't need it. Follow the same plan as bouncing things ahead when conditions get warmer during a thru-hike. It can be uncomfortable to add the technical gear since it's fairly heavy and can double your pack weight, plus make it harder to pack up each morning, and you'll likely need to pack more food. You'll need to revise your expected mileage for the technical sections down accordingly. Sometimes your travel might be down to less than 0.5 mile per hour. That being said, it's rewarding and fun and adds a whole other dimension to thru-hiking, which should probably be called multisport hiking, multisport adventuring, or thru-adventuring.

GEAR CONSIDERATIONS FOR EACH

When researching your route and the details of the equipment and what's needed, you'll often see the suggested gear. Whether it's a helmet, rope, tag line, rappel device, anchors, slings, harness, ice screws, crampons, ice ax (ice climbing versus mountaineering), etc., you'll need to keep an open mind and be comfortable with all that equipment. Just as important for these components is comfort and familiarity with climbing knots. Know your figure-eight follow through, Munter, prusik, alpine butterfly, etc. These will allow you to be safe but also creative with how you use your equipment so you can save weight. For example, using prusiks means you won't have to carry ascenders.

Tip: If you're not climbing anything super technical but are traversing or rappelling, you can use webbing or even the ultralight CAMP Alp Racing harness to save weight, at just over 3 ounces.

BIKEPACKING

Bikepacking is a fun multisport, or single-sport, alternative to thru-hiking. Thru-hiking slows you down, relaxed and decompressed at a different level, but you also need to have another level of patience. When the trip doesn't entail cross-country travel, and is on good singletrack, doubletrack, dirt roads, or even paved roads, bikepacking is a fantastic alternative. I often think back about when I hiked the Continental Divide Trail the first time in 2005. The trail wasn't nearly as complete then as it is now. There were numerous sections for fairly long distances on USDA Forest Service roads, and even some sections on paved roads. It would have been great to bike those sections and cut down some road-walking. Imagine doing the roughly 125-mile Great Divide Basin in Wyoming in a day or two

and not worrying about a 30-mile waterless stretch because it only took 2 or 3 hours to get to that next water source?

Keep in mind that rules and regulations have to allow for bikes. Bikes are not allowed on most national scenic trails or within wilderness areas. The Arizona Trail, for example, has a separate bike route that circumvents the wilderness area sections. If you like biking and don't have the time for a long thru-hike, it can be a great compromise to bikepack the trail, or mix in bikepacking sections to compress the time of a thru-hike, and mix up the activities for a change of pace. Sticking with the Arizona Trail example, the approximately 850-mile Arizona Trail will usually take people four to six weeks to hike. On a bike, it could take two to three weeks. Mixing biking into sections of the New Mexico section of the CDT and interspersing the road or dirt road sections with the Great Divide Mountain Bike Trail will have a similar effect on timing. That being said, bikepacking isn't all about timing and speeding up. It's just fun to mix it up and challenge yourself with another type of activity. Bushwhacking with a bike takes things to a whole other level of fun!

GEAR CONSIDERATIONS

Figure out where you're headed and what the trails will be like. Is it a gravel grinder you need? A mountain bike? A touring bike? You may just be able to switch out tires to make your bike work for various conditions and trips. Make sure you size your bike and your seat height correctly to prevent injuries. Twenty-nine-inch tires are the top choice for anything off-road. Bike before the trip to get your legs, legs, butt, and arms used to the riding, seat, and vibrations. The choices with bikes are similar to other gear: The lighter, the more expensive. In the case of bikes, it's the type of metal, with steel being the lowest price, then aluminum, titanium, and carbon fiber. Prices

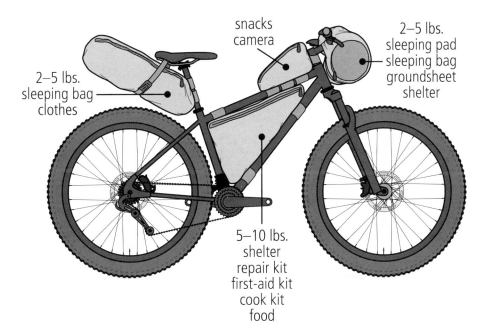

snacks
camera

2–5 lbs.
sleeping pad
sleeping bag
groundsheet
shelter

2–5 lbs.
sleeping bag
clothes

5–10 lbs.
shelter
repair kit
first-aid kit
cook kit
food

can range all the way to tens of thousands of dollars, so research and invest wisely for how you'll be using the bike. You probably don't need dual suspension. Hard-tails are more efficient, weigh less, and have less to go wrong. I've used some Salsa bikes and have liked them a lot. I don't add bar ends, but that's just my personal preference.

You can use most of your backpacking gear with your bike: tent, sleeping bag, pad, etc. You may just want to pack it differently. You will likely want to streamline your backpack so you just have a few odds and ends in there, like snacks and maybe a little water or an extra layer. You'll add in a frame back, seat post bag, and maybe a handlebar bag and some other trinkets. The old way of a trailer or panniers has gone the way of the dodo for ultralight use and bikepacking. They're way too heavy and not nimble.

A lot of the bags are made by cottage manufacturers and use DCF (Dyneema composite fabric). They're a heavier weight than most backpacking gear and feel a bit overbuilt, but they also take a fair amount of bumps and bruises. A few Voile straps can also go a long way toward saving some weight on how you strap things onto your bike versus needing to purchase or use a designated bag. Depending on how much you're packing, you may not need a handlebar bag. Food considerations should take into account that you'll be moving faster and may only need a day or two between resupplies.

Some companies, like Big Agnes, are making bikepacking-specific tents now. They're essentially the same model and design as the backpacking version but have shorter pole sections. This can be handy for packing up and stashing your tent poles on your bike, but they're not a necessity. It's another good reason to use a tarp, since it's the most packable and versatile no matter the mode of travel. Just keep in mind that if your tarp needs trekking poles to set up, you might have to get creative on the setup.

If you don't have trekking poles, you can use your bike to set up a tarp for a shelter.

A lot of cyclists like to use clip-in pedals on bikepacking trips. If I'm just mixing in a bikepacking section, I prefer to keep the same trail runners and just use flat pedals. Then I have less gear to switch out and am more comfortable when walking around town for resupplies.

I've considered a unicycling multisport. Yes, I love unicycling and thought it would be a blast and also be very convenient for throwing the unicycle on my pack if intermittent bushwhacking was needed. It's definitely a bit slower and not as comfortable for long distances, but there might be a time and a place!

PACKRAFTING

Packrafting is another way to multisport. Alternatively, you could just go on a packrafting trip down a river instead of using a raft, canoe, or kayak. The beauty of packrafting versus canoeing, kayaking, prone paddleboarding, or standup paddleboarding as a multisport is that you can easily inflate and deflate the tool and fit it into your pack. Collapse your paddle and strap it onto your pack and you're ready to start hiking or bushwhacking through the wilderness. Based on that ease and accessibility, packrafting is the clear winner in the water sports category for multi-use adventuring, so I'm not going to go into the others. Also, in my humble opinion, I don't consider canoeing and portaging a true multisport. It's fun and

Tip: Don't forget repair kits and a repair tool. You don't need much when you're backpacking, but as soon as you add some mechanical equipment, you'll need Allen wrenches, tire levers, and all that other good stuff to be able to repair your bike on the fly. Take a class, watch videos, or play around and get comfortable with doing the repairs so you don't get stuck in the middle of nowhere wishing you knew how to fix a flat tire.

no doubt an awesome trip through the Boundary Waters or Quetico Provincial Park, but to me it's a canoe trip with a little walking. You're not adjusting your gear and equipment accordingly, so I'm not going to dive into that.

PLANNING

In the planning category, it's very important to think about the purpose of the river or water travel. Is it to cross flat water? Go down Class III or IV rapids? Float down a generally flat river? Cross a large river multiple times? The answer to these questions will generally help steer you into the right shape, length, and type of packraft and paddle, and if you'll need a PFD. Do your homework online about the water features, rapids, canyons, portage spots, etc., you might hit so you're ready and prepared. It sometimes can be worthwhile and easy to portage around some larger rapid sections.

GEAR CONSIDERATIONS

A few companies make cheesy floats that don't work very well and aren't worth their weight. They won't work in rapids and don't paddle well in flat water. There's no point, since you won't need them to cross a long flat-water stretch unless it's icy cold (based on the accompanying tip). If you're going to add packrafting to your hike, get a good packraft, like an Alpacka Raft or a Kokopelli. Get a good lightweight carbon-fiber paddle that breaks down into multiple pieces, usually four sections, so it can stash on your pack relatively well without snagging on everything under the sun. You'll pay up for the carbon-fiber paddle and a good raft, but it's worth it for the performance, design, weight reduction, and durability.

Tip: If you are just trying to cross flat water or a big slow-moving river, I've often found that packrafting is overkill. If your backpack is waterproofed inside with a trash-compactor bag and then closed up, it will often float for a while. You can then easily swim behind it and push it along in front of you while you swim across the water crossing.

Getting ready to swim. Still or slow-moving water can be crossed with your pack pushed along, since it will float for a while.

The only other things you might want to consider with packrafting, depending on where you're going and what the water temperatures may be, is a dry suit, gloves—neoprene or other—and a spray skirt.

Tip: It's your call, but you may be able to get away with a silnylon or mesh vest that you can secure your empty but inflated Platypus water carry system in to give you just enough float to call it an ultralight PFD.

WINTER MULTISPORT– BACKCOUNTRY SKIING/ SNOWSHOEING

Winter multisporting takes your skills to another level. It's not just new modes of travel but also new camping, gear, and techniques to keep you warm and efficient. Even finding and getting water can be challenging. We've discussed winter camping earlier, so here we'll jump right into the planning and gear.

PLANNING

Again, proper prior planning prevents piss-poor performance.

Know the high and low temperatures you'll likely encounter as well as the weather, winds, snow conditions, and avalanche conditions, and be prepared for what you'll encounter. This is all part of being safe.

GEAR CONSIDERATIONS

Know what equipment you need and how to use it. For example, an avalanche beacon, probe, and shovel don't do any good if you don't know how to use them or haven't kept up practicing. It's not quite like riding a bike.

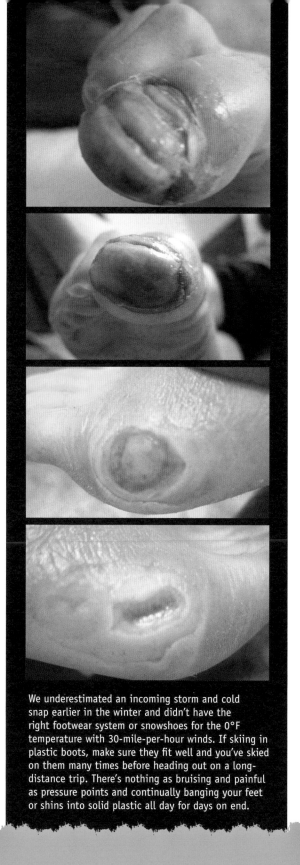

We underestimated an incoming storm and cold snap earlier in the winter and didn't have the right footwear system or snowshoes for the 0°F temperature with 30-mile-per-hour winds. If skiing in plastic boots, make sure they fit well and you've skied on them many times before heading out on a long-distance trip. There's nothing as bruising and painful as pressure points and continually banging your feet or shins into solid plastic all day for days on end.

Tip: Storm and snow conditions and terrain will greatly affect your speed of travel. So make sure to be informed and plan your food requirements accordingly. It can be important to carry at least an extra half or full day of food in the winter in case you need to hunker down to wait out a storm or heightened avalanche conditions.

I'm not going into fat biking here as a mode of travel for this purpose, because people riding fat bikes are typically on pre-groomed or compacted trails, not purely in the backcountry. Same with skate skis, even though I've done a bit of skate-skiing off piste and in the backcountry on good spring crust days.

Snowshoes don't take much additional skills to travel on. They are fairly inefficient and slow, but a lot better than postholing. The issue is that you still need to walk down hills rather than glide,

like on skis. That being said, they are very good for terrain where you may go in and out of snow line or between dirt and snow at times, since they are much more packable and lighter than skis and ski boots. Your footwear system can be planned depending on how much bare ground you think you'll hit so you can just strip off layers and have your trail runners to wear at that point.

TIP: If you are going to sidehill or go up and down steep terrain, metal-framed snowshoes with cleats around the metal frames, like the MSR Lightning Snowshoes, are recommended. I often wear the women's version and cut off the ascension bar to save a little weight.

Skis are a tough category, since there's so much variety and so many subcategories. I'm going to focus on touring and distance travel, so don't think I'm going into any resort skis or anything like that. Even though I Telemark, I'm skipping that too, since the backcountry side of it has not kept up with alpine touring in weight and performance. Alpine touring boots are light and can

Underneath these NEOS waterproof overboots, we were either wearing lightweight waterproof synthetic boots or trail runners, depending on conditions. This was a very versatile combination.

Alpine touring boots have thinner plastic to save weight, as you can see from the damage to this divot from repeatedly hitting the front of the binding during touring.

The Voile skis we used have fish scales, so we didn't need to put skins on if the terrain was rolling and conditions were good. Saved a lot of time on transitions.

perform well on the downhills. The lighter you get, the less performance on the downhills. I'm OK with that. I tend to stick to the rando racing or ski-mo (ski mountaineering) styles for the lighter weight, despite sacrificing warmth, performance, and often waterproof capabilities. I'd rather figure out a way to make up for some of that stuff and be in a lighter-weight and more comfortable boot. No boots are specifically made for long-distance lightweight overnight travel at this point, so it's all a trade-off.

Over the years of trial and error, I've found skis with "fish scales" to be the holy grail. The catch is, I also want metal edges and some width underfoot.

Depending on the snow conditions where you're headed, the width will help you have a little more floatation. Typically in the backcountry, I want at least 70-millimeters underfoot, usually at least 80 millimeters to be a little more versatile in case there's fresh snow. Only a few brands make metal-edged skis with fish scales. The Voile backcountry skis with fish scales are cutting-edge and some of the lightest on the market.

You'll also likely want to add an avalanche beacon, probe, shovel, poles, and climbing skins to your kit for the winter. You also may need a few repair items for broken skins, ski bindings, skin glue

KITE-SKIING OR KITEBOARDING

There's nothing worse or more frustrating than carrying extra weight and not getting any glide.

To be perfectly honest, I have yet to do either of these beyond a beginner level, but they're up there on my list because of the potential for interesting multi-sport trips. I have been flying a trainer kite to practice and get used to the motions of flying a kite—launching and getting in and out of the power zone. I can't wait to get on skis or a board and see how I can mix this in. I view this more as a single-sport adventure at this point, though, because the kites are fairly heavy and not super compressible in a pack, but the opportunity to travel fast and far makes it worth the weight. Plus, many kites are made out of DCF already, so we're probably close to as light as they can get. There's opportunities to cut some weight by using a smaller kite, but it will pick up less wind. It's a trade-off. I think a 3- or 5-meter kite is pretty versatile and probably the size used most often. There's a number of brands out there, but no one is focusing on the weight of the kite or how the harness system and other components pack up and compress. The opportunity to kite across Greenland and cover 100 miles per day is definitely on my list!

not working, or carrying your skis. A Voile strap is always handy for strapping on skins that aren't sticking any more. You may want to carry a small piece of hard skin wax and rub-on ski wax in case the snow starts sticking and clumping up. There's nothing more frustrating!

Bone dry

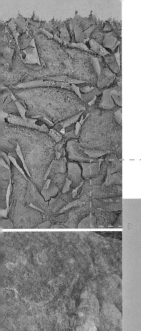

FINDING WATER ON A MAP OR IN A DESERT

Finding water is a life-saving skill. Even when you're not in trouble, you still need to know how to find water. While the best option is to fill up whenever you stop for a significant break, sometimes it doesn't work, and you may come close to running out when you need it.

Always read the legend or key on your map. Most hiking maps show seasonal creeks with dashed or dotted lines. On colored maps they're usually blue. On black-and-white maps they might be different than other dash patterns. However, you can't rely on these as likely water sources. Permanent creeks, streams, springs, and rivers are usually marked by a solid line or a blue line on colored maps. Some maps have different symbols for seasonal springs, seeps, and hot springs. Everything is explained in the map legend.

Don't assume that deeper ravines, canyons, or dried-out watercourses are most likely to have water. Look for where they originate from (lake, spring, or a big cirque with permanent snowfields) and what direction they are facing. In the Northern Hemisphere, north-facing watercourses are the most likely to hold water because they stay cooler and shadier. The opposite is true in the Southern Hemisphere.

The time of day can play a huge role in a body of water's flow. A water source fed by snowmelt can swell throughout the day. In other situations it can also shrink to the point of disappearing.

In a desert or sandy terrain and in hot weather, water can quickly evaporate and disappear. I have seen a creek disappear into the sand in a matter of minutes. In these circumstances, water may be available in the morning but not later in the day. If you're faced with such a situation, consider carrying extra water.

Look for certain types of vegetation or a long line of vegetation, like willows, when looking for water. Sycamores and willows love water and usually are near streams. They also are an indication that water may be close to the surface if no water is visible. If you dig into the ground, water may seep and pool in the cavity.

Water is often seasonal in the desert. Most deserts get precipitation in the winter. While they're mostly dry in summer, others get monsoonal rain in the middle of the summer. You may find potholes or holes in sandstone that keep water in them. It's probably not the best-tasting water, but it's water nonetheless. Don't bathe in such holes—wildlife and microorganisms need these holes to survive, so don't clean your dirty self off in them.

Sometimes all you can find is silty water, especially in desert conditions. In these conditions—if you're using a SteriPEN or filter—use your shirt or a bandana to help filter out sediment when you fill your water bottle. If you're filling up when you stop for the evening, stand your reservoirs or bottle upright before you go to sleep. That way, any remaining sediment will settle to the bottom overnight and you can drink or pour the water without getting sediment.

In desert canyons a dry pour-off or dry waterfall can lead to a pool of water below. These can last long after the rest of the canyon has dried up.

TRAUMA TIP
Sometimes you'll find seeps in the desert. They're basically springs of water coming out of the rock. They might have very little flow or be hard to corral into your water bottle or reservoir. If you're using them for water, you can use your rain gear, rainfly, or shelter to funnel the water into your container. You can also use your pot to help catch the water, since it has a larger opening than a water bottle.

SPONSOR-SHIPS

Decked out and trying to act gangster
Photo by Raina Ferran

If you're a serious outdoor athlete looking for money from a company or gear manufacturer, here's some information that can help. Sponsorships are partnerships with a company or group. They help you out, and you help them out. It has to be a two-way street. Companies want to support cool projects, but they really want sponsorships that help them sell more or develop better equipment.

It's mainly the former. They want to sell more gear. That's the reason they are in business. If they don't sell gear, they won't be around much longer. I understand this relationship through years of working closely with various outdoor manufacturers. I've also seen the industry evolve, and I'm the type of person who is less and less likely to get future sponsors. I'm not a self-promoter. I don't want to be in the press. I just want to enjoy the outdoors, see cool places, and challenge myself. In the past I have worked hard behind the scenes to help the companies design and create longer-lasting products and gear I would like to use. I'd send them photos from trips they could use in promotional material but not regularly post from my remote locations. This is no longer seen by many companies as the "value" they want. They want hashtags and social media influencers. I'm old-school. You can do less-intense trips and get sponsored if you're providing the "value" and messaging.

Some manufacturers cap the monetary amount of gear you can order.

Don't expect to walk into a full-salary sponsorship, particularly in the outdoor industry. We have our stars, but there are no Diego Maradonas in the sport. Work your way up to larger sponsorships. Build a relationship with the company or organization. Show the company how you can help them as an influencer, gear tester, public face for the company, or gear promoter. Do that, and the relationship might naturally progress.

GETTING SPONSORED

Put together a sponsorship proposal. The proposal details why you want their sponsorship, what you're

Sponsorship Tips

- Treat all your sponsors well. Do everything you can to keep them happy and maintain a good working relationship.
- The first sponsor is the hardest to get. If you keep a good relationship with them, they can help you get other sponsors. Don't burn any bridges. The outdoor industry is small, and word gets around. That's also true if you do a good job with a company.

doing, your background, why they should sponsor you, and what the company will get in return.

Most companies get thousands of requests per year. Don't expect a response right away. In fact, some companies use an automated system for sponsorships to help them streamline the process.

The best way to get started in the process is to e-mail or call customer service and get contact information for the correct person for sponsorships. Get in touch with them to learn more about their process, and submit your sponsorship proposal accordingly. Follow up after you send the proposal in. Give them time (three weeks or so) to look at it. The people who handle sponsorships and marketing programs at companies are often very busy. When you follow up with them, be polite and respectful.

Some companies like to sponsor causes, like marathons benefiting cancer research or fundraisers for developing nations. Don't attempt to support a cause just because you think it will help

you get a sponsorship. Only consider going for such a sponsorship if you really support the cause and think you can have an impact. If you're not sincere, companies will see right through your attempt to get money or free gear.

When putting a proposal together, clearly explain how sponsoring you will benefit them—how many followers you have; what types of social media you're active on; some photos you've taken. They may also want feedback on products to help them develop better products; testimonials of how well the equipment worked; high-quality pictures of their products in use; mentions of their gear and contributions in articles, interviews, blogs, and YouTube videos; placing their logo on your website, blog, or social media sites; links to their site; how you'll be a good brand ambassador; content for their websites and blogs; and other means of promoting their brand. The more engaged you are to help them out, the better.

TRAUMA TIP Don't seek sponsors just to get freebies. Seek sponsors whose gear you support and want to use. It makes for a natural fit. You can fully support them and be happy about the relationship without sacrificing performance, fit, or comfort just for free gear.

Part of me and my Granite Gear family at the Outdoor Retailer show in Salt Lake City, celebrating Granite Gear's twenty-fifth anniversary (hence the tie-dyed shirts).

SOME RANDOM CRUCIAL

- When you buy shoes at Dick's Sporting Goods you can also buy their 'No Sweat Protection Plan'. You know you're going to blow through shoes fast on a thru-hike. You can mail them home and return them and basically get your shoes for the price of the insurance.

- Learn about store return policies. Sometimes you can buy electronics like cameras at Walmart or some other big box stores, and as long as you keep the receipt and box, you can return the items within thirty days if they don't meet your needs. Note that some companies charge a "restocking fee" for electronics returns.

- Always ask hotels and motels for their AAA discounts, thru-hiker discount if on a popular long trail, or best rates. Sometimes they don't even ask for your AAA card.

- When you're new to the world of outdoor adventure and get outfitted with a bunch of stuff at a store, you are spending a good chunk of change. Ask if they'll give you a break with a discount or throw in a free pair of socks or something. It never hurts to ask.

- I have never carried bear spray, but if it makes you feel more comfortable, go ahead and do so. I would only carry the smallest-size can, since you are not likely to use it. If you are going to carry it, I think you will need it only in grizzly country. Black bears usually are more docile. If you have it with you make sure it is handy. Otherwise it is worthless. Also keep in mind that you will not be able to travel on an airplane or into another country with bear spray, pepper spray, or mace.

- I often carry two different types of insoles, Superfeet and orthotics or homemade insoles from foam clogs, like Crocs or Waldies. I switch at some point, usually about two-thirds into the day, always starting with the Superfeet and switching to the softer cushy insole in the afternoon when I'm starting to get tired. This helps keep your feet fresh.

- Keep your toenails clipped. It will help prevent pain and potential ingrown toenails

- There is nothing worse than getting sick while in the backcountry. You are most likely to get sick from being around other people. You often pick up illnesses in towns when you are around others. It's a good idea to take extra precautions: wiping down TV remotes at hotels (or putting them in a plastic bag or the shower cap that the hotel may offer for free) and wiping shopping carts and baskets at the supermarket with sanitizer when it's available.

- When shopping for a backpack, remember that the weight of the backpack isn't as important as the weight of the items that go inside the pack. The most important thing is the pack's ability to carry the load you're carrying comfortably.

- When the weather is bad, always remember to eat. You should stop for a short time, even in a torrential downpour. If you do not eat, you will feel colder. It helps to always have about a day's worth of food that is easy to eat while walking and easy to access without digging through your pack.

- If you're in a group of two or more and think a ford is dangerous, make your partner(s) go first! Just joking. Cross one at a time. That way, you won't all get into trouble at the same time.

- When you fill up your water bottle in cold weather, fill it only about three-quarters of the way. The water movement can prevent freezing.

- Don't overpack or overdress for a cold-weather trip. When you're hiking or doing something else active, you won't need too many layers—unless you're in extreme cold. You'll generate a lot of body heat, and you don't want to soak your layers with sweat.

HIKING AND LIFESTYLE TIPS

- In winter, or if you may encounter freezing temperatures overnight, carry an extra garbage bag or stuff sack to put your shoes in. You can put the sack under the foot of your sleeping bag. This way your shoes won't freeze or get everything wet.

- To preserve your rain jacket's performance for as long as possible, only hike with it on when it is raining, rain is imminent, or you really need it as a cold-weather layer.

- If you need to touch up the water sealant on equipment while on the trail, look into UV sealing products. They dry quickly when exposed to UV light, so you won't have to sit and wait for hours while the sealer dries.

- I don't usually carry a bandana, but a lot of people do. There are a ton of uses for it. Under the hat to keep the sun off, wetting it down to cool you off in the desert, keeping mosquitoes off the back of your neck or lower face, and as an ice pack with snow or for compression at night for injuries are just some of the ways to use a bandana.

- When shopping for your hiking food, you can add a pack of ramen noodles to double the size of your meal. It will be less than half the price than if you bought two Lipton Sides or other ready-made meals.

- Use Fritos to start a fire if you need some easy kindling. The corn chips contain so much oil that they burn evenly and slowly—like a match.

- Take your shoes and socks off at breaks to help your feet dry and air out. This prevents a lot of foot problems.

- If you're dealing with a lot of mosquitoes, minimize your skin exposure. Put on your rain jacket and keep your hood up. Tuck your shirt into your pants or shorts. If you're at a break and wearing shorts, pull your pants on over them, allowing the pants to hang over your feet. Set up the body of your tent or bug netting really fast, and get in there for some peace of mind.

- If your shoes untie a lot, try double-knotting them and then tucking the loops into your lower shoelaces. That should help keep them tied little longer. If you are still having trouble, make the double knot by going the reverse direction than you had been doing it.

- Turmeric, pineapple, omega-3s, and arnica are natural inflammation reducers. Arnica comes in tablets. It also is available as a cream so you can localize it to your sore spots. Turmeric also comes in pill form, so you don't have to eat a ton of it. You can add this spice to your foods. Health food stores often have anti-inflammation pills with a mixture of all of the active ingredients extracted from these plants.

- Always pay attention to the color of your urine. It tells you how well or poorly hydrated you are. The yellower it is, the more dehydrated you are.

- Homeopathic treatments: Use garlic for a tooth abscess. For an abscessed tooth, place thinly sliced garlic directly on the abscess. Leave it there for about 15 minutes and repeat. It'll likely sting. If it gets to be too much, try a garlic-water rinse.

- If your stomach is ailing, add more garlic and/ or ginger to your food. Additionally, eating pumpkin seeds can prevent intestinal bugs. If you're hiking in South America, you can chew coca leaves, which supposedly help prevent altitude sickness.

- These tips are not substitutes for proper medical attention if you're ill. They can help prevent parasites or illnesses and can help you heal faster.

Before (inset) and after—forty-seven days of hiking through Nepal, hundreds of thousands of feet of elevation changes, and major calorie deficits *Photos by Shawn Forry*

MAJOR TRAILS IN THE US

The United States is blessed with some great long trails, three of which—the Appalachian Trail, the Continental Divide Trail, and the Pacific Crest Trail—make up the Triple Crown of hiking. There are shorter trails and regional trails in the United States. The Hayduke and Colorado Trails are in these categories. These trails are a great place to see a part of the country that you might otherwise never see.

APPALACHIAN TRAIL

The AT was the first National Scenic Trail and is the most popular long-distance hiking trail in the United State.

Don't expect to be alone on the AT or in a very remote wilderness setting. Most AT hikers love the trail because they enjoy the lifestyle, meeting people, and making new friends along the way. Many Triple Crowners consider the AT the most difficult of the three trails because it is steeper than the others. Here are some facts and FAQs about the trail:

AT FACTS

- Distance: 2,174 miles. (The International AT adds 1,900 miles of hiking in Maine and Canada).
- High point: Clingmans Dome, Tennessee, 6,643 feet above sea level.
- Low point: Hudson River, Hudson, New York, 124 feet above sea level.
- National Parks: Great Smoky Mountains National Park and Shenandoah National Park.
- First official thru-hike: Earl Shaffer, 1948.
- States the trail goes through: Georgia, North Carolina, Tennessee, Virginia, West Virginia, Maryland, Pennsylvania, New Jersey, New York, Connecticut, Massachusetts, Vermont, New Hampshire, and Maine.

AT Q&A

Q: Do I need to carry maps?
A: No, you probably don't need detailed topographic maps for the AT, unless you're hiking in the winter. The best thing for an AT thru-hike is a good data book, or an app with data tables, that has distances between shelters, towns, and water sources. You will need information on the services available in each town. The trail is well trodden, well established, packed down, and well-marked with white blazes that are highly visible—except in a snowstorm. You should be fine without maps.

Q: How is the weather?
A: Weather on the AT can range from cold and snowy to hot and humid. Plan accordingly. If you hike during thru-hiker season (spring to fall), start the trip prepared for cold conditions. If you're going north on the trail, switch out to warmer-weather equipment after passing the Grayson Highlands in Virginia and switch back to cooler-weather equipment in Glencliff, New Hampshire.

Q: When should I change to summer gear?

A: It depends on when you leave, but generally after Trail Days, around the end of May. Most people wait until they clear the Grayson Highlands to switch out to a summer sleeping bag.

Q: How much water do I need to carry?

A: Not much. You can usually find water on the AT at least every 7 miles, usually much more often. Almost all the shelters have some sort of water source.

Q: What type of shelter should I use?

A: This is up to you. Three-sided shelters are spaced out along the length of the trail. If you plan on staying in the shelters, you can save some weight on your own shelter and get by with a tarp or bivvy—if you need it. Sometimes the shelters are full, so you should have your own. The answer also depends on your mosquito and blackfly aversion; you may want to camp instead of staying in the shelters if the bugs are bad.

Q: How often are there shelters?

A: Throughout the AT, shelters are available about every 7 miles. In southern Vermont the AT and LT (Long Trail) overlap, and there are shelters roughly every 3–4 miles.

Q: What are trail angels and hostels?

A: A lot of people along the AT help out the hikers—be grateful for this. Some trail angels will let you stay at their house for free or for a donation. Other trail angels put soda or cold drinks on the trail; others have big barbecues. When you come across such people or things, enjoy them—don't take them for granted.

Hostels are accommodations that are generally cheaper than hotels. You'll find them along the AT, along other trails, and in some cities (more likely in other countries). Those along the AT are primarily for hikers. Some offer a shuttle service so you can slackpack. Some offer services for hikers as well. Laundry is a nice bonus.

Q: Are bears and venomous snakes a concern on the AT?

A: On the AT I worry more about ticks and Lyme disease in the summer. Yes, there are bears. Take precautions with your food and other items that have an odor. Hang them up at night, particularly where there are poles or other hanging systems for bear protection set up. There's no reason not to.

Rattlesnakes and copperheads are found mainly south of Massachussets in summer. You can avoid them. Be mindful when you come out on sunny open rock ledges, like there frequently are in Pennsylvania.

More of a nuisance than all of these are mice. Some shelters on the AT have a healthy mouse population. They will try to get into your food bag at night, so, again, use the shelter's food hanging system.

Q: What degree sleeping bag do I need?

A: This depends on how you sleep. I sleep pretty warm. I use a 20- or 30-degree bag to start the trip and switch to a 50-degree bag during the height of summer.

Q: What are some helpful websites?

Appalachian Trail Conservancy (ATC): appalachiantrail.org

The AT-L archives at National Scenic Trails Mailing Lists: backcountry.net/mailman/listinfo/at-l

WhiteBlaze.net: whiteblaze.net

PACIFIC CREST TRAIL

The PCT is an amazing trail. It's well graded and incredibly scenic. A few hundred people hike the trail in the summer and leave from the PCT Kickoff, which usually occurs at the end of April. If you're looking for a hiking community like on the AT, start your hike from the event. If you want a quieter hike, leave before or after PCT Kickoff; the crowd will be more spaced out.

PCT FACTS

- Distance: 2,650 miles.
- High point: Forester Pass, California, 13,153 feet above sea level.
- Low point: Bridge of the Gods, Cascade Locks, on the Oregon-Washington border, 180 feet, 140 feet above sea level.
- National Parks: Sequoia National Park, Kings Canyon National Park, Yosemite National Park, Lassen National Park, Crater Lake National Park, and North Cascades National Park.
- First official thru-hike: Eric Ryback in 1970.
- States the trail goes through: California, Oregon, and Washington.

PCT Q&A

Q: Do I need to carry maps?

A: Yes. I highly recommend carrying maps for this trail, not just a data book. Some junctions aren't marked as well as the AT. The biggest issue is that you're likely to hike on snow, which can obscure the trail. It's very helpful to have a map in hand to navigate—especially from Idyllwild, California, north over Fuller Ridge, and from Kennedy Meadows north. Without a map through these often snow-covered regions, it's easy to head up the wrong pass or into the wrong drainage. Also, sometimes water sources are just off the trail and may not be marked.

Q: Do I really need an ice ax, crampons, and sunglasses?

A: Sunglasses are mandatory! I have heard that a few hikers have gone snow-blind from UV rays bouncing off the snow. This can take time to recover from and can end your trip prematurely.

Regarding the other equipment: It depends on how early you get to the High Sierras and how much snow fell over the winter. I enjoy getting to the Sierras early and the challenge of snowy passes. The first time I hiked through, I didn't use an ice ax or crampons. The second time, I arrived even earlier and used both. I recommend an ice ax. I think you can get away without crampons. With an ice ax you can self-arrest if you slip. Alternatively, I think just having something like Vargo Pocket Cleats and not carrying an ice ax, would work just as well for even less weight and volume.

Try to plan your hikes over passes to coincide with the best time of the day for the snowpack. South-facing sides soften up early and north-facing sides a little later. North-facing passes can be scary, steep, and icy if you hit them too early. Hence, it's nice to have the safety of an ice ax to self-arrest, or the Pocket Cleats. You can also use the ax to cut steps if you need and as a tent stake.

SUNGLASSES TIP: If you break your sunglasses and can't get them to work on the PCT or in snowy or other extremely bright places, try to cover your eyes with duct tape. Make thin slits in the tape so you can see through. You can also wrap a piece of a T-shirt or other clothing around your head to cover your eyes. This will block enough sun so you won't go snow-blind. Pick up some new sunglasses when you get to the next town.

Q: How much water do I need to carry?

A: The longest (natural) waterless stretch in Southern California is about 30 miles. Those lengthy stretches are often shortened by trail angels, who leave gallons of water out for hikers. Most of the time you're only dealing with a 15-mile stretch without water.

If you don't really need the water caches, try not to use them. Somebody else with more need may be passing through the area after you. Trail angels at the Third Gate in the San Felipe Hills have to pack in the water.

Q: How hard is hiking through the Southern California desert?

A: The Southern California desert on the PCT can get very hot—especially if you leave later in the thru-hiking season. Plan accordingly. Wake up early and get some early miles in. Get to a water source before it gets hot. Then take a siesta until it cools down a bit in the evening.

In other parts of Southern California on the PCT, you're at an elevation that can also be cold and snowy. You may encounter snow and snow-covered ground in Southern California. Be prepared for 20°F nights in some areas.

Q: How much snow will there be?

A: It depends on the year and time when you head out. The earlier you head out in spring or summer, the more snow you'll encounter. You will walk on some snow. Monitor the snowpack before you head out, and plan accordingly. When you're in snowy areas, wake up early and try to hit the snow while it is firm.

Q: Are there tough river crossings? If so, what should I do?

A: Yes, some river crossings can be tough. Crossings in Kerrick Canyon, some fords in the High Sierras, and Yosemite are some examples of difficult crossings. The best thing to do is try to reach them early in the day and scout out a good place to cross.

Water levels in these locations rise dramatically in the afternoon. If you don't think you can cross where the trail does, go upstream until you find a place where you can ford. Follow the creek back to the trail and go on. You can also camp by the crossing and wait until the next morning. For more info, refer back to the section on fording techniques.

Q: Are there hostels and trail angels on the PCT?

A: Yes, there are some hostels and trail angels. There are not nearly as many as on the AT. Yogi's Pacific Crest Trail Handbook has a lot of information about towns, hostels, and trail angels on the PCT.

Q: What degree sleeping bag do I need?

A: Be prepared for cold weather in Southern California and through the High Sierras, especially at the start of thru-hiking season in early May. I used a 20- to 30-degree bag, but I sleep warm. After a couple of months on the trail, around late June or July, you may get away with a lighter bag, something in the 35- to 45-degree range depending on your comfort range. Then be prepared to switch back to your heavier bag as fall approaches and you get into Washington.

Q: Can I really hike more miles on the PCT than the AT?

A: Yes! Most people's daily mileage increases on the PCT because the trail is well graded. Then again, most people on a PCT thru-hike have more experience than on the AT and are carrying less weight. Don't plan on increased mileage through the High Sierra section though.

Q: Do I need permits for the national parks?

A: You can get what I refer to as "The Golden Ticket" on the PCTA (Pacific Crest Trail Association) website. You can register for free, or pay the recommended donation as a thru-hiker and get an all-inclusive PCT permit. There is also an add-on option to summit Mount Whitney if you would like to tag that peak as you pass by. This covers almost all the permits you need for the entire trail! Access will be determined by your start date, since they are capping the number of people starting the trail each day. Make sure to get your permit and start on your assigned date. Once you start on that date, you can go as fast or slow as you'd like,

Q: What are some helpful websites or books?

- Pacific Crest Trail Association (PCTA): pcta.org
- The PCT-L archives at National Scenic Trails Mailing Lists: mailman.backcountry.net/mailman/listinfo/pct-l

- Post Holer: postholer.com
- Yogi's Guides: yogisbooks.com/pacific-crest-trail/pct-yogis-pacific-crest-trail-handbook
- USDA Forest Service Active Fire Mapping Program: data.fs.usda.gov/geodata/maps/active-fire.php
- Pacific Crest Trail Water Reports Southern California: pcta.org
- NOAA National Snow Analyses: www.nohrsc.noaa.gov/nsa
- USDA National Water and Climate Center—Snow Telemetry (SNOTEL): www.wcc.nrcs.usda.gov/snow/
- Latest snow information: postholer.com

CONTINENTAL DIVIDE TRAIL

The CDT is some people's favorite of the three US long-distance trails. It can be a really fun adventure and take your hiking skills to the next level. It's also the least traveled and isn't officially complete. It's a bit more wild than the well-blazed trails of the AT and PCT, but its use and signage increase each year. Be prepared to use your navigation, map, and compass skills.

CDT FACTS

- Distance: Between 2,500 and 3,100 miles, depending on the route you choose.
- Highest possible point: Grays Peak, Colorado, 14,270 feet.
- Lowest possible point: Columbus, New Mexico, 3,900 feet.
- National Parks: Glacier National Park, Yellowstone National Park, and Rocky Mountain National Park.
- First thru-hike: Not available.
- States the trail goes through: Montana, Idaho, Wyoming, Colorado, and New Mexico.

CDT Q&A

Q: How long is the trail?
A: The CDT has historically been a "choose your own adventure" type of trail. It can range from 2,500 miles to 3,100 miles. Most people's CDT routes are between 2,600 and 2,800 miles. The route is now getting more defined and the trail getting more complete each year.

Q: Do I need to carry maps? Which are the best?
A: Yes, maps are crucial for this trail. You need both the maps and the skills to use them. Consistently check your location at random intervals so you can more easily figure out where you are if you get lost or come to unmarked junctions.

I recommend Jonathan Ley's map set for the CDT. It's a great system and includes a lot of fun options and alternate routes. Yogi's Continental Divide Trail Handbook will give you more information on places to resupply and what town amenities to expect. Many people are also using Guthook's app.

Q: Are there multiple routes for this trail?
A: Yes, there are multiple routes, especially if you use the Jonathan Ley maps or CDTS (Continental Divide Trail Society) guides. It's a younger, more open trail than either the AT or PCT. A formalized route has not yet been established, so you can choose your own route in some places. This can lead to your own adventure. The few who try to thru-hike the CDT each year do not hike the exact same route between Mexico and Canada.

Q: How much navigation is necessary?
A: Some navigation and cross-country travel is likely. It depends on the route you choose to take. More often than navigation, you'll run into tricky unmarked junctions and intersections. Again, it's helpful to pay close attention to where you are so when you reach an unmarked intersection of trails, you will know your location. However,

every year the route is getting better marked and more defined.

Q: Is it hard to resupply on the CDT?
A: Some resupplies are harder on the CDT. It's definitely harder than on the AT. A lot of the towns along the trail are smaller, and you might have to resupply at a general store or convenience store.

There are also fewer hiker-specific amenities. There are fewer outfitters and hostels. Hitchhiking to resupply on the CDT can take a while. It generally takes longer than on the AT.

Q: Do I need permits for the CDT?
A: Yes, you will need backcountry permits to camp in national parks (Glacier and Yellowstone, and possibly Rocky Mountain—if you do one of the routes that goes through it).

Q: What direction should I go and when should I go?
A: More people travel the CDT southbound from the Canada-Montana border and leave around mid-June. Those going northbound from New Mexico usually leave in April. Southern Colorado's San Juan Mountains can be difficult for northbound travelers if they hit them before mid-June. Some people flip-flop and hike north through New Mexico in April before it gets too hot and travel up to Canada before hiking back to New Mexico.

Q: What degree sleeping bag do I need?
A: It partly depends on your shelter. I recommend a 20- to 30-degree bag to start. You can probably switch out to a warmer bag in the middle of summer.

Q: What are some helpful websites?
- Continental Divide Trail Coalition (CDTC): continentaldividetrail.org
- The CDT-L archives at National Scenic Trails Mailing Lists: mailman.backcountry.net/mailman/listinfo/cdt

- USDA Forest Service Active Fire Mapping Program: data.fs.usda.gov/geodata/maps/active-fire.php
- NOAA National Snow Analyses: www.nohrsc.noaa.gov/nsa
- USDA National Water and Climate Center Snow Telemetry (SNOTEL): www.wcc.nrcs.usda.gov/snow/
- Latest snow information: postholer.com

HAYDUKE TRAIL

The Hayduke Trail is an awesome backcountry route. It uses trails, dirt roads, cross-country travel, and a little road-walking. You see many of the spectacular highlights of southern Utah and Arizona. It's more wild than the AT and PCT.

Q: Do I need maps? What do I need for navigation?
A: Yes, you definitely need maps for the Hayduke Trail. This trail requires even more navigation skills than the CDT. You can use a GPS unit. With solid map and compass skills you'll be fine without a GPS.

Q: How technical is the Hayduke? Am I going to be scared?
A: It's as technical as you make it. There are a few areas that the guidebook considers Class 3, but I didn't find them sketchy at all. Like the CDT, you can choose your own adventures with the Hayduke Trail. There are many ways into and out of the canyons, and you can make those side adventures as challenging as you want.

Q: What's the water situation?
A: The trail has decent and consistent water sources. There were only a few situations when I carried more than 3 or 4 liters of water.

Q: What should I do about permits?
A: You really need to plan your permits for the Hayduke Trail. Grand Canyon permits can be very

hard to get. If the dates you plan to be in the canyon change, you can change your permit, which is easier than getting a new one. When Pepper and I got to the national park boundary, we were actually a week ahead of schedule. Our permit was worthless. We hiked to the Grand Canyon Village backcountry office. They were much more helpful in person than on the phone. They changed our permit on the spot, and on we went.

Other national parks you will go through on the Hayduke, like Bryce and Arches, can be hiked in one day. If you can hike through the park in one day, you won't need permits.

INFORMATIVE WEBSITES

- Backpacking Light: Latest ultralight gear reviews and hiker forums: backpackinglight.com
- Fastest Known Time: Speed record information: fastestknowntime.proboards.com
- Maps and planning: Caltopo.com
- Planning: Google Earth

SITES FOR INTERNATIONAL MAPS

- OmniMap (recently acquired by East View Companies): omnimap.com
- Stanfords: stanfords.co.uk
- The Map Shop: themapshop.co.uk
- Maplink: evmaplink.com

A ford near Kakwa Lake Provincial Park, British Columbia, Canada *Photo by Shawn Forry*

Acknowledgments

Thanks to everyone who's helped me along the way: trail angels, friends, mentors, and fellow ultralighters and hikers. I too started out with a 50-plus-pound backpack when I set off on the AT. The friendships with other hikers and amazing support of the trail angels have been a blessing; and the journey has been unbelievably rewarding. Without the valleys and low times, there wouldn't be the amazing moments.

My eternal gratitude goes to my mom and dad, who are OK with anything I want to do—well, almost. They weren't too happy about my setting off to hike through Africa by myself. They've always pushed me to follow my own path. Thanks to Raina, who puts up with me even though I leave for months on end to seek out adventures to satisfy my wanderlust. You have done all I could ask for; including watching Yoni, updating my website, and stocking the freezer with countless pints of Ben & Jerry's upon my return.

Thanks to Yoni for being by my side and sticking with me for tens of thousands of miles. You will be with us forever.

justin lichter

Ascending a steep snowfield in the High Sierras on the PCT

Glossary [TERMS TO KNOW FOR HIKING]

A-frame: Shelter, tarp, or tent setup that resembles an "A."

Ablation valley (lateroglacial valley): A valley on the side of a glacial moraine.

Active protection: Protective climbing device with moving parts, like a cam (used to be called a friend and was originally invented by Ray Jardine).

ADT: American Discovery Trail.

Alcohol stove: A stove that uses alcohol as its fuel.

ALDHA: Appalachian Long Distance Hikers Association; aldha.org.

ALDHA West: Western sister of ALDHA, many Triple Crowners register with ALDHA West. Hosts a West Coast gathering in early fall/late summer.

Alluvial fan: Fan-shaped accumulation of silt, sand, gravel, and boulders deposited by fast-flowing mountain rivers on flatter land.

Alluvium: Sediment deposited by flowing water, including riverbeds, floodplains, and deltas.

Alpine: Above tree line in a mountainous area.

Alpine start: Getting up and heading out early—usually prior to sunrise.

Alpine-style hiking: Hiking with no outside support or help. Also referred to as Alpine style. Some say it only refers to solo trips.

AMC: Appalachian Mountain Club. Some AT hikers call it the Appalachian Money Club because they charge for hut use.

Animal trail: Trail created by the frequent travel of animals. Sometimes helpful on cross-country treks.

Anti-bott (Anti-balling) plates: Hydrophobic plates, usually of flexible plastic or rubber, that attach to crampons, preventing snow and ice buildup in conditions close to freezing. Balled snow adds weight and reduces the usable penetration distance of a crampon.

Arroyo: Canyon with a dry riverbed.

AT: Appalachian Trail.

ATC: Appalachian Trail Conservancy. Governing body of the AT with offices in Harpers Ferry, West Virginia, about 1,000 miles up the AT; appalachiantrail.org.

AT Trail Fest: Mid-March annual hiker gathering in Dahlonega, Georgia.

Ax mark: Trails were once blazed with ax marks in tree bark. Often shaped like an upside-down exclamation point.

AZT: Arizona Trail.

Backpackers: Refers to hostels in New Zealand.

Basalt: Fine-grained, dark igneous rock. The most common form of volcanic rock.

Basin: Natural depression in land, especially in mountainous land. Often with a lake at its low point or points. As in the Rae Lakes Basin in the High Sierras.

Belay: 1. Securing a climber to mountain, rock, or ice-face with a rope via a rock, tree, piton, other person, etc.; safeguarding them in the event of a fall. 2. The act of using rope to aid another climber in the act of climbing.

Bench: Flat area, similar to a plateau but smaller. Often found above rivers. Can be nice to find during cross-country travel.

Bergshrund ('Schrund): Crevasse dividing moving glacial ice from stagnant ice. May extend to bedrock below.

'Biner: Short for carabiner. Oblong metal ring with a spring clip. Used in mountaineering and rock or ice climbing to attach running rope to a piece of protection.

Bivvy spot: Small spot to camp. Usually has some shelter or protection. Possibly under a large, stable boulder or rock ledge.

Blaze: Mark indicating where a trail is. The AT is blazed with white paint marks roughly the size and shape of a dollar.

Blue blazer: Someone who takes blue-blazed trails on the AT. Blue-blazed trails often bypass sections of the main white-blazed trail for scenic views or shortcuts.

Bonk: Crashing or getting tired from not eating and/or low-blood sugar.

Bounce box: A package that you mail to yourself and "bounce" up the trail as you go. The package often contains maps, batteries, extra or spare gear and clothing layers, or food.

Braided river: River with a number of channels. Channels and braid bars are usually highly mobile. River layout can change significantly during floods. River braids are a good place to cross a tough river.

Burn: Means a stream in some locations, like New Zealand. Also referred to as a branch, brook, beck, creek, crick, gill (occasionally ghyll), kill, lick, rill, river, sike, bayou, rivulet, streamage, wash, run, or runnel.

Bushwhacking: Going off-trail where the terrain is thick with brush. Occurs on lesser used or ill-maintained trails. Bushwhacking is somewhat interchangeable with cross-country travel.

Butte: Conspicuous isolated hill with steep—often vertical—sides and a small, relatively flat top. Term is used often in the Desert Southwest. A butte's top is not as wide as its height. Similar to mesas, which are wider than they are tall.

Cable car: Cart attached to a cable used for crossing a river.

Cairn: Rock pile used to mark a trail or a route. Also called a duck or stoneman.

Carabiner ('biner): Oblong metal ring with a spring clip. Used in mountaineering and rock or ice climbing to attach running rope to a piece of protection.

Cathole: Hole for human feces.

CCT: California Coastal Trail.

CDT: Continental Divide Trail.

CDTC: Continental Divide Trail Coalition. Governing body of the CDT.

CDTS: Continental Divide Trail Society. Mission: "To help in the planning, development, and maintenance of the CDT as a silent trail and to assist users plan and enjoy their experiences along the route"; cdtsociety.org.

Chaparral: A type of shrubland found in California, northern Baja California, and Mediterranean climates; often has impenetrable dense thickets of stiff, thorny plants. The plants are often highly flammable, and these areas have a history of wildfires.

Chute: Break in the rock or cliff band where you can get through. Sometimes snow-filled.

Cirque: Amphitheater-like valley head formed by the erosion of a glacier. Also known as a corrie or cwm.

Cirrus clouds: High, level clouds. Often referred to as "mare's tails." Usually wispy, but many can connect to cover large areas. Cirrus clouds often signify an upper-air disturbance or approaching frontal system, which can bring storms. They also are often the remnants of a thunderstorm.

Col: Mountain pass or a low point on a ridgeline.

Contour: Hiking from one spot to another along a hillside or slope without losing elevation. Same as contouring.

Cornice: Overhanging ledge of snow formed by wind on the edge of a mountain ridge, cliff, or corrie. Cornices are usually leeward of prevailing winds.

Corrie: A round hollow in a hillside. Also a steep-walled semicircular basin in a mountain. May contain a lake. Also known as a cirque or cwm.

Corrie loch (Tarn): Mountain lake or pond formed in a cirque. A moraine may form a natural dam below a corrie loch.

Cowboy camping: Camping under the stars without setting up a shelter.

Crampons: Outdoor footwear attachments with metal parts to provide traction on snow and ice.

Crevasse: Crack in a glacier that may or may not be covered.

Crevice: Crack in a rock.

Cross-country: Traveling off-trail.

Crux: Crucial point or hardest part of a route.

CT: Colorado Trail.

Cumulus clouds: Clouds with noticeable vertical development and clearly defined edges. "Cumulus" is Latin for "heap" or "pile." Cumulus humilis clouds, small or medium-size puffy clouds, often occur during fair weather. Cumulus clouds can grow into cumulonimbus clouds. They can produce heavy rain, lightning, severe and strong winds, hail, and even tornadoes. Cumulus congestus clouds, which appear as towers, often grow into cumulonimbus storm clouds.

Cwm (pronounced COOM): Welsh word for "valley." A bowl-shaped valley, also known as a cirque.

Datum: Point, line, or surface used as a reference for surveying, mapping, or geology. GPS units use datum points to orient the unit to maps.

Denatured alcohol: Fuel for hikers using an alcohol stove. It burns slowly. Also a solvent for lacquers, polishes, and for industrial purposes. Found in paint sections of hardware stores.

Denier: Unit of weight by which the fineness of silk, rayon, or nylon yarn is measured. Equal to the weight in grams of 9,000 meters of the yarn.

Ditties: Small, random items or accessories like a notepad, card with contact information, etc.

DNT: Den Norske Turistforening: Norwegian Trekking Association. DNT has offices throughout Norway. You can buy a key to access the Norwegian hut system. They paint red Ts on cairns and rock walls to mark trails. In forested areas (e.g., around Oslo) and along the coast, huts are marked with blue strips painted on trees or poles; turistforeningen.no/english/

Duck: 1. A variety of waterfowl. 2. Rock pile used to mark a trail or a route of travel; also cairn or stoneman.

Dynamic rope: Rope that stretches. Used for trad (traditional) climbing and sport climbing. Helps absorb shock of a falling climber.

ECT: Eastern Continental Trail. Connects numerous trails from Key West, Florida, to Cap Gaspé, Quebec. Connected trails include the IAT, AT, Benton MacKaye Trail (BMT), Georgia Pinhoti Trail, Alabama Pinhoti Trail, road-walking, and the Florida Trail.

Erratic: Rock that differs in composition, shape, etc., from nearby rock that was transported from its origin. Usually transported by glacial action.

Exposure/Exposed: Potential for injury on technical or tough terrain (as in "exposed rock face"). Also, lack of shelter from weather elements.

Fastpacking: Term coined by Jim Knight during a 1988 traverse of the Wind River Range in Wyoming. In a 1988 article in *UltraRunning Magazine*, Knight wrote, "We were wilderness running. Power hiking. Kind of backpacking, but much faster. More fluid. Neat. Almost surgical. Get in. Get out. I call it fastpacking." Now used for backpackers that take backpacking to a physical and mental extreme.

Filler: Trail connecting scenic places but not in itself interesting or scenic.

Flash flood: Sudden localized flood of great volume and short duration.

Flip-flop: Hiking a complete trail, but not from terminus to terminus. Usually flip-floppers start at one terminus, stop at a certain point, travel to the other terminus and hike back to previous stopping point.

Floodplain: Flat or nearly flat land adjacent to a stream or river. Stretches from the body of water's banks to the base of the enclosing valley. Can experience flooding during periods of high discharge.

Foot: Lower end of a valley, lake, base of mountain, or glacier. Also toe or snout (for a glacier).

Footprint: Material placed under a tent to protect the floor of the tent.

Ford: Cross a river by wading.

Fork: Branch or tributary of stream or river. Also trail split.

Front-pointing: Technique for ascending steep or overhanging ice or snow with crampons. In this technique, the front teeth of crampons are used to dig into the ice by kicking into it. The dug-in crampon is used as a step.

FT: Florida Trail.

GA–ME: Georgia to Maine. A northbound thru-hike on the AT.

Gathering: Annual October hiker event with presentations and awards. Draws many hikers.

GDT: Great Divide Trail route through the Canadian Rockies using existing trails, cross-country travel, dirt, and paved roads.

GET: Grand Enchantment Trail through New Mexico.

GHT: Great Himalaya Trail.

Gill (Ghyll): Stream. Depending on its location and characteristics, may also be referred to as a branch, brook, beck, burn, creek, crick, kill, lick, rill, river, sike, bayou, rivulet, streamage, wash, run, or runnel.

Glacial river/stream: Waterway with glacial origins. Different from other water sources because they are often cloudy or milky. Hard to see the bottom of the water sources. Glacial rivers fluctuate in flow volume depending on the time of day.

Glacier: Slow-moving mass of ice originating from an accumulation of snow. Spreads either from a central mass (continental glacier) or descends from a high valley (alpine glacier).

Glissade: Controlled slide used to descend a steep icy or snowy incline in either standing or sitting position.

Goat track: Faint trail.

GPS: Global Positioning System. Computerized navigational system that determines location, longitude, and latitude by gathering data from multiple satellites.

Granite: Light-colored, coarse-grained igneous rock. One of the most common rocks in the continental crust. Formed by the slow, underground cooling of magma.

Grommet: Fastener consisting of a metal or plastic ring lining a small hole. Allows for attachment of cords or lines to a piece of equipment like a backpack.

Ground cloth/groundsheet: Material put on the ground with a tarp or shelter to prevent wet ground from saturating campers' sleep systems.

Guy out: Setting up guylines. Makes a shelter sturdier.

Guyline (aka guy): Cord used to keep a structure upright in various weather conditions, like wind or snow.

Hanging glacier: Glacier on a shelf or wall above a valley or another glacier. May be joined to the lower glacier by an icefall or be separate from it.

Hanging valley: Tributary valley entering the main valley at a much higher elevation. Deepening of main valley most likely because of glacial erosion.

Hayduke Trail: Inspired by the works of Ed Abbey. A route from Arches National Park to Zion National Park in Utah. Connects many national parks in Utah and the Grand Canyon using preexisting trails, cross-country travel, and dirt and paved roads.

Head: Upper end of valley, lake, or glacier.

HEET: Brand-named alcohol-based gas line antifreeze and water remover suitable for alcohol stoves. Found in gas stations throughout United States and Canada—particularly in cold climates. HEET comes in two varieties, yellow and red. The yellow bottle is methyl alcohol, a cleaner burning alcohol than the isopropyl alcohol in the red HEET bottle. Knockoffs exist that use the same color scheme as HEET.

Hiker trash: Nickname for hikers in towns. Refers to their dirty, smelly nature and their tendency to loiter. Pepper's hiker trash slogan: "Scope it out. Lay it out. Spread it out." Refers to how hikers dry wet gear and prepare for future sections.

Hut: Shelter for hikers. Ranges from a fully staffed hut with meal service—like in New Hampshire's White Mountains—to a shepherd's cabin in rural New Zealand. Many regions known for hiking have hut systems. These include Europe, parts of the AT and New Zealand, and others.

IAT: International Appalachian Trail. Picks up at northern terminus of the AT and extends into Canada's Belle Isle. Current efforts are being made to extend it into Europe to follow the historic range of the Appalachian Mountains.

Ice ax: Mountaineering, ice-climbing tool used for climbing and cutting steps in snow and ice. Also used to self-arrest.

Icefall: Steep part of a glacier with deep crevasses. Resembles a frozen waterfall.

ICT: Idaho Centennial Trail.

In the alpine: Above tree line.

Isobutane: Pressurized fuel used for fuel canister stoves.

Kicking steps: Refers to kicking shoes or crampons into snow when ascending or descending to get purchase.

Kickoff: ADZPCTKO or Annual Day-Zero Pacific Crest Trail Kickoff. Hiker gathering in mid- to late April on the PCT in Southern California.

Kill: Stream. Depending on its location and characteristics, may also be referred to as a branch, brook, beck, burn, creek, crick, gill (occasionally ghyll), lick, rill, river, sike, bayou, rivulet, streamage, wash, run, or runnel.

Kit: Gear with you.

Lateral moraine: Ridges of debris deposited along the sides of a glacier.

Lean-to: AT shelters in Vermont, New Hampshire, and Maine are sometimes referred to as lean-tos. Also a type of shelter or means of setting up a tarp where the roof is angled to the ground on a flat plane, creating shelter underneath.

Ledge: Exposed rock, rock layer, or flat area on a rock face.

Leeward: Direction downwind from point of reference. Side sheltered from the wind. The term "lee" derives from the Old English *hleo,* meaning "shelter."

Lenticular clouds: Lens-shaped cirrus clouds can mean the approach of a storm in the next 24 to 48 hours.

Lick: Stream. Depending on its location and characteristics, may also be referred to as a bayou, branch, brook, beck, burn, creek, crick, kill, rill, river, sike, rivulet, streamage, wash, run, or runnel.

Lightweight hiker: No standard for the term. Generally someone whose base pack weight is less than 20 pounds (9.1 kilograms).

LNT: Leave No Trace. The practice of outdoor rules and ethics to help alleviate human impact.

Loch: Lake. Partially landlocked sea inlet.

Lollipop loop: Loop hike shaped like a lollipop. It is not a true loop, since you have to hike part of the trail in both directions.

Long-distance hiking: There is no set definition as to the amount of distance you must travel before it's considered long distance.

LT: Long Trail.

Meadow: Area where environmental factors restrict the growth of woody plants indefinitely.

ME–GA: Maine to Georgia. A southbound thru-hike on the AT.

Mesa: Elevated landmass with a flat top. Sides are usually steep cliffs. The top is typically wider than the height of its sides. "Mesa" means "table" in Spanish. In Spain such a landmass is called a meseta.

Moraine: Mass of debris, carried by glaciers, forming ridges and mounds when deposited.

Muds: Mindless ups and downs on a hike.

NCT: North Country Trail. A trail that travels through North Dakota, Minnesota, Wisconsin, Michigan, Ohio, Pennsylvania, and New York.

Nero: Near-zero day. A day you hike a few miles or have a short day.

Nobo: Northbound hiker.

OR (Outdoor Retailer Show): Biannual outdoor industry event showcasing new products to prospective retailers. Open only to retailers, manufacturers, and media. Not open to the public.

Pack explosion: When you get to a motel room, take everything wet out of your pack and hang everything around the room to dry.

Pass: Point on a ridge where you can cross—usually from one watershed to another. Similar to a saddle but usually at a higher elevation.

Passive protection: Climbing protection without moving parts. Includes chocks, stoppers, nuts, or any other wedge-shaped pieces that fit into cracks. Also Hexentrics and tricams rotated in to fit tightly into cracks and holes.

PCT: Pacific Crest Trail.

PCTA: Pacific Crest Trail Association. Governing body of the PCT; pcta.org.

Permanent snowfield: Snowfield that doesn't completely melt in summer. Not a glacier because it is not glacial ice.

Pink blazer: Male hiker looking for trail tail.

Plateau: High plain or tableland with relatively flat terrain. Similar to a mesa.

PNT: Pacific Northwest Trail. Trail through Washington, Idaho, and Montana.

Postholing: When your legs punch through snow while walking.

Pour-off: Seasonal desert waterfall. When the waterfall is dry, it is called a pour-off. It can be a tough obstacle for a hiker or canyoneer.

Privy: Outhouse.

Puds: Pointless ups and downs on a hike.

Purist: Hiker or thru-hiker who has to walk every step of the trail. Specifically, an AT thru-hiker who chooses to walk past every white blaze without taking any blue-blazed routes.

Quiver: Hiker's stock of gear for trips. For example, I have three sleeping bags in my quiver—a 20-degree bag, a 0-degree bag, and a 30-degree bag.

Rainfly: Waterproof material covering the outside of a tent.

Ramp: Ascending or descending area that will help you move on the trail.

Ray Jardine: Considered a pioneer of ultralight hiking. Likely the first to write about the phenomenon. Taking the ultralight revolution to a new level within the long-distance hiking community. Published *Pacific Crest Trail Hikers Handbook* in 1996. The book advocated hiking the PCT in a much shorter period than traditionally expected by using homemade, lightweight gear and techniques that included earlier start times, longer days, and more mileage at a slower pace. The book was revised and retitled *Beyond Backpacking* in 1999, and again in 2009 as *Trail Life*.

Rill: Stream. Depending on its location and characteristics, may also be referred to as a bayou, branch, brook, beck, burn, creek, crick, kill, lick, river, sike, rivulet, wash, streamage, run, or runnel.

Rime: Frost formed by freezing supercooled water droplets in fog onto solid objects.

Riparian areas: Plant habitats along river margins and banks.

Rivulet: Stream. Depending on its location and characteristics, may also be referred to as a bayou, branch, brook, beck, burn, creek, crick, kill, lick, rill, river, sike, streamage, wash, run, or runnel.

Rotten snow: Snow you punch through when hiking in, requiring postholing. Often happens on spring afternoons as things warm up throughout the day. Also occurs in cold, continental climates in winter.

Run or Runnel: Stream. Depending on its location and characteristics, may also be referred to as a bayou, branch, brook, beck, burn, creek, crick, kill, lick, rill, river, rivulet, sike, streamage, or wash.

Saddle: Low point between two peaks or along a ridgeline.

Sandstone: Medium-grained sedimentary rock consisting of fine to coarse sand-size grains compacted or cemented together. Varies in color from yellow or red to gray or brown.

Saw marks: Sawn logs are a sign of trail maintenance. Good indication that you are on a trail or old trail.

Scree: Mass of small loose rocks that cover a slope on a mountain.

Scree running: Scree often moves when you step on it. When traveling downhill, you can often run or slide down it as if on snow.

Sea-to-Sea Route (C2C): Amalgamation of trails including IAT, AT, NCT, road-walking, and the PNT. Connecting Cap Gaspé, Quebec, to Cape Alava, Washington.

Section hiker: Person hiking complete trail by hiking each individual section; not in continuity or, necessarily, in sequence.

Seep: Small spring or place where water has oozed through the ground. May or may not be flowing enough to use as a water source.

Self-arrest: Maneuver in which a climber is sliding down a snow or ice slope and arrests (stops) the slide without using a rope or other belay system. Usually done with an ice ax or hands, feet, knees, or elbows.

Self-supported: Most commonly used interchangeably with "unsupported." Taken on new meaning by people who believe that "unsupported" means that you carry all your equipment and food with you from the start. They take "self-supported" to mean that you don't carry everything you need from the start. You set up all your own mail drops or shop from stores along the way.

Serac: Block or column of ice formed by intersecting crevasses on a glacier. Often house-size or larger. Dangerous since they are prone to fall without warning. Seracs are found within an icefall or on ice faces on the lower edge of a hanging glacier.

Shelter: Three-sided building on AT for hikers. Some are fully enclosed buildings.

Shoulder: Part of ridgeline where the ridge lowers on one end.

Sidehill (Contouring): Maintaining elevation while hiking from one spot to another along a hillside or slope.

Slackpacking: Hiking without your backpack.

Slot canyon: Narrow canyon formed by the wear of water rushing through rock. Slot canyons are significantly deeper than wide.

Snout: End of a glacier. Also foot or toe.

Snowfield: Accumulation of snow and ice. Differs from a glacier. Also a wide swath of snow cover.

Sobo: Southbound hiker.

Spring: Natural outflow of groundwater.

Static rope: Rope without built-in stretch. Ideal for rappelling and top-rope climbing.

Stealth camping: Effort to camp but not be seen. On the AT, camping away from a shelter.

Stoneman: Rock pile used to mark a trail or a route of travel. Also called duck or cairn.

Stratus clouds: Cloud belonging to a class characterized by horizontal layering and a uniform base, as opposed to convective clouds that are as tall or taller than wide—cumulus clouds. Stratus describes flat, hazy, featureless clouds of low altitude, varying in color from dark gray to nearly white. Stratus clouds may produce a light drizzle or snow.

Subalpine: Upper forest zone.

Super-ultralight hiker: Base weight of less than 5 pounds. Also called überlight.

Supported: Hike supported by a team, supplying items as you need them. Hikers and trail runners attempting speed records often use this method so they won't have to carry all of their supplies.

Switchback: Zigzagging trail through a steep incline to lessen the grade for hikers and erosion for the slope.

Talus: Sloping mass of loose rocks at the base of a cliff.

Tamarisk: Originally from Eurasia, it is an invasive plant in the Desert Southwest and desert areas of California. They consume larger amounts of groundwater than native species and make the soil more saline. The native willows and cottonwoods have trouble competing against them. They are stiff and thick and not very pleasant to bushwhack through, compared to the gentle and pliable willows. They are also known as salt cedar.

Tarn: Mountain lake or pond formed in a cirque excavated by a glacier. A moraine may form a natural dam below a tarn. Also called a corrie loch.

Tea house: House in Nepalese Himalayas where you can eat and/or stay the night.

Terminal moraine: A moraine that forms at the end (snout) of the glacier. Terminal moraines mark the maximum advance of the glacier.

Terminus: End point of a trail.

Three-wire bridge: Bridge made out of three cables in an upside-down triangle or "V" shape.

Thru-hiker: Person hiking a long-distance trail from end to end.

Thru-hiker shuffle: Gimpy, stiff-legged walk that many long-distance hikers exhibit, usually at the beginning of a hike as their body gets used to the miles or immediately after a break when their muscles are tight.

Ti: Short for titanium.

Toe: Lower end of valley, lake, base of mountain or glacier. Same as foot or snout (for a glacier).

Town day: (Usually said as a happy exclamation) Day a hiker heads into a town for resupplying and carbing out on food.

Trail angels: People who perform trail magic and acts of random kindness.

Trail Days (Daze): Annual hiker gathering in Damascus, Virginia, on the AT in mid-May.

Trail magic: Generosity toward hikers. Offering a hiker a place to stay overnight, leaving candy or soda, or having a hiker BBQ.

Trail name: Hiker's nickname.

Trail tail: Getting action; hooking up during a hike.

Traverse: Travel or pass across, over, or through. Cross and recross. Go up, down, or across (a slope) diagonally.

Tree line: Zone at high altitudes or high latitudes beyond which trees can't grow.

Triple Crown (of long-distance hiking): AT, PCT, and CDT.

Trowel (potty trowel): Small shovel with a pointed, scoop-shaped blade used for digging things like catholes.

TRT: Tahoe Rim Trail. Trail that passes through California and Nevada, surrounding Lake Tahoe.

True right/left: Direction of travel while facing downriver.

Tundra: Cold, treeless, usually lowland area of far northern regions. Lower strata of tundra soil are permanently frozen. In the summer the top layer of soil thaws, supporting low-growing mosses, lichens, grasses, and small shrubs.

Tussock: Clump of grass, common in New Zealand. Often slippery when wet.

TV time: Downtime in town for relaxing, watching TV, lying in bed in a motel room surrounded by food.

Überlight hiker: Super-ultralight hiker with a base pack weight of less than 5 pounds.

Ultralight hiker: Generally someone whose base pack weight is below 12 pounds (4.5 kilograms). Commonly used to refer to someone who watched his or her pack weight and carries a lightweight pack—regardless of the actual pack weight.

Unsupported: Most commonly a hike with no outside support or help. Also referred to as alpine style. Some people refer to unsupported as an unaccompanied trip.

Wash: Canyon bottom where water flows seasonally; usually a sandy area.

Weekender/Weekend warrior: Person who works Monday through Friday and heads out camping, hiking, backpacking, or skiing for the weekend.

White gas: Fuel used in many stoves. A distilled gasoline that burns clean so it doesn't often clog a stove or get a pot dirty.

Windmill: Wind turbine that extracts usable energy from wind. Used on parts of the CDT to pump water out of the ground for cattle. They may be your only water source in some areas.

Windward: Direction upwind from the point of reference. Side facing into the wind, opposite of leeward.

Yellow blazer: Hiker who accepts car rides to skip sections of the trail.

Yogi: A vocalized suggestion for helpful trail magic. ("The weather is pretty bad. It would be great to find a good place to camp or stay tonight.")

Yo-yo: Hiking a trail from one terminus to the other and then turning around to hike back.

Zero, or Zero Day: Day off from hiking; rest day.

Index

Q&A

HOW DID YOU GET YOUR TRAIL NAME?

I got the trail name "Trauma" on my first hike in Utah. I was resisting a trail name, but, as they say, "Resistance is futile." I was dubbed Trauma following a few traumatic experiences near the beginning of the trip.

A few days into the trip, while I was hiking up a side canyon, four or five ravens started dive-bombing me. As I tried running forward, they came at me more fiercely, nearly attacking me. I tried running back, and they did the same thing. I hid behind a boulder, hoping they'd forget about me or let me make a run for it. My friends came up the canyon about 5 minutes later. When they found me they asked, "What the heck are you doing there?"

Toward the end of the same section, I was running short on food. We found old MREs (meals ready to eat) in cans in the wash. MREs haven't been packed in cans for quite a while—not since the 1970s. They were a bit beat up, corroded, and pretty much rusted through. So I popped open a can of fortified crackers and fortified cheese spread. It tasted like Cheese Whiz and I ate the whole can. I was still hungry, so I popped open a can of fortified cheese spread with jalapeños. The "cheese" in that one was lime green, so I stayed away from it. Still hungry, I opened up a third can, which was filled with fortified chocolate and ate that. It tasted like Nestlé Crunch!

My friends were aghast. They thought that I was going to get violently sick and that they would have to carry me out. Fortunately, that never happened. Nonetheless, my friends couldn't stop laughing at my affinity for traumatic situations. The trail name "Trauma" was coined, and it stuck. Since then I've been putting myself and my gear to the test.

WHAT ARE YOUR FAVORITE PLACES TO HIKE?

Everybody has their sanctuaries. In my case they include hiking in the High Sierras, Wind River Range, Canadian Rockies, New England in the fall, the Laugavegur trek in Iceland, Southern Alps of New Zealand, southern Utah, Norway, Pacific Northwest, and North Cascades. Southern Utah and the High Sierras definitely are exceptionally special places for me.

WHAT IS YOUR FAVORITE LONG TRAIL IN THE US?

My favorite of the three main trails is the PCT. As far as shorter trails go, I also really enjoyed the Hayduke Trail.

WHAT IS YOUR FAVORITE INTERNATIONAL HIKE?

There are a lot of pretty places around the world, but I really enjoyed hiking across Iceland. It's a scenic and diverse country. If you're looking for 200 to 300 miles of scenic terrain with hardly any filler, this is a great place to hike. If you have only a few days, there's an amazing 60-mile hike across from Landmannalaugar to Skogar along the Laugavegur in the southern half of the country.

WHAT WAS YOUR WORST WATER SOURCE?

The stock reservoir I came across on the CDT was the worst. It contained dead cows that had exploded in the sun. Their intestines were floating in the water along with dead mice. I also drank some really nasty water in Africa. It seemed a little better than the water in that stock reservoir.

WHAT IS YOUR FAVORITE WATER SOURCE?

Lava Spring in Washington on the PCT is an unbelievable water source. It has an endless flow of great-tasting, crisp, cold water.

IS THERE ANYTHING YOU DISLIKE ABOUT HIKING?

Dealing with permits in national parks and internationally is sometimes a real hassle. There is nothing I hate more than mosquitoes on a hot, humid day when DEET won't keep the buggers off. You have to put on extra clothes to protect yourself. You're hot and sweaty, and there's simply no escape or peace of mind.

About Trauma

Justin Lichter grew up in Briarcliff, New York, about an hour north of New York City. After college he quickly shunned the traditional career path and lived in southern Vermont; Dillon, Colorado; and Truckee, California, as he followed snow and his passion for skiing. When not hiking, Justin works as a ski patroller. Recreationally he enjoys backcountry skiing, Nordic skiing, snowshoeing, mountain biking, surfing, and anything else active and outdoors.

Since 2002, Justin has hiked more than 40,000 miles, equal to nearly one and a half times around the Earth. His passion started in 2002 when he took an outdoor education class through the University of California at Santa Cruz. In this class they mostly traveled cross-country through the canyon country of southern Utah. On this trip Justin started developing the idea of setting off on the Appalachian Trail. The following year, 2003, he hiked from Georgia to Cap Gaspé, Quebec, following the Appalachian and International Appalachian Trails.

The next year he undertook the Pacific Crest Trail from Mexico to Canada and then continued on the Pacific Northwest Trail to the Washington coast. Justin finished his first Triple Crown of long-distance hiking in 2005 upon completing the Continental Divide Trail from Mexico to Canada. He didn't stop there—he continued to hike north from the Canadian border on the Great Divide Trail to Kakwa Lake, British Columbia. Upon completing the Triple Crown, Justin looked for an opportunity to challenge himself and push the limits of human endurance—and find a good excuse to be outside and hike for a year straight. From November 1, 2005, to October 23, 2006, he completed the Eastern Continental Trail (Cap Gaspé, Quebec, to Key West, Florida, incorporating the AT), the Pacific Crest Trail, and the Continental Divide Trail in under a year, a total of more than 10,000 miles in 356 days.

The following year Justin and frequent hiking partner Pepper developed a precursor to the Te Araroa Trail in New Zealand and traversed the Southern Alps and the South Island of New Zealand from south to north.

The list continues. In 2007 he swam unsupported around Lake Tahoe without a wet suit and developed and hiked a route from Durango, Colorado, to Las Vegas, Nevada. In 2008 Justin hiked the Hayduke Trail through Utah and Arizona, traversed Iceland on foot, and hiked through Norway and Sweden. The next summer Justin ambitiously hiked 1,800 miles, solo and unsupported, through Africa, including crossing through Ethiopia and Kenya, before ending his trip after being stalked by lions. In 2011 Justin completed a traverse of the Great Himalaya Trail through the Himalaya Mountains from the eastern Nepal border to the India-Pakistan border. In 2012 Justin swam across Mono Lake. In 2013, Justin skied about 400 miles through the High Sierra, hiked the John Muir Trail, and thru-hiked the Copper Canyon in Mexico later that fall. In the winter of 2014/2015, Justin and his hiking partner, Shawn Forry, became the first people to successfully traverse the Pacific Crest Trail in the winter. In 2015 he hiked the Na Pali Coast Trail and Lowest to Highest Route in California. In 2017, he skied the Tahoe Rim Trail in the winter and in 2019 skied the High Sierra Ski Route.

Justin continues to work as a ski patroller in the winter and is constantly dreaming up new adventures.